Prais
Inviting Int

MW00612259

"*Inviting Interruptions* is a treasure trove for all who like to think with and about fairy tales. Its unique combination of texts and visuals celebrates the richness of fairy-tale material today. The editors' notes open the conversation on potential meanings for each contribution, making this collection indispensable for courses in fairy-tale studies that want to keep up with this genre's latest developments."

—Vanessa Joosen, author of *Critical and Creative Perspectives on Fairy Tales*

"*Inviting Interruptions* is a major contribution to the field: an anthology of contemporary fairy tales that seeks to match and continue—in ambition, liveliness, and ideological orientation—the promise of the great renaissance of fairy tales of the 1970s and 1980s. Matching that promise involves recognizing and responding to changes in our political climate, as well as to changes in our attitude to the very idea of a climate. *Inviting Interruptions* does so inspiringly. There simply isn't a volume of this kind currently on the market."

—Stephen Benson, senior lecturer in the School of Literature, Drama and Creative Writing, University of East Anglia, United Kingdom

"*Inviting Interruptions* is, indeed, an amazing collection of expressionist fairy tales that reflect the troublesome times in which we live. The editors of this remarkable anthology, Cristina Bacchilega and Jennifer Orme, have carefully gathered narratives, artworks, graphic stories, and photos that will cause readers to pause in astonishment. Due to the explosion of 'wonder' tales in the twenty-first century, they could have added several hundred more. As it is, their selection—bringing together Shaun Tan, Kelly Link, Rosario Ferré, David Kaplan, and Joellyn Rock among the talented writers and artists—is a significant achievement. This is a book to read and ponder in the chaotic years to come."

—Jack Zipes, University of Minnesota

"In a fairy-tale world wherein the best prevail (which doesn't include every fairy tale!) this truly innovative anthology would replace all others. Where most books of wonder tales focus on literary versions, using visuals primarily as illustration, *Inviting Interruptions* fully engages with photography, graphic novel, sculpture, film, painting, drawing, and multimedia visual art as much as with the written word. Bacchilega and Orme offer verbal-text-driven fairy-tale studies an entirely engaging disturbance."

—Pauline Greenhill, professor of women's and gender studies, University of Winnipeg, Canada

"With this vivid, rich, and thoughtful collection, the editors have created a passionate manifesto for the wonder tale. The storytellers they have chosen—and in many cases rediscovered—aren't scared off by polemical themes. They take us down bold and unexpected paths, making us smile and shiver and yes—wonder."

—Marina Warner, author of *Fairy Tale: A Very Short Introduction*

Inviting Interruptions

Series in Fairy-Tale Studies

Series Editor

Donald Haase, Wayne State University

A complete listing of the advisory editors and the books in this series can be found online at wsupress.wayne.edu.

Inviting Interruptions

Wonder Tales in the Twenty-First Century

Edited by
Cristina Bacchilega and Jennifer Orme

Wayne State University Press
Detroit

ISBN (paperback): 978-0-8143-4700-3
ISBN (hardcover): 978-0-8143-4699-0
ISBN (ebook): 978-0-8143-4701-0

Library of Congress Control Number: 2020938983

Published with the assistance of a fund established by Thelma Gray James of Wayne
State University for the publication of folklore and English studies.

Cover art by Rosalind Sayuri Hyatt Orme
Cover design by Lindsey Cleworth

Wayne State University Press
Leonard N. Simons Building
4809 Woodward Avenue
Detroit, Michigan 48201-1309

Visit us online at wsupress.wayne.edu

Contents

Introduction • ix
Cristina Bacchilega and Jennifer Orme

Part I: Inviting Interruptions

Once Upon a Time • 2
Su Blackwell

The Tale of the Cottage • 4
Emma Donoghue

Untitled • 10
Shary Boyle

Swans • 12
Kelly Link

How to Be a Mermaid • 24
Maya Kern

Birth of Commerce • 46
Shaun Tan

A Tale of a King • 48
Shaun Tan

Beast • 54
Shary Boyle

Little Red Riding Hood • 56
David Kaplan

Of No Real Account • 60
Bryan Kamaoli Kuwada

Aitu • 76
Dan Taulapapa McMullin

Part II: Interrupting Invitations

Medusa • 80
Rosalind Hyatt Orme

Fairytales for Lost Children • 82
Diriye Osman

Burdens: They Must Always Be Carried • 96
Anne Kamiya

Among the Thorns • 98
Veronica Schanoes

Shelter • 132
Shaun Tan

A Poisoned Tale • 134
Rosario Ferré

Frau Trude • 146
Miwa Yanagi

The Good Mother • 148
Danielle Wood

Lupine • 156
Nisi Shawl

Still Rather Fond of Red • 160
Nalo Hopkinson

Selkie Stories Are for Losers • 162
Sofia Samatar

Bare Bones • 171
Joellyn Rock

The Master of Nottingham's Daughter • 200
Susanna Clarke

Sources and Credits • 209
Works Consulted and Further Readings • 211
About the Authors, Artists, and Editors • 217

Introduction

Cristina Bacchilega and Jennifer Orme

As WE MAKE OUR way deeper into the twenty-first century, fairy tales continue to interest and enchant general audiences, students, and scholars. In fact, these tales may be proliferating in popular culture in new ways since the turn of the century. It is admittedly risky to say there is something "new" in the production, reception, and critical discussion of fairy tales today as the multitude of versions and tales in history and across cultures virtually guarantees some form of repetition in purportedly new stories. That said, as speculative-fiction author Octavia Butler puts it in the epigraph to her unfinished *Parable of the Trickster*: "There is nothing new under the sun, but there are new suns" (in Canavan 2014). Not only are there new media platforms to tell and retell tales of magic and wonder, but there are new creators and adapters who engage, from varied locations and desires, with the genre as a vital and transformative site for reimagining a future that is both just and sustainable. This anthology assembles a small sampling of wonder tales and images that put pressure on and reanimate the genre from perspectives that are not accounted for in its mainstream iterations; as such, these twenty-first-century wonder tales do the double work of "inviting interruptions."

Fairy tales are often disparaged as "just" for children, or "just" light reading for white women, or "just" fantasy entertainment that should not be taken too seriously; or they are "just" hopelessly outdated. Ironically, these easy dismissals point to how the fairy tale is a particularly potent genre for carrying ideology. Fairy tales are "just" in so many ways that they easily slip under the radar, and because they are so often repeated, even if with variations, their messages tend to become naturalized. Not only are many of these naturalized expectations and assumptions being more rigorously and publicly questioned in the twenty-first century, the proliferation of fairy-tale texts of all kinds and in all mediums, created by a diverse population of artists who refuse to be ignored or "justed" out of the conversation, is providing ways to actively interrupt the workings of hegemonic or normative fairy-tale ideologies. These "new" tales invite us to exchange the well-trodden paths of fairy-tale forests for threads of connection across webs of wonder.

Quite possibly, the most common discussions about fairy tales since the 1970s, both academic and public, touch upon the representation of women and femininity. When Jack Zipes's *Don't Bet on the Prince: Contemporary Feminist Fairy Tales in North America and England* first appeared in 1987, it was a breath of fresh air, sampling stories by Margaret Atwood, Angela Carter, Anne Sexton, Tanith Lee, Jane Yolen, and others who were in different ways questioning and playing with dynamics of gender, genre, and power in classic fairy tales. Anthologies of the 1990s followed suit, widening the field of fairy-tale revisioning further in Ellen Datlow and Terry Windling's fairy-tale series with, for example, *Snow White, Red Blood* (1995) and *Black Swan, White Raven* (1997) and in Kate Bernheimer's collection *Mirror, Mirror, on the Wall: Women Writers Explore Their Favorite Fairy Tales* (1998). And in the twenty-first century so far, English-language edited collections of "new fairy tales" include Bernheimer's *Brothers & Beasts: An Anthology of Men on Fairy Tales* (2007) and her literary anthology *My Mother She Killed Me, My Father He Ate Me: Forty New Fairy Tales* (2010); Stephen Jones's horror *Faerie Tales: Stories of the Grimm and Gruesome* (2013); Sandra Beckett's *Revisioning Red Riding Hood around the World: An Anthology of International Retellings* (2014); Paula Guran's *Once Upon a Time: New Fairy Tales* (2013) and *Beyond the Woods: Fairy Tales Retold* (2016); Dominik Parisien and Navah Wolfe's *Starlit Wood: New Fairy Tales* (2016), which gathers retellings of individual tales; and the collected volume *Grim, Grit, and Gasoline: Dieselpunk & Decopunk Fairy Tales* (2019). This is by no means a comprehensive list, but it suggests in Guran's words that if "fairy tales are transformative . . . the stories themselves transform and evolve even as new ones are invented" (2016, 4).

Contemporary fairy tales continue to transform. While other collections bring the renewal of the genre to readers' attention and/or continue to foreground gender as its foundational trapping, our poetics as editors identifies intersectionality as crucial to the genre's contemporary transformation: an intersectional approach that does not center our attention on gender alone, even when creative adapters may be primarily women, but points us toward the active speculation and awe inspired by the wonder tale rather than the magical enchantment enacted upon audiences by the mainstream fairy tale. Complementing the work of other collections, then, our anthology boldly gathers such inviting interruptions and showcases the variety of their intersectional and wondrous interventions.

In the internet age, more readers than ever are aware of discussions of gender oppression and realize that traditional tales and Disney films are not as "innocent" of ideology as we may like to believe from our childhood memories. Many of these readers and viewers are intrigued with the "darker" elements of fairy tales that pervade contemporary popular culture and listicles that shout clickbait headlines such as "You'll Never Believe What Your Favorite Fairy Tales Are REALLY About!," "8 Creepy Dads in Your Favorite Fairy Tales!," or "Get Ready to Lose Your Childhood: Here Are 10 Terrifying Relationship Fails of Disney Princesses!!!" Less often, however, are we exposed to new tales that directly address contemporary issues in nuanced and intersectional ways. Audiences need to actively seek out complex interventions into the genre. This book hopes to assist in that search. Overall, this collection conceives of interventions in fairy-tale culture quite broadly but is aimed at showcasing how some contemporary verbal and visual artists shake up the fairy tale's more traditional or normative expectations and take up the genre's offer to think up and explore alternatives in the twenty-first century.

Twenty-first-century wonder tales respond to older tales and traditions in light of contemporary and located interests, desires, and concerns. All readers—students, instructors, "general audiences" (a misnomer if ever there was one)—experience art in specific contexts. Our readers are, like us, living in various versions of a cultural and political "now" in the Globalized West. We are all aware of and, to one degree or another, familiar with current concerns of, in no particular order, identity; visibility and voice; invisibility and silence; surveillance; violence of many types; policing of bodies and forms of sexual expression; trauma and its many sources; who gets to tell what story in which context, who listens, and who is believed; drastic and sudden changes to social fabrics caused by the COVID-19 pandemic; and the great social divides on political and economic spectrums. We take it as a given that the mass media, social media, subcultural groups, and cultural institutions (such as schools, universities, and art galleries) all have vested interests in influencing our assumptions and expectations around these issues. We also take it as a given that the stories we tell ourselves have the potential to naturalize some positions through repetition, but interruptions to those repetitions also have the ability to contest easy and simplistic assumptions and to offer complex responses, if not absolute solutions, to the issues we experience today.

Inviting Interruptions

Invitations may be, as all stories are, polite requests for attention or time. But an invitation also implies a calling forth, providing the occasion for an action or event; in this way, a tale or an image might invite you to enter a different world or worldview. There is also a seductive aspect to any invitation; to be inviting is to allure, entice, and attract with glittering edges, enchanting language, and delightful surprises. And, of course, an invitation is only the offer. You must accept and participate for the anticipation of the invitation to be fulfilled, whether it be for good or ill. Unlike invitations, which bring to mind etiquette and polite interest, *interruptions*, we are told, are rude, impertinent, and selfish. But sometimes, to survive, to be heard, to put a stop—temporarily or more permanently—to an event, speech, structure, or problem that has already been going on too long, an interruption is exactly what is needed to change the subject or stop everything in its tracks.

Our title weaves the two actions together to make them do double duty: inviting interruptions are engaging disturbances that ask us to stop and rethink in new ways. But, then again, to invite interruptions is also to make oneself vulnerable to interrogation, to resistance. The strange situations, bold characters, and adorable creatures in this book are both alluring and arresting. These wondrous images and stories invite and provoke our imaginations while also interrupting and unsettling mainstream fairy-tale expectations.

Since transforming fairy tales into wonder tales calls for this active approach on the part of both artists and audiences, this anthology invites you as readers and viewers of these tales and images to also employ strategies of engagement that interrupt common misconceptions, received knowledges, and the kinds of limiting, exclusionary, or othering forces that can be at work within the best-known and popular-culture retellings of the genre itself.

The interruptions with which we invite you to engage in this anthology address the many ways intersectional issues play out in terms of environmental concerns as well as identity markers, such as race, ethnicity, class, gender, and disability, together with the forces that affect identity, such as nonnormative sexualities, addiction, educational opportunities and choices, abuses of power (familial and otherwise), political dispossession, religious oppression, and forms of internalized self-hatred caused by any number of external pressures. These forces have had a long-term role to play in the production and reception of fairy tales. But the interruptions in this book are, if not new, executed on different grounds and in the light of new suns. And within them we also find celebrations, whimsy, and beauty. This is important because our tales and images are selected to extend readers' pleasure as well. The invitations and interruptions these new tales offer encourage critical thinking about not only specific tales but the genre and received notions about fairy tales' relationships to lived experience. They invite us to imagine the world, not only the world of wonder and marvels but the world around us every day, differently. They invite us to see ourselves differently, interrupt complacency, and imagine Otherness. They may even have the power to temporarily and partially transform us into other kinds of Others.

In gathering these verbal and visual wonder tales, we are not only calling attention to their existence and interventions but hoping that the transformative potential of their invitations and interruptions will be further kindled by their appearing together and in juxtaposition to one another in one place. Our choices of texts and images are primarily led by our preferences as readers, teachers, and fairy-tale scholars. So, our first questions about a selection were always these: Do we both *like* it? Do we genuinely enjoy the tale and find depth enough to delve into it as well as reimagine its potential? Then came questions like, Do the stories and images we chose address different types of issues or similar ones in significantly divergent ways? Do we offer a range of voices both within the tales and of their makers in terms of gender, disability, ethnicity, sexuality, and cultural geography?

Wonder Tales

Just as Angela Carter said in the introduction to *The Old Wives' Fairy Tale Book* (1990), it is also true that in this anthology "fairies, as such, are pretty thin on the ground" (ix). But wonder abounds. It expands to fill in the spaces between the tales and the images and within the mind. "Wonder tale" is not simply another term for "fairy tale" in this collection. Rather, our privileging this umbrella term is meant to reactivate the wondrous dimension of the fully animated and in-flux storyworld of older fairy tales. Beings, objects, and events that elicit wonder populate the fairy-tale world, but, more so, its wondrous interventions and transformations extend possible ways for being and acting in the world. While magic enacts its power on us, perhaps as best visualized in the sparkling and upward-spiraling sartorial makeovers in Disney films, wonder is engendered in the acknowledgment that our powers are quite limited and, precisely because of that, exercising them to create better futures matters. Wonder tales in the Western tradition as well as other wonder genres across cultures offer possibilities for connecting or reconnecting with noncapitalist, nonhuman-centered ways of being in the world as well as for thinking through scenarios where emotional intelligence, kinship, justice, and difference make their mark on the future. Wonder tales cultivate our capacity to be humble and act humbly; as such, wonder is both the trigger and the product of transformation, ours and the world's. Wonder tales in the twenty-first century do not look nostalgically back to the past but ask questions, enact relationships, and build hope based on ways of being and knowing that are too often either dismissed or violently crushed in the twenty-first century, in the real world as well as in the sanctioned fantasy world of franchises.

In the Twenty-First Century

This last part of our title implies that our volume is a collection of images and texts published in English with*in* the twenty-first century. We like how the temporal phrase grounds the wonder tales we collected in the contemporary world while signaling how they reach into imagining and affecting the future. But like the texts and images we have chosen, we too are rule breakers, on occasion, and refuse to be held in absolute terms to including wonder tales only produced in the twenty-first century. We have included three late twentieth-century texts in part to underscore the ways that, culturally at least, the twenty-first century did not begin on the stroke of midnight, January 1, 2000. We see these tales as fitting well with the interventions that the more recent anthologized texts make. In fact, they might be seen as "seeds" that have only fully germinated in the twenty-first century cultural context, which has the language and conceptual understanding to recognize and cultivate them in ways that were still nascent at the end of the last century.

Rosario Ferré's story, "El cuento envenenado," was published in its original Spanish in 1985 and in its English translation first by the author and Diana Vélez in 1991 as "A Poisoned Tale" and again the following year as "The Poisoned Story" in Ferré's English-language collection *The Youngest Doll*. Emma Donoghue's *Kissing the Witch* was published in 1997 and David Kaplan's short film *Little Red Riding Hood* also first appeared in 1997. What matters to us is that they all read aptly as wonder tales in the twenty-first century. Ferré's "A Poisoned Tale" demonstrates the power and dangers of gossip, rumor, and even "fake news" in times of sociopolitical upheaval and has yet to be read widely in English. Emma Donoghue and David Kaplan are probably more recognizable in fairy-tale circles, but Donoghue's cognitively different narrator in "The Tale of the Cottage" and Kaplan's transbiological wolf have yet to be widely read for a more intersectional queerness.

This book is also the product of limitations, some we imposed and others we had to contend with. We decided to stay with prose narratives and comics, no poetry or drama. The publication's formats, hard-copy book and e-book, meant still images only, with the experimental exception of an online link to one short film; video games, board games, role-playing games, music, performance, or other cultural products do not readily fit between the pages of a book. In addition, the need to acquire publishing permissions for world rights in English meant that some art and stories we would have liked to include, and some translations, were beyond our budget constraints.

We raise the issue of budget not as an excuse to cover for lacunae—this is a small volume by design—but to call attention to the economic, material reality of creating a book that includes the creative labor of a number of contributors in collaboration with the editors. In a culture that places a premium on the value of cultural products but not on the labor that produces them, it behooves us to raise the topic rather than ignore it. The book you are reading is only possible because of the very generous creative people who agreed to allow us to include their work within it, who agreed to play a part in the project of "inviting interruptions."

Engaging with Wonder Tales in the Twenty-First Century

We could have turned to some other alliterative terms to group these wonder tales and wondrous images: *interventions, interrogations, insubordinations, transgressions*. But the mix of pleasure and curiosity that an invitation can provide with the discomfort and excitement that may come from an interruption seems best to fit how fairy tales and other wonder tales appeal to audiences as *both* entertainment and knowledge. The book has two sections. We start with "Inviting Interruptions" for texts and images that seem to suggest new ways of thinking; we then move on to "Interrupting Invitations," which features images and texts that appear to us to be a little more explicit in their use of wonder to intervene in the assumed "innocence" of fairy tales.

Interspersed throughout the book are wondrous or marvelous images from the visual arts: drawing, painting, photography, porcelain and paper sculpture, film, and mixed media. You will note the majority of the images are not illustrations of specific tales. Rather, each of these images is a stand-alone creative piece that we recognize as embodying a quality of the wonder tale, if not always an explicit reference. In other words, these images provoke us to see and think with wonder and across a multimedia fairy-tale web.

For instance, Nalo Hopkinson's mixed media *Still Rather Fond of Red* refers visually and textually to her story "Riding the Red," her dramatic monologue "Red Rider," and the fairy tale "Little Red Riding Hood," but it is not an illustration of any of those per se (see Bacchilega 2013, 26). Just like the stories and comics, these artworks are very much a part of the fairy-tale web. We encourage you to discover threads that link the individual images, as well as that connect the images and our verbal texts, and to draw upon intertexts available to you beyond this book. In doing so, you too are participating in weaving the web.

Each tale is followed by brief notes, reading questions, and publication information. Our notes follow the stories because we want them to add to *your* own first impressions rather than influencing them beforehand. For the artwork we have a different take. Preceding each image are notes and questions for contemplation when taking in the image; these questions are meant as starting points that, from our perspectives, allow for attending to the image's invitation and interruption. You will, of course, read the book in the way you want, and perhaps not linearly at all, but we chose this structure to encourage and inform a pleasurable and critically curious reading practice for thinking with wonder tales.

In our editors' notes, we sometimes quote the author or artist; these are comments that contributors offered to us about their works during our process of putting this collection together; because the comments were intended specifically for this volume, no published source is given. At the end of the book you will find a Sources and Credits section that lists each story or artwork alphabetically by the creator's last name; there you will find copyright and previous publication information for each work. Following this is the Works Consulted and Further Readings list. It includes critical resources, and we hope that your curiosity will have been whetted enough to check some of them out. The About the Authors, Artists, and Editors' section closes the book with brief entries that will give you additional information about any of the creators you may like to learn more about.

Editors' Notes

Our notes, as you will see, do not necessarily move toward specific interpretations. Rather, we take our cue from the authors and artists and look to nonrealistic stories as vital resources for being in the world and enacting change in it. Agreeing with the Michi Saagiig Nishnaabeg scholar, poet, and artist Leanne Betasamosake Simpson that theory "in its most basic form is simply an explanation for why we do the things we do" (39), we recognize how these wonder stories function as theory: theories that envision ways for us to abide in the world and that challenge the status quo. Attending to how old and new wonder tales envision the lives and place of humans in the world does not require assigning a meaning to the tale but rather demands thinking through, questioning, and acting on what the tale affords us ethically, esthetically, philosophically—via the relationships, choices, and outcomes it maps out. This approach led us to another practice as editors who want to encourage thinking with tales of wonder. Our characters, tales, images, tellers, and artists offer no apologies for their difference. The invitations and interruptions they have produced come from, to one degree or another, the outside. Often outsiders are expected to explain themselves to the in-group; they are made to offer translations into the dominant language and culture. As compilers and editors, we too offer no explanations or translations to help readers along. To do so could be read as speaking for the artists or authors, and we do not wish to "step in" for them or to "smooth over" unfamiliarity, unknowing, or discomfort in the audience. Rather, our approach has been twofold: to trust our readers to divine information from context or research and to provide at least some intertextual links to other tales of wonder and enchantment.

In our notes, these links primarily take on two different forms. One is to tale types, according to which folklorists have classified folktales and fairy tales, identifying characteristic plot and thematic elements in variants and versions collected internationally in primarily pre-twentieth-century works. It is common for folklore scholars to identify these tale types by name and number from *The Types of International Folktales*. This index accounts for more than 2,000 tale types, 449 of which are fairy tales or tales of magic. For instance, "Red Riding Hood" is included in the subcategory "Supernatural Adversaries" and listed as ATU 333, with ATU standing in for Aarne-Thompson-Uther, the editors whose work is represented in the latest edition of the index. A tale like "Hansel and Gretel" is referred to as ATU 327A, grouped under the umbrella tale type "The Children and the Ogre" ATU 327 with other clusters of tales such as "The Brothers and the Ogres" ATU 327B.

While this is undoubtedly an imperfect and even biased system of classification, it works for us as shorthand to place a tale within an extended family of stories that share affinities across cultures and time, based on their enactment of analogous conflicts. Our pointing to a twenty-first-century wonder tale's connection to a tale type does not necessarily suggest the centrality of that intertextual relationship; rather, it gestures to the broader web in which tales and tellers respond to and interact with one another within and across traditions. Approaching a wonder tale in the twenty-first century as one-to-one adaptation is a gamble: can it really be referring back to one source text? Of Kelly Link's "Swans," we note that in their collection the Grimms alone published three different versions of "The Maiden Who Seeks Her Brothers" ATU 451, the tale type that Link clearly invokes; furthermore, the storyworld of "Swans" includes Rumpelstiltskin as fairy godfather, a king whose photo is in the newspaper, and a microwave, as well as a haunted bowling alley. Tale types for us then are not given sources but rather links in a web of relations, some given, some in the process of becoming, that ground the tale in specific social struggles and pursuits of the imagination.

The other intertextual link in our notes is to critical resources. As Vanessa Joosen convincingly detailed in *Critical and Creative Perspectives on Fairy Tales: An Intertextual Dialogue between Fairy-Tale Scholarship and Postmodern Retellings* (2011), the confluence of fairy-tale revisions and fairy-tale scholarship has been a productive force for rethinking the genre from the 1970s on. Thus, in showcasing the transformative creativity of wonder tales in the twenty-first century, this anthology invites us to think of them as emerging in connection with recent critical approaches to the genre that do not supersede gender considerations but reconstitute and reframe them. We hope our notes and critical links will productively inform your reading rather than didactically state how these images and texts *should* be read.

We agree with Pauline Greenhill and Kay Turner's emphasis on the role of the reader in responding to a tale's queer invitation:

> Readers are central to queer and trans folktale and fairy-tale theory. Regardless of their sex/gender or sexual orientation, they willfully turn away from the conventional. The written fairy tale impels the labor of dialogic interaction. Reader and text participate in a making of meanings similar to those associated with the oral precedents of teller and story. (2016, 846)

Thus, no one theoretical approach will or should work for all readers/viewers or stories, but we invite you to consider media studies, eco-criticism, disability studies, and Indigenous studies as relevant to your understanding of wonder tales. Studies like the *Routledge Companion to Media and Fairy-Tale Cultures* (Greenhill, Rudy, and Hamer 2018) offer invaluable and multiple insights from both media and fairy-tale studies to approach fairy-tale iterations and adaptations in the contemporary world. Sara Maitland's *Gossip from the Forest* (2013) offers just one model for thinking about how nature and storytelling are more intertwined than we normally think. Moreover, no matter where the wondrous image or story is set, its melding of human and animal or its blurring of rural, suburban, and urban spaces invites us to contemplate the ravages of human influence upon the planet and/or to imagine ways to heal our ecosystems. In thinking about how wonder tales and images can take the view of disability as "a cultural interpretation of human variation rather than an inherent inferiority, a pathology to cure or an undesirable trait to eliminate" (Garland-Thomson 2005, 1556), we look for ways a tale's "inviting interruption" might shift away from the pattern that Ann Schmiesing has noted is common in fairy tales, where "able-bodied protagonists are . . . contrasted with antagonists who exhibit or are punished with impairment" (2014, 1). Another productive link that informs our notes is to a critical understanding of various forms of the fantastic as offering opportunities for addressing issues of decolonization and self-determination in that, while Euro-American wonder tales are not to be confused with what Daniel Heath Justice calls "Indigenous wonderworks," both speculative genres participate in "imagining otherwise" as a "moral imperative" (2018, 142).

Our practice then is to make connections and to encourage you to connect with multiple, intersecting, and even contradictory reading strategies for approaching the tales and images in this anthology—and to suggest that collectively the wonder tales in this volume also call for new readings and transformative thinking.

We employ these reading approaches for both texts and images, but there are some additional strategies that we bring to visual wonder. The drawings, paintings, photographs, and sculptures engage with wonder in some similar and some different ways from how narratives do this. An aura of the marvelous, magical, and enchanting surrounds all of these images. Content also can be similar to that of a story: each image has a setting, even if it is a relatively plain background; human and nonhuman figures project personalities and emotions; we can imagine what has happened just before this moment or what will happen next. Nevertheless, we do not mean that every picture is a story. So while we certainly do not discourage reading narrative into the images, it isn't the only way to look at the wondrous images in this book.

These visual texts do not "support" or "expand upon" the written texts but rather are their own iterations of wonder. Just as we invite you to make connections between the tales in the book, we encourage the same with these images. Do any of them stand out to you as perhaps belonging to similar worlds as one of the stories? Do they remind you of other intertextual nodes on the fairy-tale web? Each image is quite distinct in style, form, and content from all of the others, and we have suggested some points of comparison in our notes, but are there other ways to put them in relation to one another?

Some people who consider themselves to be good book readers feel they don't know how to look at art; they are unsure of what they are *supposed* to see or do. They wonder in anxious tones, "But what does it *mean*?!?"—as though an image should have a single, unambiguous meaning that you should be able to understand all in one gulp. As with a story or a film, reading visual art takes time. Allow yourself to savor the experience of looking. Then again, you don't want to just sit there staring at a page feeling ¯_(ツ)_/¯. So allow us to suggest some aspects of visual art to take into consideration when pondering these wondrous images.

When you are not sure how to think about an image, you may begin with the deceptively simple question: *What am I looking at?* Literally take note(s). How you describe the image to yourself will tell you quite a bit about it. "I'm looking at a rock in the sky." Or, "I'm looking at a house with a rock hanging over it." Both describe the content of Shaun Tan's *Shelter*, but they privilege different aspects of it. Or you might say to yourself: "I'm looking at a book with pages cut out and made into objects." Or, "I'm looking at a girl and boy walking through the woods toward a cabin." Both are, again, correct, but the fact that one focuses on the form of the piece and the other on the subject tells us something about Su Blackwell's work and your response to it.

Another technique is to consciously follow your own gaze. Lines, light and shadow, space, forms, colors, and textures can draw the viewer's gaze in particular ways. Become aware of how your eyes move across the page. Unlike with reading English-language text (Joellyn Rock's "Bare Bones" being a partial exception that highlights the rule), when viewing images we are not stuck with a left to right, top to bottom eye movement that written/printed English demands. But that does not mean our gaze just flits about any old where. Images will provide you with gentle direction: pay attention to it, and you are likely to see more, and more clearly, than otherwise.

As in writing, music, and other art forms, there are a number of specific elements and principles of organization in visual art. You should not expect yourself to just "know" how to read an image. In what follows, we briefly discuss composition, color, texture, and the gaze, but you should also take into consideration line, shape, light and shadow, space, form, and the title of the work, as we do briefly in the Blackwell example below. In addition, the questions we raise for each image will also help focus your thinking with these tools.

Composition and Relationships

Composition is the placement of elements in relation to each other. Composition can balance or discombobulate. It provides rhythm and movement. It draws the eye. It is not the same as the content or subject of the piece. The content of Su Blackwell's *Once Upon a Time* would include the two child figures, trees, the cottage, a wolf, and the book/forest floor. How those elements are placed in relation to each other is an aspect of composition. The child figures are both closer to the front of the book/forest floor and larger than the house, and this tells us that the house is in the distance. They are also the "natural" starting place for our eyes to begin. The whole piece stands before a deep black background and is lit from the left, which also guides our gaze via the direction of the shadows. Direction and movement are guided by the lines of text on the children's bodies and the forms of the trees, which are all directed toward the right and back of the page. So, we read this sculpture as we would the book it is made from, left to right. The work's title is also a piece that ensures the image's cohesion: the fairy-tale links, and specifically the literary fairy-tale links, are the subject of this piece.

Color

Shaun Tan's *Shelter* and Shary Boyle's *Beast* are very different paintings. One is a landscape and the other a portrait. Nevertheless, they provide us a way in to talking about color. The backgrounds in each are on the blue spectrum, but they provoke different kinds of responses. In *Shelter*, this blue background is clearly the sky in the evening or early morning. How we read this sky—as the moments before night covers the land in darkness or as the stillness before the sun rises—will influence how we read the image. Is the blue behind Boyle's Beast also sky? Maybe, but it also seems possible that the blue here, with the halo around the Beast's head, is pure background; its function is to surround and not distract from the portrait's subject. Why blue then? How does this shade make one feel about the Beast? What if it were darker, as in the Tan image? This contrast shows us that we must also consider light and darkness, their cultural coding, and their effects upon color composition.

Texture

Textures are particularly important to sculpture and mixed-media material objects such as the smooth porcelain, lace, and fine thread of Boyle's untitled spider-woman and the plastic flowers and gems and paper cutout wolves atop a painted-over photograph in Nalo Hopkinson's *Still Rather Fond of Red*. If only we could reach through the pages of this book, we could feel each of these textures with our fingers. In contrast, the feathers of the birds and the soft fur of the animals in *Burdens, They Must Always Be Carried* and *Beast*, the rock's surface in *Shelter*, and the scratchy, dusty land of the world in *Birth of Commerce* all are conveyed by visible pencil or brush strokes; and yet we can imagine the feel of these too. The photograph *Frau Trude* contains a kaleidoscope of visual textures: the plush rug and rough wood; the damp, stained walls and the dry heat of the fire; the smooth skin of the girl and the wrinkled face/mask of the old woman. Like color, visual textures convey less literal meaning than they evoke sensual memory and, yes, "feelings." Imagine them as you view the images: rough, smooth, damp, dusty, and sharp all convey a wealth of information. Just as metafiction calls attention to the fictionality of a text, signs of the artist's hand, such as obvious brushstrokes or juxtapositions of material or style, draw attention to the constructed nature of the art object.

The Gaze

In relation to our solo figures in particular, we must also consider the gaze, meaning who is looking at whom? Hopkinson's woman in red and Boyle's Beast both look out at us, their expressions enigmatic and not giving anything away. But certainly, there is much to think about as we gaze back into their eyes. The gaze is related to power: who is doing the looking and who is being looked at? When the look is reciprocal, as with these two, we cannot avoid our relationship with the subject. But a human or human-like figure who is looking elsewhere or whose eyes are closed is different. This figure often has less subjectivity, becomes more of an object of our gaze or a type than a figure who engages with us. But where and in what manner the figure looks away also matters. What is the difference between looking down and away from looking up or toward an object in the distance? It is often through the figure's gaze that we learn about relationships and emotional states.

It is wise to also take in one's position as the gazer, as it were. Our subject positions and identities inform how we see and even what we perceive and what we deem important or unimportant. The fact that the images appear in this book and were chosen by scholars implicitly provides them with value in this context. Note that we chose a range of images in different media, from very different artists at different places in their careers and geocultural locations. Some of these pieces hang in important museums or galleries, others have appeared in other fairy-tale studies books, and some are more personal works. And one was created when the artist was just nine years old. What are your expectations when viewing these images in a collection of wonder tales in the twenty-first century? Do they provoke you to see wonder tales differently?

Finally, we acknowledge and ask you to briefly consider the limitations of presenting artwork in the pages of a book. The most obvious loss is to sculpture. We lose information and entire perspectives when three-dimensional objects are flattened to two dimensions and a single angle of vision. But it is not only the sculptures that are distorted by the medium; all of the images, no matter the choice of materials or the size of the original object, appear here on flat, glossy paper or a flat, glossy screen, and all of them now appear the same size as this book rather than as they do in "real life." And, regardless of how suggestive the stills from *Little Red Riding Hood* are, to experience Kaplan's short film, you must activate the Vimeo link to it. We have had to accept these limitations and have deemed them acceptable, if not ideal, because we are excited to share these images with you.

We have spent more time on reading strategies that apply to visual wonder because, while the dominance of visual culture in the twenty-first century is indisputable, the fairy tale and other wonder genres are usually conceived of as narratives, and foremost as verbal narratives first, no matter what their current medium. Regardless of how new you are to these reading strategies, we invite you to think with the images and tales in this collection. We gathered them together to underscore how their intersectionality and appeal to wonder inform them as interruptions of mainstream fairy-tale normativity and as invitations to reimagine a future that is both just and sustainable. To accept the invitations and interruptions of these wonder-tale artists, you need only read on. . . .

Part I

Inviting Interruptions

Notes on *Once Upon a Time* by Su Blackwell (2016)

The lights of the story house are on: Who is invited?

THE SUBJECT OF BLACKWELL's book sculpture is probably the most fairy tale-ish of our collection. It is called *Once Upon a Time*, after all. The image of children approaching a cottage in the woods recalls early twentieth-century illustrations for children's books and as such is familiar and comforting. It is the materials that are surprising and intriguing. The image inspires delight in the viewer, but why is that? What is it about a familiar fairy-tale image sculpted from the pages of a book, indeed the whole book, that is so delightful? As pleasing as it is, is this image entirely light-hearted? Is this a cozy or cold environment? A scene of innocent happy homecoming or danger? The title might give us a clue.

The pure black background creates infinite space behind and around the scene like a night sky. It focuses attention on the action, but it is also like a void. How does the negative space behind the sculpture influence the feeling of the scene? And what of the light in the cottage window? What does the yellow glow tell us about the house?

Notice the wolf in the far right corner, its posture and position. And the owl flying out of the forest and the books in the tree branches: what roles do they play in this "once upon a time" tale?

As Blackwell explains it, "Fairy tales and folklore are rich subjects." She is "often drawn to the figure of a lone girl, in a vulnerable setting like a forest, expressing the wonders and fears of childhood. Choosing characters that are in flight or on the verge of discovering something adds urgency and potential to the scenes. Often a small light source illuminates the diorama, creating shadows, which add to the psychological intensity of the scene." Let's not forget that, cut out with a scalpel, the book sculpture also uses the words on the page to "create drama and atmosphere." Blackwell says, "I employ this delicate, accessible medium and use irreversible, destructive processes to reflect on the precariousness of the world we inhabit and the fragility of our life, dreams and ambitions." We think we know this story; we think we know what will happen next; but do we *really*?

Once Upon a Time

Su Blackwell

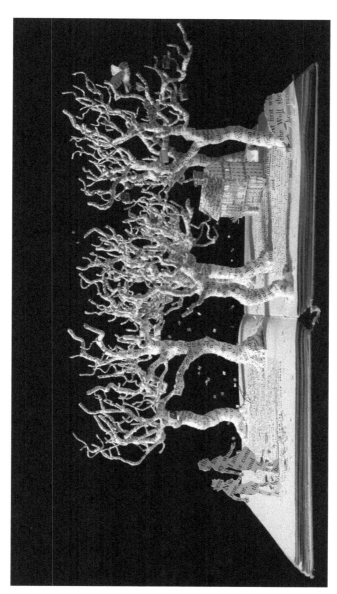

Su Blackwell, *Once Upon a Time*, 2016, paper, 50 x 300 x 220 mm.

The Tale of the Cottage

Emma Donoghue

I ONCE HAD BROTHER that mother say we were pair of hands one fast one slow. I once had father he got lost in woods. I once had mother.

Huntman had wonderful beard. Let me and brother come too into woods with gun. Brother let me help little house of branches till broke and he push away.

Things changed after we held broom behind our hut and they jumped. Things went sour milk in churn all forgotten. Sky went far off and leaves went *scrish scrish*. Too cold for snow, say mother. Put brother and me sleeping with chickens not annoy him.

One night hit her harder *whap whap* so her voice went big into rafters woke chickens say, Curse you.

Then on no luck for huntman. Means no meat for us. Brother say mother eat her words. I see only nuts and old bread. She say, Sorry sorry. She put last drops holy water on huntman gun. Still no luck. One night he come home snowed like pine. Next day lie in smelly furs all day bellyache. Bang fist on wall angels witness. Say, How can we feed your children when we can't even feed ourselves?

Moonrise I holding chicken for warm hear him through wall. They talking small not like *whap whap*. She say, It's their home. He say, What's a home with a bare table?

Later after sounds like running I hear him say, Pick one. You can't feed two birds with a single stone. The little one's no earthly use not right in the head.

After mother cry and gone quiet like sleeping I hold my head like apple shake it for see what sick. Sound all right. Never can tell.

Morning huntman let us come too into woods for rabbits brother and me. I dance like appledust. Trees come thicker round till no sky left. He tell

Emma Donoghue, "The Tale of the Cottage," in *Kissing the Witch*, 1997.

brother go look at snare. He sit me behind tree for game. Make little fire give bread say, No sound good girl.

I suck bread soft and wait for them come back. Cold. Sound like crows. Good girl. Want home. Cry.

Lots hours later fire gone small. Hear feet think maybe lost father coming with acorn teeth and ivy where eyes were. Try run fall on root.

Brother it was whistling. I call out. Don't cry little nut I found you I'll bring you home, he say. Twice as old and ten times as clever. I put legs round waist and hold on.

Hut shine light. I feared. Stop at door. Seem like dark inside. Brother say, Home again little hen. Lift latch mother cry cry like happy. Huntman angered say, Why did you get yourself lost you halfwit girl. He not remember game. No food on table. Mother face wet salty.

Night they talking low again. Brother sleeping. I push nosy chicken away put ear on wall. Huntman say, You want to watch them starve? You want to wait till the cramps buckle them up? Mother cry Nonononono like punched out. He soft voice now say, Don't take on so woman. Don't fight fate. You can have more when times are good again.

I think of having more more food more fire more shoes till sleep.

Morning mother not get up. I want into furs with. Huntman say Woods again today.

Walk lots hours. Where trees thickest he make small fire say, Rest now like good children while I go deeper in to chop wood for a while.

Brother want to go with. Huntman say, Look after your sister or I'll beat the skin off you.

We wait. Lots hours later trees so thick no light at all outside fire. Sound like wolves. Fire tiny. Brother go for wood I cry so he come back curl round me. Warm fart. Then no fire. He say, Don't worry half-pint I'll bring you home as soon as it gets light.

Wake all covered snow cold laughing. Throw ball brother. Home home home like song loud through snow. When brother wake face like old bread. Say he can't find way when all white. I say, Follow me dance like snow home to mother.

Snow thicker feels like no feet no hands no noses. Brother follow me cry try hide it.

Get dark again. Brother go up tree see wide round. Slither down say, There's a light, little loaf. We walk walk walk. When ground dip all dark again I not cry. I not cry. Brother find light again.

When we see up close dazzle I think morning. When we see cottage I think dreaming. Windows shine like sugar walls brown like gingerbread.

Brother say, Home. Not home. Then brother say, Come. I feared. I known wormy apples with shiny skin. I seen rotted teeth behind handsome beard. Brother go knock knock.

When door open I think mother then no. Young. Woman say, What brought you here? No words from brother no words from me. Woman say, Stop here with me tonight and no harm will touch you.

Bed so soft I think hot snow.

She wake me blowing on nose. I tell her walls gingerbread. She say, And the door is toffee and the chimney is licorice and the beds are chocolate. I not know words. Laugh anyway. She make pancakes two each me her and brother. Her eyes red like crying. Face smooth like girl.

We can stay if work. She know all that grow in woods. She know how talk rabbits into big cage in kitchen so never starving. Brother chop logs laugh like grown man ask kiss get slap. She teach me roll dough for baking into shapes of woman tree star.

Only bad nights. Wrap round brother like bread before oven. Very quiet say home like would get me there.

One night brother gone out bed. I look sugar crystal window. No steps in moon snow all swallowed up. Too feared to cry. Then woman scream like mother old nightmares say, Get out of my bed. Brother fall on floor. Say, Just for a warm. She hit something. Brother say, Lonely.

Morning woman wake me stroking say, Bonny red cheeks what will we do? I look brother out axing wood. Bake bread, say I. She laughing.

Days on days go by snow shrinks to nothing. I dance like white flowers pushing through cold headfirst. Brother has hair chin instead of smile. Woman make him chop all trees died in winter till hands red like robins. I pick moldy seeds from good.

One day we baking brother walk in call her name I never heard lift her skirt behind. Woman no scream this time. Put skinning knife to chin make drop of blood till he get in rabbit cage. He laughing as she chain it. I laughing I feared. He shake cage. It hold fast.

Night I cold so woman let me in with her. Make like she not hear brother shouting. I say, He cold. She say, Not for long.

I sleep warm between arms. Wake up understanding she go to skin him like rabbit.

Slip into kitchen heart banging like churn. Brother sleep till I find key in drawer open chain put hand over mouth.

He climb out stretching. Come on, he whisper. You're safe with me little nut.

Not safe anywhere.

He shake my head to wake it. Don't you understand? Now the snow is gone I can find our way home to mother.

No, I crying quiet. Home not home if mother not mother.

But you can't stay here, she's mad, she's got a knife.

Take my chances, I say.

He look for long while then nod. I give him fresh bake loaf shape like me. Tell him no come back with huntman gun. No come back ever.

I watch him run through trees. Snow begin falling cover tracks. I lean head in door wait for woman to wake.

Notes on "The Tale of the Cottage" by Emma Donoghue (1997)

> An often silenced voice interrupts notions of who gets to tell their own story.

This "Hansel and Gretel" tale (ATU 327A, included in the larger tale type "The Children and the Ogre" ATU 327) invites us into the mind of an unnamed girl with cognitive difference. Where Gretel in the Grimms' and other traditional versions of the tale is the one who saves Hansel and does so thanks to her quick wit, this narrator and her brother are characterized by their mother as a "pair of hands one fast one slow," and yet it is the girl, not her brother or an authoritative external narrator, who tells the tale. It is still fairly unusual for fictional stories to be narrated by characters with nonnormative cognition, that is, by characters who may be considered developmentally delayed or challenged, yet here we as readers are challenged to understand the narrator's world from her perspective and in her language.

David T. Mitchell and Sharon L. Snyder's (2001) concept of "narrative prosthesis" is a twofold artistic device: it accounts for the pervasiveness of disability in literary narrative and acts as a material metaphor for something else. The flatness of characters in fairy tales often means that disability becomes metaphoric shorthand for villainy. Otherwise, disability is imposed on a character as punishment or "cured" as a reward for good behavior. As Ann Schmiesing says, disability as metaphor for something else is "a form of erasure, because it abstracts the disabled individual and her or his impaired body" (2014, 13). Another common concern with disability in literature, the naming and categorizing of difference according to medical classifications, speaks primarily to and for nondisabled subjectivities, rather than exploring impairment from the character's perspective and experience (13).

We do not need a medical diagnosis to immediately recognize the difference in this narrator's voice as compared to the other first-person narrators in Emma Donoghue's *Kissing the Witch* or even to companion narrators in this book. Her voice is unusual, but her cognitive difference is neither the cause of her and brother's ills nor a sign of moral turpitude, stupidity, or vacuity. Like the other narrators in Donoghue's collection, she tells her story without apology, explanation, or translation for reader comfort or ease. Instead, we must learn to understand her. She does not conform to our linguistic expectations but speaks for herself, and no other character interrupts or "explains" what is "really" going on for her.

As we see with other tales in this anthology, first-person narration and viewpoint can create a feeling of intimacy between narrator and reader. The experience of reading from the "I" perspective may even produce the illusion that we are experiencing the events of the tale ourselves, rather like a virtual reality mind game. This illusion breaks down, of course, the moment we begin to think about it, but while we are immersed in the tale, the feeling of closeness prevails. First-person narration then is another way to ensure that disabled storytellers are neither erased nor spoken for; rather, the subjective "I" both refuses objectification and becomes the center to which nondisabled perspectives are different and marginal. And yet, the narrator of "The Tale of the Cottage" is a fictionalized character; the author, Emma Donoghue, creates her speech for her. Is this appropriation? How are we to think about cognitively typical authors representing the voices of those who are so often left out of the conversation?

Of course, there is much more to this tale than its narration. Gender and power are crucial to the ways characters interact with each other. Brother is a particularly interesting character; he is neither entirely a "good guy" nor a simple villain, and the narrator's choice at the end of the story shows her own complex understanding of his nature as well as the limited possibilities available to her in a world where "Home not home if mother not mother." Nevertheless, she asserts her autonomy and right to determine her own future. What does her final decision tell us about the kind of world and the kinds of relationships she imagines for herself?

Notes on *Untitled* by Shary Boyle (2004)

Weaving an invitation to the fairy-tale web.

BOYLE'S UNTITLED SPIDER-WOMAN LOOKS down and away from us in this photograph, but what if we were able to see her in person, as it were, in her full three dimensions? And in any case, where are her other eyes looking? Is she looking back at you, even as she looks away? Who controls the gaze if the subject has eight eyes and can look in multiple directions at once, while we can see her only from one angle at a time?

Portraits and landscapes count as "art" with a capital *A*, but just as tales of magic have traditionally been dismissed from the annals of great literature, porcelain figurines of pretty white women in pretty lace dresses have been dismissed as mere ornamental knickknacks for working-class or middle-class mantles. This untitled spiderlike woman, sitting on her stump and weaving her pentacle web, is very much part of that tradition. And yet she embodies a number of interruptions to it.

What are we to make of the pentacle she has woven with her web? The pentacle is a symbol of protection: whom or what does she protect? Arachnids have had mixed reception by humans, and images of them carry different meanings. What do this figure's spiderlike aspects tell us about her or about our notions of beauty? The way she holds her thread in her many hands is very similar to a child's game of cat's cradle. Does that make her childish? Or might it indicate something about girls' and women's pastimes that we dismiss, as we do fairy tales and porcelain figurines?

Untitled

Shary Boyle

Shary Boyle, *Untitled*, 2004, lace-draped porcelain, thread, and china paint, 27 x 24 x 18 cm. National Gallery of Canada, Ottawa. Photo: NGC.

Shary Boyle, *Sans titre*, 2004, dentelle de porcelaine, fil et peinture à porcelaine, 27 x 24 x 18 cm. Musée des beaux-arts du Canada, Ottawa. Photo: MBAC.

Swans

Kelly Link

MY NAME IS EMMA Bear, and I am eleven years old. I live on Black Ankle Road beside the Licking River. I live in a palace. My father is a king. I have a fairy godfather. This summer I read *The True Confessions of Charlotte Doyle* and learned how to make blue dye from a flower called woad. I have six brothers. My mother is dead. I'm in the seventh grade. My father remarried this summer. My favorite class is home ec. I love to sew. I make all my own clothes. My mother taught me how to sew. I can also knit, crochet, and quilt.

Yesterday my stepmother pointed her pinkie finger at my brothers and turned them all into swans. They were being too noisy. I'm never too noisy. I don't talk at all.

This year I was failing choir. I opened my mouth to sing, and nothing came out. I hadn't been able to say a word since my mother died. In my other classes, it was okay. Homework was okay. Math was okay, and English. Art was okay. I could write down answers on the black board. I carried around a pad of paper and a pen. You'd be surprised how often you don't actually have to say anything. Mostly if I just nodded, it was okay. But choir doesn't work that way. You can't sing by writing on a pad of paper. But nothing came out of my mouth when I opened it.

Last year I had lots of friends. This year I didn't have any. What happened in between? My mother died. I stopped talking. No more friends. Really, I've been too busy to have friends, I suppose.

When I first stopped talking, no one noticed. Not until Mom's funeral, when we were all supposed to stand up and say something. I stood up, but nothing came out when I opened my mouth. First my father sent me to see a psychologist. I just sat on her couch. I looked at pictures, and wrote down

Kelly Link, "Swans," in *A Wolf at the Door and Other Retold Fairy Tales*, edited by Ellen Datlow and Terri Windling, 2000.

what they looked like. They all looked like flowers, or birds, or schnauzers. Then my fairy godfather came to the palace.

My fairy godfather is a little man with red hair. His name is Rumpel-stiltskin. He was a friend of my mother's. He'd been away on business for a few months—he'd missed the funeral. His eyes were all red, and he cursed a lot. He'd loved my mother a lot. He sat with me for a long time, brushing my hair, and patting my hand.

Finally he said, "Well, you certainly don't have to talk until you want to. Keffluffle. Excuse my French. What a mess this is, Emma."

I nodded. I wrote down on my pad of paper, *I miss her*.

"Fudge, I do, too," my godfather said. "Excuse the French."

He tapped me on the nose gently. "You know your father is going to have to get married again."

I wrote, *I'll have an evil stepmother?*

"That evil stepmother stuff is just a pile of horsepucky," he said, "excuse me. It's just baloney. Whoever he marries will be just as afraid of you and your brothers as you are of her. You keep that in mind."

To my father, he said, "Emma just needs a piece of time. When she needs to say something, she'll open her mouth and say it."

He hugged my father, and he hugged me. He said, "I have a commission for you, Emma. I have a godchild who is going to a ball. All she's got to wear are rags. She needs a fancy dress. Not pink, I think. It wouldn't match. She's got lovely red hair, just like me. Maybe a nice sea-foam green. Right down to the ankles. Lots of lace."

I wrote, *When do you need it?*

"When she turns seventeen," he said. "That's not for a bit. I'll send you her measurements. Okay?"

Okay, I wrote and kissed him good-bye.

When my mother was young, she was famous. She could spin straw into gold. Her name was Cleanthea. A year ago, she went jogging in the rain, and then she caught cold, and then she died.

My mother's quilts were famous. Famous quilts have their own names. She made crazy quilts, which are just bits of scraps sewn together, and then decorated and embroidered with fancy stitches—wheat stitches, briar stitches, flowers, birds, little frogs, and snowflakes. She made Log Cabin quilts and Wedding Ring quilts, and she also made up her own patterns. Her quilts had names like Going Down to the River and Snakes Fall in Love and Watering the Garden. People paid hundreds of dollars for them. Every bed in the castle has a quilt on it that my mother made.

Each of my brothers had a quilt that my mother made just for them. She made my brother Julian a *Star Wars* quilt, with X-Wing Fighters and Death Stars. She made my oldest brother an Elvis quilt. Up close it's just strips and patches of purple cloth, all different patterns. But when you back away, you can see that all the bits of different colors of purple make up Elvis's face—his eyes, his lips, his hair. For my youngest brother, she made a Cats Eat Birds quilt. She sewed real feathers into the cats' mouths, and little red cloth-patch birds into their stomachs.

She never finished my quilt. We were working on it together. I'm still working on it now. I don't really want to finish it. In fact, it's gotten a little bit big for my bed. When I spread it out, it's almost as big as a swimming pool. Eventually, it will fill up my whole room, I guess. Every night now I sleep on a different bed in the castle, under a different quilt. I pretend that each quilt is a quilt that I have never seen before, that she has just finished making, just for me.

I should tell you about my father and my brothers. I should also tell you about my stepmother. My father is very tall and handsome, and also very busy with things like affairs of state and cutting ribbons at the grand openings of grocery stores and presenting awards to writers and musicians and artists and also going to soccer games and football games so that photographers can take his picture. That was how he met my stepmother. He was at the zoo, which had just been given a rare species of bird. He was supposed to be photographed with the bird on his shoulder.

When he arrived, however, the keepers were distraught. The bird had disappeared. Even worse, a naked woman had been found wandering around the grounds. She wouldn't say who she was, or where she came from. No one could find her clothes. The keepers were afraid that she might be a terrorist, or an anarchist, come to blow up the zoo, or kill my father. It would be bad publicity for everyone.

"Nonsense," my father said. He asked to meet the woman. The zookeepers protested, saying that this was a bad idea. My father insisted. And so my father's picture appeared in the papers, holding out his hand to a woman dressed in a long white T-shirt and a pair of flip-flops that one of the keepers got out of the lost and found. The picture in the paper was blurry, but if you looked closely you could see the look in my father's eyes. He looked like he'd been hit on the head. He looked like he was falling in love, which he was.

The woman, my stepmother, looked small and fragile in the photograph, like a Christmas tree ornament. She had long, feathered hair. The T-shirt hung on her like a tent, and the flip-flops were too big for her.

We still don't know much about my stepmother. She was from a faraway country, we thought, because she had a slight but unrecognizable accent. She was a little bit cross-eyed, like a Siamese cat. She never brushed her hair. It stuck up in points behind her ears, like horns. She was very beautiful, but she hated noise. My brothers made too much noise. That's why she turned them into swans.

They came and stood on the lawn this morning, and I fed them dried corn and bits of burnt buttered toast. They came back early, while my stepmother was still sleeping. They honked at me very quietly. I think they were afraid if they were loud, she'd turn them into something even worse. Snails, maybe, or toads.

Some of the other girls at school thought I was lucky to have so many brothers. Some of them said how handsome my brothers were. I never really thought so. My brothers used to pull my hair and short-sheet my bed, and they never helped with my homework unless I gave them my allowance. They liked to sit on top of me and tickle me until I cried. But when my mother died, they all cried. I couldn't.

My brothers' names are George, Theodore, Russell, Anthony, William, and Julian. George is the oldest. Theodore is the nicest. Anthony is the tallest. Russell has freckles, and he is allergic to milk. William and Julian are twins, and two years younger than me. They liked to wear each other's clothes and pretend that Julian was William, and William was Julian. The thing is, all of them look alike now that they're birds. They all look like twins.

My father told us that my stepmother didn't like noise. They got married at the beginning of the summer. We got to throw rice. We'd only seen my stepmother twice before—once in the newspaper picture, and once when my father brought her home for dinner. There were a lot of important people at that dinner. We ate in the kitchen, but afterward we stood in the secret passageway and spied through the painting that has the eyes cut out.

My future stepmother didn't eat much dinner, but she had three helpings of dessert. This is when I first became suspicious that she was magic—a witch, or else under an enchantment. Witches and people under spells, magic people, always have sweet tooths. My fairy godfather carries around sugar cubes in his pockets and stirs dozens of them in his coffee, or else just eats them plain, like a horse. And he never gets cavities.

When my father and stepmother came back from their honeymoon, we were all standing on the palace steps. We had all just had baths. The palace steps had just been washed.

My father and stepmother were holding hands. When they saw us, my stepmother let go of my father's hand and slipped inside the palace. I was holding up a big sign that said, welcome home, dad. There wasn't any room on the sign for stepmother.

"Hey," my brother George said, "what did you bring me?"

"Anthony stole my rocket launcher," Russell said. "It wasn't me," Anthony said, "it was Theodore."

"It was NOT me," Theodore said, and William and Julian said, "Emma made us brush our teeth every night."

Everyone began yelling. My father yelled loudest of all.

"I'd really appreciate it if you all tried to be quiet and didn't yell all at once. Your stepmother has a bad headache, and besides, she's very shy, and not at all used to loud children," he said, looking at my brothers. Then he looked at me. "Emma," he said, "are you still not talking?"

I took out my notepad and wrote *yes* on it. He sighed. "Does that mean 'yes, you are talking now,' or 'yes, you still aren't talking'?"

I didn't say anything. I just smiled and nodded. "Maybe you'd like to show your new stepmother around the castle," he said.

My stepmother was in the library, reclining on a sofa with a damp cloth over her eyes. I stood there for a bit, and then I tapped my foot some. She didn't move. Finally I reached down and touched her shoulder. Her eyelids fluttered.

I held up my pad of paper. I wrote, *I'm Emma. I don't talk.*

She sat up and looked at me. She wasn't very big. When she stood up, I bet that we would have been the same height, almost, except she was wearing pointy black shoes with tall heels to make her look taller.

I wrote, *Dad asked me to show you the castle.*

I showed her around the castle. I showed her the kitchen with the roasting spit that the dogs turn, and the microwave, and the coffeemaker. I showed her the ballroom, which is haunted, and the dungeon, which my father had converted into an indoor swimming pool and squash court, and I showed her the bowling alley, which is also haunted, and the stables, and the upstairs bathroom, which has modern plumbing. Then I took her to my mother's room. The quilt on the bed was Roses and Cabbages Growing Up Together, all pieced together from old green velvet hunting coats and rose-colored satin gloves.

My new stepmother sat down on the bed. She bounced experimentally, holding her head. She stared at me with her slightly crossed eyes. "A nice bed," she said in a soft, gravelly voice. "Thanks, Emma."

My mother made this quilt, I wrote. *Her quilts are very valuable. Please be careful when you are sleeping.* Then I left her there on my mother's bed. The next day she turned George into a swan. He was practicing his saxophone.

George is my father's heir. George doesn't want to be king. George wants to be a saxophonist in a heavy metal band. I was listening to him in the ballroom. He isn't very good yet, but he likes to have an audience. I sit and listen to him, and he pays me five dollars. He says someday it will be the other way round.

I was embroidering the back of a blouse with blue silk thread. I was trying to embroider a horse, but it looked more like a crocodile, or maybe a dachshund.

My stepmother had been swimming in the pool. She was still in her bathing suit. She came into the ballroom and left puddly footprints all over the waxed and polished black walnut floor. "Excuse me," she said. George ignored her. He kept on honking and tootling. He smirked at me. "Excuse me," our stepmother said, a little bit louder, and then she pointed her pinkie finger at him. She flicked her pinkie up at him, and he turned into a swan. The swan—George—honked. He sounded surprised. Then he spread out his wings and flew away through an open window.

I opened my mouth, but of course nothing came out. I stared at my stepmother, and she shrugged apologetically. Then she turned and left, still dripping. Later that afternoon when Anthony set off Russell's rocket over the frog pond, my stepmother turned him into a swan, too. I was up in the tree house watching.

You're probably wondering why I didn't tell someone. My dad, for instance. Well, for one thing, it was kind of fun. My brothers looked so surprised. Besides, at dinner no one missed Anthony or George. My brothers are always off somewhere, camping with friends, or else sleeping over at someone else's house, or else keeping vigil in the haunted bowling alley. The ghost always shows up in the bowling alley at midnight, with his head in his hand. The pins scream when he throws his head down the lane.

My stepmother had three helpings of pineapple upside-down cake. After dinner, she turned Theodore and Russell into swans. They were banging down the grand staircase on tin trays. I have to admit this is a lot of fun. I've done it myself. Not turning people into swans, I mean, sliding down on trays.

I had to open up a window for Theodore and Russell. They honked reproachfully at me as I pushed them out over the windowsill. But once they opened up their wings, they looked so graceful, so strong. They flew up into the sky, curving and diving and hanging on a current of air, dipping their long necks.

How do you do that? I wrote down on my pad. My stepmother was sitting down on the staircase, looking almost ashamed.

"I don't know," she said. "It just seems to happen. It's just so noisy."

Can you turn them back? I wrote.

"What an excellent inquiry," she said. "I do not know. Perhaps and we shall see."

William and Julian refused, as usual, to brush their teeth before bedtime. Loudly. I told them, *Be quiet, or else.*

"Or else what?" Julian screamed at me, his face red with temper.

New stepmother will turn you into a swan.

"Liar," William said loudly. He said it again, even louder, experimentally. My stepmother, wearing pink flannel pajamas, was standing there, just outside the bathroom door. She stuck her head in, looking pained. Julian and William pretended to be afraid. They screamed and giggled. Then they pretended to be swans, flapping their arms. My stepmother waved her finger at them, and they sprouted wings. They sprouted feathers and beaks, and blinked their black beady eyes at her.

I filled up the bathtub with water, and put them in it. It was the first time they ever seemed to enjoy a bath. Even better, they didn't have any teeth to brush.

Then I put them outside, because I wasn't sure if they were house-trained.

The next morning I woke under my favorite quilt, the Rapunzel quilt, with the gray tower, and the witch, and the prince climbing up the long yellow braids. I ate breakfast and then I went outside and fed my brothers. I'd never had pets before. Now I had six. I tried to decide what I liked better, birds or brothers.

When I went back to get more toast, my father was sitting in the kitchen, reading the morning paper. He was wearing the striped purple bathrobe I'd made him for Christmas three years ago. Mom had helped with the cuffs. The hem was a little bit frayed. "Good morning, Emma," he said. "Still not speaking? Where are the rest of you, anyway?"

I wrote down, *New stepmom turned them into swans.*

"Ha," he said. "You're a funny girl, Emma. Don't forget. Today I'm dedicating the new school gymnasium. We'll see you about two-ish."

First there were speeches. I sat with the rest of my grade, in the bleachers, and looked at my new stepmother. I was thinking that the smart thing would have been to buy her earplugs. Whenever my principal, Mr. Wolf, put his mouth too close to the microphone, there was a squeal of feedback. My stepmother was looking pale. Her lips were pressed tightly together. She sat behind Mr. Wolf on the stage, beside my father.

Sorley Meadows, who wears colored lip gloss, was sitting next to me. She dug her pointy elbow into my side. "Your stepmother is, like, tiny," she said. "She looks like a little kid."

I ignored her. My father sat with his back straight, and his mouth fixed in a dignified, royal smile. My father can sleep with his eyes open. That's what my mother used to say. She used to poke him at state occasions, just to see if he was still awake.

Mr. Wolf finished his speech, and we all clapped. Then the marching band came in. My father woke up. My stepmother put her hand out, as if she were going to conduct them.

Really, the band isn't very good. But they are enthusiastic. My stepmother stood up. She stuck out her pinkie finger, and instead of a marching band there was suddenly a lot of large white hissing swans.

I jumped down out of the bleachers. How mortifying. Students and teachers all began to stand up. "She turned them into birds," someone said.

My father looked at my stepmother with a new sort of look. It was still a sort of being hit on the head sort of look, but a different sort of being hit on the head sort of look. Mr. Wolf turned toward my father and my stepmother. "Your Royal Majesty, my dear mademoiselle," he said, "please do not be alarmed. This is, no doubt, some student prank."

He lifted the little silver whistle around his neck and blew on it. "Everyone," he said. "Please be quiet! Please sit back down."

My stepmother did not sit back down. She pointed at Mr. Wolf. Mrs. Heliotrope, the French teacher, screamed suddenly. Mr. Wolf was a swan. So was Mrs. Heliotrope. And as I watched, suddenly the new gymnasium was full of birds. Sorley Meadows was a swan. John Riley, who is someone I once had a crush on until I saw him picking his nose in the cloakroom, was a swan. Emma Valerie Snope, who used to be my best friend because we had the same name, was a swan. Marisa Valdez, the prettiest girl in the seventh grade, was a swan.

My father grabbed my stepmother's arm. "What is going on here?" he said to her. She turned him into a swan.

In that whole gymnasium, it was just me and my stepmother and a lot of swans. There were feathers floating all over in the air. It looked like a henhouse. I pulled out my pad of paper. I jumped up on the stage and walked over to her. She had just turned my whole school into a bunch of birds. She had just turned my father into a bird. She put her hand down absentmindedly and patted him on the top of his white feathery head. He darted his head away, and snapped at her.

I was so angry, I stabbed right through the pad of paper with my ballpoint. The tip of the pen broke off. I threw the pad of paper down.

I opened my mouth. I wasn't sure what was going to come out. Maybe a yell. Maybe a curse. Maybe a squawk. What if she turned me into a bird, too? "WHAT?" I said. "WHAT?"

It was the first word I had said in a whole year. I saw it hit her. Her eyes got so big. She threw her arm out, pointing her pinkie finger at me. I was pointing at her. "WHAT?" I said again. I saw her pinkie finger become a feather. Her arms got downy. Her nose got longer, and sharp. She flapped her wings at me.

She wasn't a swan. She was some other kind of bird. I don't know what kind. She was like an owl, but bigger, or maybe a great auk, or a kiwi. Her feathers looked fiery and metallic. She had a long tail, like a peacock. She fanned it out. She looked extremely relieved. She cocked her head to one side and looked at me, and then she flew out of the gymnasium.

"WHAT?" I screamed after her. "WAIT!" What a mess. She'd turned my family, my entire school into birds, and then she flew away? Was this fair? What was I supposed to do? "I want to be a swan, too! I want my mom!"

I sat down on the stage and cried. I really missed my mom.

Then I went to the school library and did a little research. A lot of the swans came with me. They don't seem to be house-trained, so I spread out newspaper on the floor for them.

My fairy godfather is never around when you need him. This is why it's important to develop good research skills, and know how to find your way around a library. If you can't depend on your fairy godfather, at least you can depend on the card catalog. I found the section of books on enchantments, and read for a bit. The swans settled down in the library, honking softly. It was kind of pleasant.

It seems that to break my stepmother's pinkie spell, I need to make shirts for all of the birds and throw the shirts over their necks. I need to sew these shirts out of nettle cloth, which doesn't sound very pleasant. Nettles burn when you pick them. Really, I think linen, or cotton, is probably more practical. And I think I have a better idea than a bunch of silly shirts that no one is probably going to want to wear again, anyway. And how are you supposed to sew a shirt for a bird? Is there a pattern? Down in the castle storerooms, there are a lot of trunks filled with my mother's quilting supplies.

I miss my mother.

Excuse me. I just can't seem to stop talking. My voice is all hoarse and croaky. I sound like a crow. I probably wouldn't have gotten a good grade in choir, anyway. Mrs. Orlovsky, the choir teacher, is the swan over there, on top of the librarian's desk. Her head is tucked under her wing. At least I think it's Mrs. Orlovsky. Maybe it's Mr. Beatty, the librarian. My father is perched up on the windowsill. He's looking out the window, but I can't see anything out there. Just sky.

I think I'm going to finish the quilt that my mother and I started. It's going to be a lot bigger than either of us was planning on making it. When I finish, it should be big enough even to cover the floor of the gymnasium.

It's a blue quilt, a crazy quilt. Silk, corduroy, denim, satin, velvet. Sapphire, midnight blue, navy, marine, royal blue, sky blue. I'm going to patch in white birds with wide white wings on one side, and on the other side I'm going to patch in little white shirts. When I finish, I'm going to roll it up, and then throw it over all the swans I can find. I'm going to turn them back into people. This quilt is going to be as beautiful as sky. It's going to be as soft as feathers. It's going to be just like magic.

Notes on "Swans" by Kelly Link (2000)

> Enforced silence can be a useful way to avoid unwanted
> interruptions or to invite the silent to find their own voices.

Recounting her experience as a younger writer with reading and rereading Angela Carter, Kelly Link writes in her "Introduction" to a recent edition of the 1979 *The Bloody Chamber and Other Stories*: "I needed to see how playfulness and generosity and friction—of ideas, in language, in the admixture of high and low, the mythic and the psychologically realistic—were engines for story and structure and point of view. . . . What a relief to see how much stretch there was to stories" (2015, x). Link also comments on how quarreling with stories matters; she concludes, "The girls and women in *The Bloody Chamber* remake the rules of the stories they find themselves in with their boldness. Angela Carter, too, was bold. I tried to learn that lesson from her" (xiv).

In Link's "Swans," the eleven-year-old I-narrator and protagonist Emma Bear finds herself living a specific fairy tale, the Grimms' "Six Swans"; once she recognizes it, thanks to her research skills in the library, Emma makes a bold plan to transform the swans—her family and school community—back into humans, a plan that, based on her experience and knowledge, cleverly adapts the given fairy-tale plot, changes its rules.

Rehumanizing one's relations following trauma and loss is difficult, but Emma knows her strengths and puts them, the quilting and sewing she learned from her mother, to work in ways that unmake the poetics of sacrifice and silence in the Grimms' tale. While Emma did not at first know the power of her questioning and angry voice—"WHAT?"—by the end of the story she understands the problem with enchantment imposed without one's consent. She believes instead in the transformative and healing powers of her creative stitching.

The focus in Link's fiction and the Grimms' versions of ATU 451 ("The Maiden Who Seeks Her Brothers") is on interspecies transformation, but notice how there are several bird-humans—the swans but also the rare-bird stepmother and crow-like Emma—in Link's tale, making it somewhat "species queer" (Greenhill 2014). What other features distinguish Link's wonder tale?

In "Swans," the stepmother has little control over her powers and is not scheming as she is in the Grimms' tale; and Emma communicates through writing when she can't talk, continuing to ask questions and express herself. If there is a trace in "Swans" of the sequence that has the silent heroine of ATU 451 marrying a king who never really understands her, it's in the step-mother's experience. But unlike the ATU 451 heroine, Emma's stepmother is not sentenced to death for witchcraft; and there is no mother of the king—another jealous fairy-tale mother figure—to plot against her.

The swans' sister in the Grimms' version is defined, as a girl and a woman, by her quest to save them, but Emma is not. Has Link perhaps split that Grimms' heroine into the adult stepmother/new queen and the child Emma? And to whom is this wise child telling her story in a "hoarse and croaky" voice?

Maya Kern, "How to Be a Mermaid," 2012.

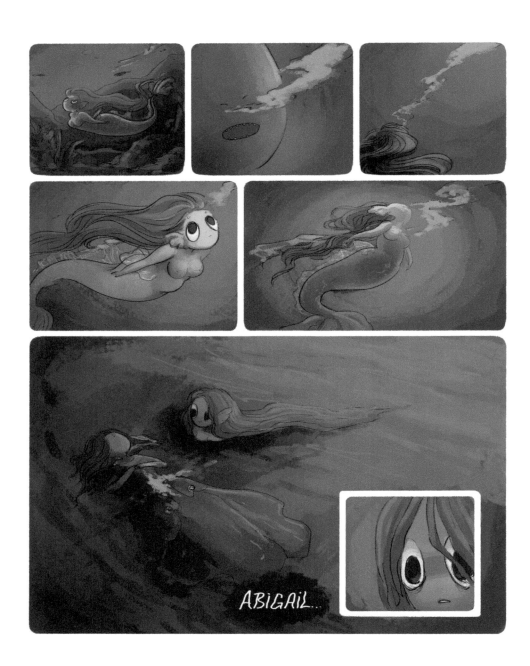

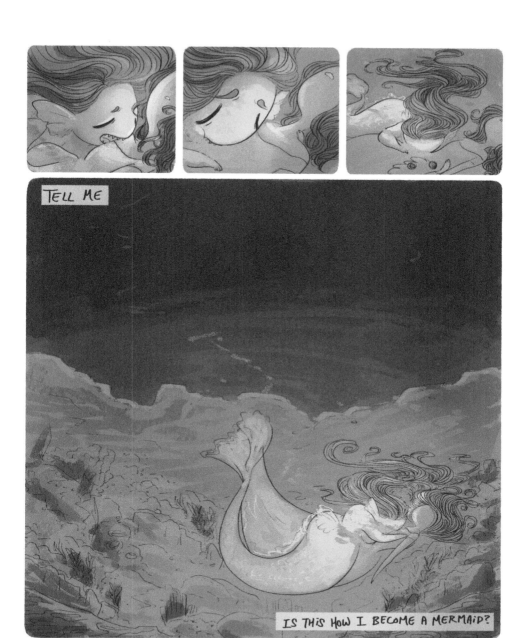

How To Be A Mermaid
by maya kern

Notes on "How to Be a Mermaid" by Maya Kern (2012)

> An invitation to ponder how to become what we most desire . . .
> or how not to become what we do not desire.

IN "HOW TO BE A MERMAID," Princess Abigail is being exchanged in a politically orchestrated royal marriage, and she knows it. When she tries to explain her predicament and the important role that money plays in it, Abigail shows a coin to Yaya: the sharp-toothed mermaid bites into it and, realizing it is no good to eat, rejects it in disgust. Abigail's reaction articulates her newly felt desire, which is at odds with the story scripted for her: "Being a mermaid must be nice. I wish I could be like you." This also signals her desire not to be like the people of her new home who are bigots that reject her "filthy blood." The transformative process of becoming a mermaid demands blood—drawn from an erotic kiss-bite between Abigail and the mermaid but then also spilled violently when a hired assassin knifes Abigail on land. But, while in the plot of court intrigue the princess is a pawn, the mermaid—who refused from their first encounter to see her simply as meat—resourcefully brings Abigail's desire and transformation to some fruition in the end.

"How to Be a Mermaid" is introduced on Maya Kern's website (www .mayakern.com) as "a reimagination of 'The Little Mermaid' and other mermaid lore," immediately signaling how Hans Christian Andersen's well-known literary tale participates in a web of stories and beliefs that stretches back in time and across cultures. In Andersen's tale ("Den lille havfrue" in the original Danish), the mermaid—like her story ancestors, the Sirens—has the most beautiful singing voice, but she chooses to trade it for shapely legs in order to join the human world, hoping to marry the prince she cannot put out of her mind. Her love for the prince ends unhappily, but, unlike other water spirits such Mélusine and Undine in older European tales, Andersen's little mermaid never experiences actual romance and remains nameless. Her final transformation into an air spirit brings her closer to having a soul, exemplifying self-sacrifice as a form of self-fulfillment. Kern's comic rewrites the path of female desire in the story: the mermaid falls for a human princess, and this human wants to be a mermaid. Kern's tale also flips the ancient Japanese legend "Yao Bikuni," in which a woman who eats mermaid meat ends up living for hundreds of years. Affirming the mermaid's fleshy and appetite-filled way of being, her sympathetic and erotic act of devourment works to fulfill Abigail's desire, extend Yaya's life, and question what is human.

As Amy Carlson (2019) insightfully notes, Kern's intertextual web extends across media to the manga entitled *Mermaid Saga* (*Ningyo shirīzu*) by Takahashi Rumiko, which retells the longevity legend of Yao Bikuni, and to the Walt Disney Company's 1989 animated film adaptation of Andersen's "The Little Mermaid," in which the mermaid acquired a name and took back her voice. Of her comic—a multitrack narrative that functions economically and esthetically quite differently from film or forms of nonsequential visual art—Kern wrote: "There's something wonderful about taking stories that are so steeped into our culture that their influence is seemingly ubiquitous, and reexamining them. The perspective thru which a writer chooses to reimagine an old story is telling both of their own beliefs and of the shifting attitudes of modernity."

There is much to be gained by thinking of the affordances of visuality in Kern's (web) comic. How do Yaya's visual representation and words play with received notions of how to be a mermaid? Note how much information emerges from the illustrations and how even the passing of time is represented in visually specific ways. For instance, when Abigail and Yaya interact in their blue surroundings, the panels depicting life in the palace are interspersed throughout their conversation, thus acting as a montage of Abigail's daily life, contrasted to her time with Yaya. How does the mixing of warm and cool colors work to reinforce or disturb the verbal narrative?

Notes on *Birth of Commerce* by Shaun Tan (2016)

Invitation to a bright new world or an interruption to a world that needs change?

SOME OF THESE BEINGS are adorable, some are frightening, and others are just plain weird. They seem to be trading objects between them. The bright colors dotted around the page convey cheerfulness, but the dull scratchy ground and what appear to be industrial smokestacks and pollution in the background are ominous. Do we take this as a warning of the dangers of trading baubles while the land and atmosphere around us are being polluted, as hope for continued life and community and cooperation even in the face of environmental degradation and change, or as something else altogether?

The creatures are certainly the least recognizable beings we have encountered in this anthology. Kern's Yaya, Kamiya's snail-human hybrid, and Boyle's Beast, while not exactly human, are at least recognizable as "transbiological," which, as Pauline Greenhill and Kay Turner tell us, "includes animals or humans who masquerade or transform into another species (in whole or in part) and/or who otherwise mess with hard-and-fast distinctions between species, including between human and nonhuman" (2016, 845). Some of these creatures seem organic, such as the big lizard in the top left; others seem wholly mechanical, such as the button-bartering pot and the pipe; and still others, like the two in the foreground, appear to be cobbled together from both organic and inorganic elements. How are we to take these beings? As cyborgs? As aliens? As us?

Birth of Commerce

Shaun Tan

Shaun Tan, *Birth of Commerce*, 2016, pastel and charcoal on paper, 50 x 60 cm.

A Tale of a King

Shaun Tan

A LONG TIME AGO, when there were no clocks or maps or ordinary things, the birds called out to twilight with a chorus loud enough to wake the sun. That great solar eye peered across a strange and ancient landscape, its enormous wings opening upon a new blue day, and it saw below a great family of wondrous creatures, all crawling, floating, slithering, swimming, flapping or walking about, each with their own daily business to attend to.

Among them lived a king, but not the kind that live in castles, sit on thrones or make laws, for such things did not yet exist. This king looked much like other animals, walking comfortably on all fours, wandering the landscape, fascinated by the smallest detail of everything he saw, always finding some new inspiration each day. The other animals loved him very much, and he loved them too.

In the evenings, all would gather in the shadows of hills to hear the king reflect upon his long walks. He would describe things he had seen, things that he might have seen, and things that he had not seen at all, only imagined. The last of these entertained his audience most of all, as there seemed no limit to the king's inventiveness. Every day ended the same way, the animals returned to their burrows, nests, lairs and hives, the sun slowly folded its wings and the grass whispered quietly to itself.

ONE MORNING THE KING wandered further than he had ever done before, drawn to something glinting in the distance. He came across an old woman kneeling by the shore of a black lake. A light breeze carried away small pieces of her once beautiful robes, and her face seemed made of ash, with lines carved into her cheeks by the long passage of tears. But what struck the king's eye most of all was a golden crown atop her bowed head, shining bright against the greyness of this mysterious scene.

Shaun Tan, "A Tale of a King," previously unpublished.

"Who are you?" he asked.

"I don't know," she uttered in a voice like sliding stone, a small plume of dust leaving her barely moving lips. Puzzled, the king asked after her crown, as he could not draw his eyes from it.

"A wonderful and cursed thing," whispered the despondent figure. "It sees every dream of the wearer and brings it forth into the world."

Compelled by a powerful and nameless desire, the king asked the woman to let him place the crown upon his own head, if only for a moment. She turned away. "If I remove the crown, I will surely die. I have worn it so long, become so consumed by its promise as to have forgotten all else. I cannot even remember myself—all the things that made me who I am. I exist now only because I imagine myself so, upon seeing my reflection in this pool."

Bewildered, the king left the old woman alone and continued his wanderings. Yet he could not stop thinking about the crown, and walked by the woman each day, even though she was too absorbed in her own reflection to pay him any notice. And each day a single tear ran down her face, fell into the pool and broke that visage into a hundred ripples. Thereupon her already faded figure would fade a little more, and the wind would pluck more pieces from her ragged gowns. This continued until one day there was nothing more than a pile of ash where she once knelt, and on top of it the golden crown.

Seeing his chance, the king hurried down to the shore and took the crown.

As soon as he placed it upon his head, he realised that the old woman's words were indeed true. Marvellous creatures of his imagination emerged from the earth and walked about as if alive, much to his astonishment. Later that evening, as the king revealed this new magical object to all the animals that had gathered by the hills, they were together overcome by laughter, joy and wonder that continued well into the night. Even the sun woke briefly at this noisy jubilation, but soon closed its great eye again, and none saw the tear that fell beyond the horizon.

The next day, everyone returned to their usual occupations, crawling, swimming, flying and so on—all except the king. He was content to sit upon a hill all day, imagining one fanciful thing after another and watching them climb out of the earth as the sun looked on silently. So it was that he spent more and more days alone working on his own creations, and less time wandering the land or communing with the other animals. He became obsessed with creating new things, each more elaborate, more beautiful, more impressive than the last. At the same time, the other animals grew less and less interested in these inventions. "They move and speak, but are not truly alive," they complained. "They come from the earth but do not belong to it."

The king grew angry at this. "You are all just stupid animals!" he cried, and he stood up tall on two legs to show how different he was from lowly creatures. "You know nothing!"

And with that he imagined a huge tower in which he could create without criticism. He imagined bigger and more beautiful animals than those he had known, animals that would work for him, admire his achievements and tell him how great a king he was. The place around the tower became a kingdom, and that kingdom grew, drawing all that it needed from the earth to build a vast domain of marvellous creation. The king's ingenuity and ambition seemed to know no bounds, even as it was always surrounded by a high wall, erected to silence the objections of other animals.

ONE DAY A SINGLE bird from beyond the kingdom managed to breach the wall and fly all the way to the king's tower. The king had become so absorbed in his own world that he didn't recognise the animal that now flew through his window until it began to talk. It told of the land he had left behind, which was disappearing as more and more earth was consumed to build what had now become a sprawling folly.

This news was so unsettling that the king could not bear to hear it. Without thinking, he imagined something to eat the bird, and the messenger was promptly devoured by a pouncing beast. Despairing at what he had done, he imagined another creature to sweep up the scattered feathers into the darkest corner of the tower's keep, and so it was done.

Many more birds came to visit the king, but none returned to report what they had seen. Eventually, there were so few birds in the land that they could no longer wake the sun, and everything fell to darkness. This did not concern the king too much, however, for he simply imagined a sun of his own, one that hung above his kingdom like a glowing silver ball. Having been away from the world for so long, however, he could no longer imagine all the colours that had once captivated him, and the kingdom was illuminated by a cold and unchanging light.

MANY YEARS PASSED, NOT that the king noticed, for time, along with everything else, had lost its meaning for him. As memory and inspiration dwindled, his subjects became increasingly monotonous copies of each other, a dull parade that praised his genius in a single droning voice. That they built great statues in honour of their master only added to his misery.

Alone, bitter and frustrated, he began to despise everything he had made. In a dark rage, he imagined a monstrous dragon that would consume everything. No sooner had the thought crossed his mind than a fire-blackened creature crept forth from the ground with a terrible moan, billowing cinders and clawing its way through the kingdom. Startled by the power of his own deep despair, the king could not imagine how to quell it. The dragon twisted and turned, devouring the kingdom's buildings and animals by the thousands. It chased the king himself and he imagined higher and higher towers in a desperate bid to escape. When the dragon began to gnaw on the foundations of the final tower, the king crawled into the furthest, darkest corner of the keep, cowering hopelessly.

There he noticed a single feather that had been swept aside so long ago. It was the most beautiful thing he could ever recall having seen, and as he held it between his fingers, he remembered the form of a bird, and suddenly great feathery wings began to unfold from his back. The walls around him cracked and split; the dragon thundered and the tower began to fall, but the king leapt through the nearest window, spread his wings, and narrowly escaped the fiery snapping jaws.

He flew across the dark sky for what seemed an eternity, far beyond his kingdom's ruins, and when he could no longer imagine his own passage, he fell to the dark desert below. There were no hills or forests anymore, only dusty craters from which the material of his kingdom had been mined; and only a handful of pale, subterranean animals crept forth to investigate the strange thing that had landed before them. The king had been gone for so long that none recognised him. They could only look on curiously as this creature, overcome with sadness, could no longer imagine his own existence. His wings were plucked apart feather by feather in the breeze, his robes dissolved into a pile of threads revealing nothing more than shadows beneath. The crown tumbled to the ground.

The animals returned to their quiet business in this dim world; only the few surviving birds remained to collect all the feathers and threads, taking them away to build nests for their eggs. Not long afterwards there were enough birds to call out and awaken the sun, and its great sleepy eye opened once again. Plants began to grow, flowers bloomed, insects came, and other animals too; forests spread and rivers resumed their ancient courses, carrying all that remained of a once mighty kingdom to the sea.

What became of the crown? Nobody knows, but such powerful things will never vanish from the world so long as there are those who so desire them. And the dragon? It is still there, somewhere in the darkness. You can hear it hissing and thrashing on a windless night, waiting restlessly to be imagined once again.

Notes on "A Tale of a King" by Shaun Tan (2021)

> Accepting a seductive invitation too wholeheartedly can lead to unforeseen costs.

"A Tale of a King" is brief and, unlike most of the narratives included in this volume, written in the manner of a folktale. Rich in interpretive possibilities, it invites many kinds of readings.

We might read it as ecocriticism: the story begins with a natural world in harmony, where all of the land's beings have their "daily business to attend to." It is the king's business to tell the animals about their world as he observes and imagines it to be. He creates the stories that shape a culture's unity, but he does not change or exploit the land. As such, the king is *a part* of a human/nonhuman world and community until his obsession literally moves him *apart* from the land and its inhabitants. Eventually, the world balance is so off-kilter and the sun's alarm clock birds are so denuded that the sun does not wake at all. Yet the king continues to extract more and more products from the land.

He is seduced by the crown, the ultimate metonymy, a sign of political power and colonialism, particularly in countries of the British Commonwealth.

The fading woman who is dependent on its consumption of resources can no longer remember, or even imagine, how to live without the crown's devouring power. She will "surely die" even though it is the crown that is consuming her own being. The king's obsession with the crown's creations causes him to create an exclusive tower that prevents him from participating in or even recognizing the natural world he used to love, at the same time that he drains its resources for each new imagined wonder and relegates his former friends to the outer reaches of his new kingdom.

Another reading might approach the king's use of the crown and the visions it brings into being as a form of addiction or destructive dependence. Eventually, like the woman who had the crown before him, he can no longer remember how to live without it. If we read the king's story as a metaphor for addiction, must it be to a drug? Might the object of obsession/ dependence/ addiction be akin to a technological marvel, such as a so-called smart phone that is so hard to put down that we ignore the terrible polluting and poisoning effects of its mass production and disposal?

Shaun Tan says, "I suppose it's a fable about being an artist to some extent, and the importance of basing most creativity on the observation of external things, not just one's own imagination. I feel there are some parallels here also with politics, where inward looking ideologies can lose touch with reality or eschew verification (on both the right and the left) as much as any other creative or interpretative act might do, including religion."

So this little tale does invite multiple, intersecting readings and interpretations. We leave you with a few more questions. Considering the ending, do you see this as a hopeful tale of possible renewal? A warning of what our current consumerist ways have lead us into? A lament for our own destructive tendencies? Is the dragon a danger or a savior? Does the dragon align with humanity or with nature? Or does its inexorable existence demonstrate that the human/nature binary cannot hold? Does the dragon's presence posit some other kind of relationship between the natural and cultural worlds?

Notes on *Beast* by Shary Boyle (2007)

What invitations are made by the gaze of a beast?

IN A FAIRY-TALE CONTEXT, many viewers will associate any beast with the tale "Beauty and the Beast." But this is not the Disney Beast, or even Jean Cocteau's *bête*, or any of the famous illustrated walrus, boar, or lion beasts we may have seen. Maybe this Beast is only called a "beast" because that is how others see it. Maybe this Beast's steady gaze and busy tongue are telling us that beastliness comes from without—not from within, as in the famous tale—that it is in the eye of the beholder. Like Kern's mermaid Yaya, this Beast is beautiful, a little frightening, and kind of adorable. How can it be all three?

In a discussion about her work for the Canada Pavilion at the 2013 Venice Biennale, Boyle said: "Sensitivity is born out of compassion, compassion from empathy, empathy from personal experience. Art is serious to me, a real, active, living language. It is a responsibility. I can't speak for others yet my consideration of those not invited influences how I see and make. Regardless of the art world's collective absorption with money status or fashion, I will insist on tenderness, silence and meaning. Plus mischief" (Drouin-Brisebois 2013, 86). We think this stance is an interesting lens through which to see *Beast*.

Beast looks back at us (you) (me). With an enigmatic expression. How do we read it? Whose responsibility is it to define this figure? Whose right is it? Do we have to know who/what Beast is? And perhaps most importantly, how do we answer these questions compassionately? Our ability to do so in relation to a wondrous creature will tell us something about our ability to do so for other humans and for nonhumans as well.

Beast

Shary Boyle

Shary Boyle, *Beast* (Highland Series), 2007, oil on panel, 40 x 35 cm. Collection Musée d'art contemporain de Montréal.

Notes on *Little Red Riding Hood* by David Kaplan (1997)

Who is inviting whom?

ATU 333, "LITTLE RED Riding Hood," is possibly one of the best-known stories across the globe. We all know the characters: a girl, her granny, a wolf. In some versions, the wolf will be a tiger, an ogre, or a werewolf. The girl will be slightly older or slightly younger, usually depending on the amount of sexuality attributed to her, and sometimes granny will be mother or will even be absent. Nevertheless, we all know this ultimate tale of "stranger danger." Don't we?

David Kaplan's *Little Red Riding Hood* takes as its primary intertext "The Story of Grandmother," an early French oral version collected in the late nineteenth century and published in English in 1956. More recently, this version has been widely anthologized and is often taught in fairy-tale courses in universities along with the Grimms' "Rothkäppchen," or "Little Red Cap," and Charles Perrault's "Le petit chaperon rouge."

The most dominant interpretations of the tale are focused on either stranger danger stemming from the Grimms' version or the more adult-themed victim-blaming rape narrative following Perrault (see Zipes 1993). Kaplan takes "The Story of Grandmother," which already has an intelligent and active girl, and gives her more agency over her own sexuality in a more modern context. But that is only one thing the film does.

The multitrack nature of film is integral to meaning making. In classical narrative cinema, the tracks blend together to create the illusion of a seamless whole. Here, the juxtaposition of the action on the visual channel, voice-over narration, and nondiegetic soundtrack produces disjunctures that shake up our received notions about "Little Red Riding Hood" and offers what Jennifer Orme has called a "queer invitation" (2010, 2012, 2015, 2016).

The invitation comes in the form of a complex layering of cultural intertexts on various tracks of the film. Quentin Crisp, self-described as "one of the stately homos of England," is the voice-over narrator. The soundtrack is Claude Debussy's *Prélude à l'après-midi d'un faune* (1894), itself a musical

(continued on page 58)

Little Red Riding Hood

David Kaplan

David Kaplan, *Little Red Riding Hood*, 1997, film, 12 minutes, 20 seconds. Dir. David Kaplan, perf. Christina Ricci, Timour Bourtasenkov, Evelyn Solann, and Quentin Crisp.

https://player.vimeo.com/video/100666128

(continued from page 56)

interpretation of Stéphane Mallarmé's poem "L'Après-midi d'un faune" (1876). This music, in conjunction with the wolf as dancer (Timour Bourtas-enkov), raises the specter of Vaslav Nijinsky and his infamous choreography and performance set to Debussy's music in 1912.

More than just the dance, Bourtasenkov's wolf costume also draws links to Nijinsky in his similar costume as the faun. Pauline Greenhill might call these "transbiological characters," as she argues "that relationships between humans and non-human animals, particularly when they super-sede those between humans; and transformations, whether embodied or costumed, between humans and non-human animals, offer the possibility of deeply transgressive pleasures" (2014, 30). Greenhill is talking about our pleasure at considering the sexual attraction—and action—between human and transbiological fairy-tale characters, for instance, between the girl and the wolf, as in Kaplan's film and Nalo Hopkinson's multimedia image *Still Rather Fond of Red*, neither of which leaves us in doubt of the pleasure taken between "Wolfie" and "Red."

By no means do transbiological relationships appear only in "Little Red Riding Hood." In fact, as Greenhill shows, they are relatively common in won-der tales and indeed even in this anthology. Thinking of the relations between human and transhuman in the tales and images in this book can be yet another fruitful way to think about humans and our environments and to help us ques-tion and que(e)ry assumptions of human supremacy on this planet.

In addition to the queer invitation of the film, we might also turn to Kaplan's own statement in a 2009 interview about the film: "One of the fun things about adapting these stories is that an audience approaches them with so many preconceptions. It appeals to my mischievous side to subvert those expectations" (Kohn 2009). Kaplan's subversion of expectations might also bring us to the mise-en-scène. How do we interpret the shift from the naturalistic forest setting into the German Expressionist–inspired cottage with its hilter-tilter perspectives? And how may this shift possibly relate to the mischievous, slut-shaming puppet cat?

David Kaplan, *Little Red Riding Hood*, 1997, film, 12 minutes, 20 seconds. Dir. David Kaplan, perf. Christina Ricci, Timour Bourtasenkov, Evelyn Solann, and Quentin Crisp.

https://player.vimeo.com/video/100666128

Of No Real Account

Bryan Kamaoli Kuwada

THE DAMNED TĪWAIWAKA WOULDN'T stop chirping. Even worse was the amused glint in the fantail's eye, like it was laughing. Sure, Māui was trying to win immortality for humankind by crawling into the giant Hine Nui Te Po's massive birth canal and out of her mouth while she was sleeping. And sure, that might look a little odd, especially because he couldn't figure out if he should go in head- or feet-first. But if that bird made any more racket, Māui was done for. No more songs would be sung about him, no more stories told of his feats. It was terrifying enough to be near the giant obsidian night goddess while she was sleeping; Māui couldn't imagine what it would be like if she were awake. As the bird's tittering increased in volume, Māui braced himself for his entry into the next life.

Hine Nui Te Po's drowsy red eyes fluttered open, lazily glancing down to see an insignificant lump of a man trying to crawl into her vagina. Yawning unconcernedly, Hine Nui Te Po rolled over and snuggled back to sleep, with a great and resounding snapping shut of her thighs, ending humankind's quest for immortality, along with the life of its greatest hero.

Word spread quickly through the peoples of Aotearoa, and a great pall blanketed the land, as keening wails could be heard echoing from the snow-capped peaks to the wide swathes of sand at the shore. Even the animals took up the cry, forest birds and great creatures of the deep adding their calls to the rising din. Swarming black clouds of birds fell from the sky in grief and great silver shoals of fish beached themselves in sorrow. So it was that the news was passed from island group to island group, atoll to atoll, the piercing and painful sounds of sadness growing and resounding until finally reaching Hawai'i, in the furthest northern reaches of the vast ocean of Kāne.

Though Hawaiians were in the midst of the worst drought anyone could remember for generations, they too immediately took up the cries of wailing

Bryan Kamaoli Kuwada, "Of No Real Account," *Hawai'i Review*, 2015.

and lamentation; Māui was, after all, the single greatest Hawaiian hero of all time. The eerie sound of abject sorrow could be heard coming from each house in every single kauhale throughout the entire string of islands. The drought had caused kalo to shrivel and rot in stagnant loʻi and bananas plants to wither and fall in the uplands. Even fishing was affected as the lack of fresh water running into the sea depleted the populations of ʻamaʻama and awa. Still, they too put aside their own troubles for an entire anahulu to grieve for their greatest son.

Yet once the mourning period was over, they came back to a stark reality. Māui was gone and the rain had yet to fall. Who would save the people? Who would bring back the rain? Who would be the people's hero? Who *could* be the people's hero?

Keaka was the people's next best hope. But no one else knew it. *He* didn't even think so sometimes. And despite the fact that he had gleefully rejoiced in private over Māui's death, he was a pretty nice guy who only wanted to help his people. He never really got the chance though. Māui hogged all of the really prestigious heroic deeds, such as fishing the islands from the sea and snaring the sun, while Keaka was left with such "heroic" acts as carrying scaly Old Man Kahiolo home after he drank too much ʻawa and saving Old Woman ʻEleua from the tiny moʻo that crawled on the walls inside her house and clicked at her. No matter how hard he tried, he could never best that gods-damned Māui.

Keaka hadn't always cursed Māui's name though. Quite the opposite, in fact. Anytime word of Māui's newest exploit reached his family, the entire compound buzzed. The men would gather to mend their fishing nets and discuss Māui's manly and heroic attributes. The women would beat their kapa and giggle about what other types of heroic attributes Māui might have. The elders would sit around reminiscing about heroes of the past, such as Kāna and Kaululāʻau, but they would always agree that, when it really came down to it, no other hero ever even came close to Māui in skill and bravery.

Keaka grew up loving all of these stories as well. His family had even named him Keaka, the shadow, because he quietly followed all the storytellers around, soaking in every aspect of their stories and mele. He had been entranced by accounts of the traveling gods Kāne and Kanaloa getting into scrapes and tussles, all the while shaping the geographic features of the islands. He had thrilled to the tales of the brothers Kāna and Niheu, one of whom could stretch to any height while the other stood brave in the face of any foe. Keaka had even traipsed across the landscape with his best friend Liko, searching for the wahi pana that Hiʻiaka created in her epic travels to fetch her sister Pele's lover, Lohiʻau.

Yet it was the Māui songs and stories he loved best. The bravery, the daring, the acclaim. He had for a time wanted to *be* Māui, but as he got older he soon began to come into his own. And then he desired nothing more than to be worthy of having stories of his own told about him. Each recounting of Māui's deeds began to sting, serving only as a reminder of how inadequately heroic he was. To top it all off, Keaka's own birth mother was the biggest Māui fan of them all. Whenever she heard a new tale of Māui's amazing feats from Old Lady Wahakale, she'd come rushing home to pass on her gossip to the entire kauhale and would even travel to their other relatives' compounds in order to tell them. It finally got to be too much and the aspiring hero moved out to live on his own.

As it turned out, however, since his mother loved him so much, she decided to add his house in the dry and desolate Honouliuli to her gossip tour of the district. Her footsteps would awaken him, and she would call out, "E Keaka, Old Lady Wahakale told me that Māui saved a double-hulled canoe that got swamped in that last storm," or "E Keaka, Old Lady Wahakale told me that Māui slew a giant moʻo that was attacking travelers." Most recently, he had been awakened by her grief-stricken wailing and the thump of her beating her breast in sorrow over Māui's death. She had knocked out three of her front teeth in mourning, and confided with a somewhat superior air that Hina, Māui's own mother, had only knocked out two. Slightly aghast, he had pressed his nose to his mother's as she took her leave of him to carry the news to the rest of her gossip circuit.

That night, he had dreamt that *he* was Māui, and it was *he* who pushed up the sky, and *he* who took the secret of fire from that old mud hen, Kaʻalaenuiahina. It was a nice dream and Keaka had felt a sense of contentment while it was going on, but when he was awakened the next morning, the warm, happy feeling went away because he knew he was still Keaka and still had not done any of those things. The drought still raged, and there was still nothing Keaka could think to do about it.

Keaka had initially not tried to help with the drought situation because he too assumed that Māui was going to do something about it. Even after Māui's death, Keaka still wandered fruitlessly around the vast and dusty expanse of coral plain of his home Honouliuli, seeking something sufficiently heroic to do. What could he do? He wasn't a real hero, or at least he hadn't proven himself yet. He had succeeded only in helping a few farmers tend their sweet potato mounds. It was hot and sweaty work that, while helpful, was hardly a deed worthy of a hero. At the end of the day, no throngs of adoring fans fawned over his every move or composed chants that commemorated his deeds. All he ever had to show for his crusade was a few lumpy sweet potatoes, and not very big ones at that.

"Eh, Keaka, you got any food or what?" It was Liko, as usual. He woke Keaka up with the same question every morning.

Keaka and Liko were together so often that people often mistook them for brothers. The pair *did* look similar. They both had long, ʻehu hair that they kept tied back, dark brown skin, the same build from surfing and swimming all the time. And although Keaka was about a handspan taller than Liko and had put on a little weight since they were younger, which he did not appreciate anyone mentioning, the two of them could indeed pass for brothers.

Keaka flung one of the scrawny sweet potatoes at Liko and sat up, not yet out of the hazy state between waking and dreaming.

"Auē, all you ever have is sweet potato! You need to start farming for yourself so you can have something else to eat besides sweet potato every day," Liko grumbled while examining the shrunken tuber that Keaka had gotten the day before.

"I don't have time to farm. I'm a hero, and I have to go around performing heroic deeds all day," came Keaka's wounded retort.

Liko snickered, "Yeah, like the time you helped Kānekoa by digging an eight-foot-wide ʻauwai to irrigate his loʻi? Didn't he and his family almost starve to death that year when all their kalo got washed away?"

Keaka cringed at the memory. "I just assumed that more water would mean more kalo!"

"You know what you need to do?" Liko asked intently, with a certain mischievous light in his eye. Keaka groaned to himself because he knew one of Liko's crazy schemes was coming. Another reason that everyone thought they were brothers was that they had been getting in trouble together since before they could even wear malo. Liko's plans usually ended with Keaka loudly cursing himself for listening to his friend's foolish plans, and Liko laughing hysterically in exhilaration or fear, while the two of them ran from whatever calamity was on their heels. "If you really want to do something about this drought, we need to go to the big city where you actually have a chance of doing real hero kind of stuff. There's no chance of that out here in the kua'āina, the very back of the land, helping farmers and fishermen."

Keaka knew he didn't have any responsibilities that would keep him in Honouliuli, but he wasn't too sure about Liko. "Eh, how can you leave? Don't you have crops to take care of?" ventured Keaka.

"If I had crops of my own, do you think I'd be here every day eating your scrawny little sweet potatoes? Come on, go get your stuff together and I'll have the canoe ready to set sail on tomorrow's morning high tide."

So it was that the two koko'olua went their separate ways, each packing what they thought they would need in the "big city" of Kou. Liko packed a couple of fresh malo and some food, which consisted of the rest of Keaka's sweet potatoes. Along with his own fresh malo, Keaka made sure to pack his war club Ku'ipē, just in case. Keaka mainly used it for mashing up his sweet potatoes, but a hero never knew when he might be called on to fight off a marauding mo'o or rescue a kidnapped beauty.

The first rays of the sun coming up over Lē'ahi the next morning found the two of them on Keone'ula's rust-colored sand, where they loaded up the canoe. When they were almost ready to shove off Keaka noticed something. "Uh, Liko, aren't we sailing on the morning high tide?"

"Yup," replied Liko briskly, as he continued to work.

"But this canoe has no mast or sail," persisted Keaka.

Liko brought out the canoe's one paddle, tossed it to Keaka and said, "Well, you're a hero, right? Here's your sail."

So they set off for Kou, with Keaka manning the canoe's one paddle and grumbling the entire way.

Keaka did not have the amazing paddling ability of the legendary Kaweloleimākua, so it took him more than just a single stroke to get to Kou from Kalaeloa, but he did post a respectably heroic time of one hour and forty-three minutes. "And that was into the wind," Keaka reminded Liko when they pulled into the harbor of Māmala.

What greeted Keaka's eyes the first time he saw Kou from the sea were the great throngs of people. He had never seen so many in his life. And the riotous noise of it all! There were traders hawking their wares on the ocean and sailors yelling at each other to get out of the way on shore. And two silent country bumpkins in a canoe wondering what they had gotten themselves into.

When they tried to barter for some lumpy poi and dried fish, the trader barked out a rough laugh. "Where have you fools been? You haven't been able to get poi for what you're offering since before the drought." He looked at their crestfallen faces, and relented a bit, not giving them the food, but softening his tone, saying, "Look, boys, there's not much we can do; if Kūlanihākoʻi doesn't tip some water out of his ʻumeke and let it rain soon, we won't even have this." The trader was talking about the giant calabash in the sky that held all of the world's rainwater.

Iron surged through Keaka's spine as he straightened with a cry. The trader's eyes showed white at what seemed like proof that Keaka was indeed some sort of fool, but Keaka merely declared in his deepest and heroic voice: "People of Kou! Fear not! I am Keaka, and I have come to save you!"

The few people in the market who had turned at Keaka's speech went back to what they were doing.

"What exactly are we going to do?" Liko asked in a low voice.

Keaka drew a great breath and replied, "Fear thee not, my doubting and inquisiturient compatriot. I shall ruminate henceforth on this present dilemma and return forthwith with a fitting stratagem to resolve the conundrum and—"

"Why are you talking like that?" interrupted Liko loudly. He'd had to shout to be heard over the rising volume of Keaka's ranting. Everyone in the market turned to look at them.

"Don't heroes talk like that?" Keaka asked somewhat sheepishly.

"Nobody talks like that. Can we just figure out a plan?" came Liko's tired reply.

"Well, if Kūlanihākoʻi refuses to let any water flow out of his giant ʻumeke, I say we just make him."

"What do you mean? Fight him? You can't fight a god."

"No, not fight him. Just make the water flow out of the ʻumeke. And I've got the perfect plan. Not some hump-or-thump Kamapuaʻa-style plan like you're suggesting; I'm talking about a Māui-level intelligent and well-thought-out kind of plan."

Before Liko could remind Keaka that he always railed at how dim-witted Māui was, Keaka grasped his war-club Kuʻipē, set his sights on the sky, drew his arm back, and with a mighty grunt flung his club straight into the air. Everyone craned their necks in wonder to watch the dark speck of the club disappear in the distance before a faint but resonant "tok!" was heard. The amazed murmurs of the crowd slowly turned into panicked shouts as everyone, including Keaka, came to the realization that Kuʻipē was now plummeting right back at them and gaining velocity as it fell thousands of feet through the sky. The gathered crowd all dove out of the way and the red-hot war club slammed into the ground, just missing Liko's head.

The club lay steaming in a small impact crater as a light rain began to wet the dusty earth. Everyone stood in mute wonder as they felt the cool water falling from the heavens.

The trader leapt to his feet and crowed, "He did it! He did it! The big fool did it!"

A huge smile split Keaka's face as the crowd began to cheer and people ran off to tell their friends what they had witnessed. Liko lifted Keaka in his arms and the two friends roared with laughter and delight, runnels of clean fresh water streaking down their faces.

Keaka had basked in his new-found fame after that, as people from all over the islands came by sea or by land to thank him for returning the rain, for bringing life back to the land. They brought gifts from their meager remaining food supplies and raised their voices to chant mele of praise for him. Some even sang songs and brought offerings for his war club, renaming it Laweua, the Rainbringer, in honor of the occasion. Keaka passed his days bedecked in lei of tī-leaf or the odd maile that had survived the drought deep in the upland forests, suffused in their clean, green fragrance. Though they took only what they needed of the food offerings and were able to return the rest, Liko spent most of his time eating and chatting animatedly with the people who came by. It was like a celebration out of the stories Keaka loved so much.

But as time passed and the tribute continued, Keaka began to get a little uncomfortable with all of the attention. Liko told him to just enjoy it while he could, because something would probably come up that would change things.

"After all," said Liko, "sending a flood to help people suffering from a drought might not be so heroic for much longer."

Liko was right. The steady patter of rain that had seemed like such a blessing at first had now begun to overflow the streams and rivers, washing away crops and homes. Even when the rivers began to flow normally again, the rain fell. Even when the slopes of Lēʻahi became verdant with green again, the rain fell. Even when the water began to overflow the banks of the loʻi, the rain fell. And even when farmers who had desperately called out to the gods for water now cried out for the water to stop, the rain still fell.

The tribute slowed to a trickle and then ended altogether, and the people who had once been so happy with him glared and muttered whenever he passed. The trader would still call out, "He did it! He did it! The big fool did it!" when he saw Keaka, but it had changed from a cry of celebration to one of accusation and denunciation.

Standing ankle-deep in floodwater, staring mutely up toward the hole he had made in Kūlanihākoʻi's ʻumeke, Keaka did not know what to do. How could he fix the Kūlanihākoʻi's ʻumeke in the sky if he couldn't even get there? He had tried throwing large handfuls of mud and clay into the sky to plug the hole, but they just got sodden from the rushing water and fell back to earth, splattering everyone's houses with dirt. People jeered his every failure, and Keaka could not help but agree with them. There was nothing he could do from down here.

As the rainfall continued to plaster his long hair to his face, Keaka regretted his glee over Māui's death. As much as he hated to admit it, Māui would have saved everyone from the drought. Māui wouldn't have flooded the whole damn island chain. Keaka shook his head to himself. He'd failed at his one opportunity to be the new number one hero.

He had to fix this, but how?

LIKO'S COMPANIONSHIP WAS THE only thing that kept Keaka from giving into despair. He smiled, thinking about his friend's rough jests and pragmatic nature. He thought fondly of them sitting at the shore in Puʻuloa, listening to stories with all the adults. He remembered Liko's dad pointing to Waolani in Nuʻuanu, telling his favorite story about Keaomelemele. He chuckled as he remembered the lumpy ducks he and Liko had unsuccessfully tried to craft from driftwood after hearing the story. Why had they tried to make ducks? He couldn't quite remember all of the story, but suddenly the recollection flashed into his mind: The god Kāne had given the boy Kahānaiakeakua a giant duck named Kamanuwai to take him wherever he desired. And the duck was said to live at Kunawai Spring, below Waolani. Less than a day's walk from where he was in Kou!

Keaka rushed back to tell Liko, who dashed cold water all over his enthusiasm. "But that story happened hundreds of years ago! That means Kamanuwai would be hundreds of years old! And ducks don't live that long." He added the last part just in case Keaka missed what would have been perfectly obvious to anyone else.

Keaka was not swayed in the least. "If the story lives on, Kamanuwai must live on," he said resolutely.

Liko and Keaka did not know how long it would take to find Kamanuwai—if he still lived, as Liko made sure to point out—so they packed their extra malo and enough food and water to last them a few days. They also packed offerings of food for the duck—which probably didn't exist, Liko pointed out again. Before setting out, they asked around for the landmarks to use in finding their way to the fabled spring, and while no one knew exactly where it was, everyone's stories overlapped enough that Keaka and Liko felt they would still be able to find their way.

The way was relatively easy and the two made good time. The sun was only a few hours past its zenith when they began to feel the coolness of the spring on the Moaʻe breeze. They emerged into a wide clearing with Kunawai in the middle. Keaka and Liko approached the edge of the spring to drink from the cool waters, when from out of the dark green neke and uki surrounding the pond arose a giant and fearsome creature.

The biggest duck they had ever seen.

He was nearly three arm spans in height, and though the wild and tangled feathers on his face and neck were nearly white, the speculum on his wings remained the vibrant blue of the ocean. He preened his mottled wings in the afternoon sun, casting a giant shadow over the two cowering men. Upon closer inspection of his face—though they didn't dare stare too long—they noticed that he only had one good eye, and the other socket was stuffed with leaves. Jagged scars crisscrossed his body where it looked like chunks of his flesh had been torn away, giving him the look of a mountain after a rock slide.

"*Kwek!* 'Tis altogether meet when your meat comes to you," thundered the ancient duck, his voice like the crash of boulders falling from a cliff. The gray-feathered mountain peered at them with his one good eye. "Draw closer, my delectable little fish, *kwek, kwek*. I have not supped on tasty land-fish like you in many ages," he rumbled, drawing out the last s.

Keaka and Liko stood there trembling, their mouths gaping open, as Kamanuwai closed the gap between them with his waddling steps. The duck stood there peering at them again, his head cocked slightly.

"Duck! Duck exists! Duck exists!" stammered Liko.

Keaka knew his friend was on the verge of breaking into fits of hysterical giggling, which happened when he was scared, so he began to speak quickly, "Uhhh . . . my name is Keaka and this is my friend Liko. We have come seeking your aid and beg of you not to indulge your appetite for land-fish upon us, O great duck of legend."

Kamanuwai continued his one-eyed stare at them for another second before he began to clack his beak together in a loud quacking sound that they soon recognized as laughter. "*Kwek, kwek, kwek!* The pair of you actually fell under the impression that I was going to eat you!" he cried gleefully. "'Great duck of legend' indeed, *kwek, kwek*! I am nothing more than a duck, *kwek*, and I eat nothing more than a duck eats. *Kwek, kwek*, I have never tasted the flesh of a man, good sirs. I apologize for the fun I had at your expense. But to see the look upon your faces!" Kamanuwai continued to quack to himself contentedly under his breath, as he waddled to a more comfortable position on the banks of the spring. Keaka and Liko heard the creak of his joints as he resettled his wings.

"Now, what current has brought you two shards of gourd floating my way, *kwek, kwek*?" Kamanuwai asked companionably, ducking his beak into the large ʻumeke of paʻi ʻai and cooked lūʻau leaves that they had brought with them as offerings. As Keaka and Liko explained their situation, Kamanuwai *kwekked* and quacked sympathetically, but made no commitment.

"I have a surefire idea to fix everything though," Keaka hastily reassured the duck.

"I don't know," cut in Liko, his misgivings about Keaka's plan resurfacing. "Your ideas don't always work out that well. Remember that ʻauwai fiasco? Or the time that you thought it'd be faster to just make one giant kapa beater out of a log of koa and beat everyone's kapa all at once? We all ended up having to walk around naked for a week! Maybe we should just ask ourselves what Māui would do in this situation." Liko's statement was greeted with an offended silence. He had mentioned the "M" word. Liko braced for the verbal tirade that he knew was coming.

"Māui? Māui?! You know that guy took all his ideas from me! It was my idea to snare the sun, but he stole it from me and did it first!" bellowed the irate Keaka. Kamanuwai cocked his head appraisingly at Keaka, who continued in a rush, "His mom was visiting with my mom one day, and she was complaining about how the sun set too quickly, before her kapa could even dry. So I sat and thought a little bit, then I realized that if I could tie up the sun and make it slow down, then everyone's problems would be solved.

"So I got my rope ready and I was heading for the top of Kā'ala when I passed Māui, who was busy stealing sweet pīlali candy from little kids. 'Eh, Keaka, where you going?' he asked me in that slow, dim-witted voice of his. So I told him my plan."

Keaka looked somewhat embarrassed at this point, but continued on, "Then he told me that my aunty was looking for me and wanted to meet at her house near Mākua, which was about a day's walk away. So I figured I'd see my aunty first, then get down to business, but when I got there she had not given any message to Māui about wanting to see me. She had, however, just heard that he snared the sun yesterday and made the days longer so his mother could dry her kapa." Keaka stopped to draw a calming breath, before continuing.

"'What a good boy he is,' she beamed, and then asked sweetly, 'and what have you been up to lately, Keaka?' And everybody thinks he's a hero because of that. But you know what? He's a thief! That's what he is, a thief!"

Keaka's story was interrupted by Liko's disbelieving roar of laughter, and even Kamanuwai's eye glinted with humor as he chuckled and shook his head to himself, though he was polite enough not to guffaw in quite the same manner as Liko. "I promise! That story is true. It's not funny!" Keaka cried out as he punched Liko in the arm. Kamanuwai smiled graciously as he finished eating; Keaka and Liko helped him wipe the last of the pa'i 'ai and lū'au from his beak, and looked at him hopefully.

"*Kwek*, as the small stick kindles the flame on the larger, so you have convinced me to assist you. I have been acquainted with Māui since he was no more than a blood clot floating in the sea. And even before he choked the secret of fire from my cousin, the mudhen Kaʻalaenuiahina, he was as insufferable a little *kwek* as you have made him out to be in your story. So even though I lack the strength of my beardless youth and have not flown any great distance for many turnings of the moon, I shall carry you forth into the lofty heights to the great water-bearing vessel of my divine brother Kūlanihākoʻi."

"As the koa bug shimmers in the sun only because of the height of the tree it perches upon, you do us great honor, O Kamanuwai," Keaka pronounced formally, stringing together an awkward metaphor that still earned him a pleased grin from the aged duck.

"*Kwek, kwek*, let us leave this very instant then, as we have no time left to fritter away. Make sure you settle yourselves securely upon my back though, my little friends, for I will suffer no harness and my feathers are quite slick from all of this rain."

And with a triumphant *kwek*, Kamanuwai flapped his creaking wings and carried them off, slowly rising into the sky. Though Kamanuwai was not as strong a flier as he used to be, he was expert at finding the warm currents that would lift him higher into the air with less effort on his part. Just as the sun began sinking towards the horizon, they crested the edge of the ʻumeke. Liko and Keaka were awestruck by the beauty of what lay before them. Even Kamanuwai, who was witness to many wondrous things in his life, could not tear his one-eyed gaze away from what he flew over.

The reddening sun glittered on an expanse of fresh, clear water that seemed to be as vast as the ocean that lay far below it. The ʻumeke itself was made of some sort of unearthly wood that was the deep brown of fecund soil but grained with pearlescent whorls that sent thousands of rainbows playing across their sight. The mirrored surface of the water was undisturbed by the winds swirling in the atmosphere, but a definite current slowly spiraled through it.

Kamanuwai glided over the water, obviously fatigued, tracking the center of the watery gyre below, with Keaka and Liko leaning out as far as they could to act as spotters for the one-eyed bird.

Liko cried out, "There's the center! That must be where the hole is!" Keaka leaned farther out to see where Liko pointed, and Kamanuwai banked jerkily to take them closer to the water's surface. The unexpected movement made Keaka lose his grip and he was swept from his seat on Kamanuwai's back, tumbling through the air.

"Aaaaaaaaaahhhhh—!" Keaka's cry of dismay was cut off by his impact with the water, to be replaced with the burble of his panicked gulping of water. He surfaced frantically, trying to cough and breathe at the same time, waving his arms wildly before he remembered that he actually knew how to swim and did not need to panic. What did worry him as he took a deep breath, however, was that the whirlpool of water draining out of the 'umeke was pulling him inexorably down, down, down. Keaka shuddered at the thought of being sucked through the gaping crack in the bottom of the 'umeke and possibly drowning, and *then* plummeting to the earth thousands of feet below where his bones and guts would burst upon impact like an overripe breadfruit.

As he was drawn closer to the bottom, he braced himself mentally and physically for the sudden acceleration that would signal the beginning of his fall through the large hole he had made in the 'umeke. Keaka almost gasped out all of the air in his lungs in surprise when he came to an abrupt halt, a sharp pain on his rear end. He reached down to feel the source of the pain on his buttocks. It took him a moment to realize what had happened.

His butt had plugged the hole.

He thought he had made a huge crack in the 'umeke with his mighty throw, but it turned out that the opening was just the size of his war club Ku'ipē. The weight of the water and the awkward angle of his body kept Keaka from being able to extricate himself from the hole, however. Keaka laughed bitterly to himself. All his notions about being a hero seemed so silly now. He would die saving his people in perhaps the most ignominious way possible. Drowned, with his butt stuck in a hole he himself had made. Mooning the entire world. He could imagine the elders of his family, gasping with laughter, telling and retelling his story to explain the presence of the bright full moon that hung above them.

As Keaka began to run out of air and he resigned himself to his fate, he felt Liko's arms wrap around him roughly. Together, they levered Keaka out of the hole. The two of them pushed off from the bottom and back to the surface, where Kamanuwai flipped them up on his back. They lay with their chests heaving, gulping down air. The duck *kwekked* concernedly over them, but save for a huge painful, dark-red bruise on Keaka's butt, they were uninjured.

When Keaka unwrapped his malo to examine the bruise as best he could, an idea struck him. He stood there holding the sodden barkcloth. He balled up the malo and looked at it closely. "E Liko ē, take off your malo!" Keaka yelled excitedly.

Liko gaped uncomprehendingly at Keaka, but began to unwrap his malo slowly.

"Quick! Quick!" shouted Keaka, and grabbed the end of Liko's malo, spinning him around in his haste to take it off his confused friend. Once he balled up the two malo together, he dove back into the water before Liko or Kamanuwai could stop him. He swam down with powerful strokes, aided by the downward spiral of the water.

This time he smiled for real, as he shoved the wadded-up malo into the hole, the absorbent barkcloth slowing the draining water to a trickle.

He swam back up to the surface and collapsed on Kamanuwai's broad back. Liko looked down appraisingly at the now-plugged hole. "Well, that's not how Māui would have done it, but I think you saved the day." Keaka regarded Liko silently for a moment, before the two naked, sopping wet friends hugged each other and chuckled in disbelief at all that had taken place.

The exhausted Kamanuwai flew them to Kou. The giant duck did not have enough strength to carry the two of them all the way back, so he set them down several miles out of town. They made their farewells and Keaka and Liko trudged through the mud back to Kou as the sun was slipping below the horizon.

When they walked into the market, no one believed that they had plugged the leak, because the rain still fell. It didn't help anyone take them seriously that they were both naked and muddy, and Keaka had a giant bruise on his ass.

Liko took offense at their indifference, bellowing, "You should be celebrating Keaka! What he did was genius! Better than just plugging the hole like you ungrateful idiots would have done!" He shouted at them about how the wadded-up malo allowed the water to flow through sporadically, meaning it would rain every so often without them having to wait on Kūlanihāko'i anymore. But no one paid attention to his explanations.

Keaka said nothing, merely throwing his arm around Liko and leading him towards their canoe to go back to Honouliuli.

Even when several weeks had passed and Keaka's mother came on her gossip tour of the district, smiling her gap-toothed smile, to tell him that Old Lady Wahakale told her that Māui had come back from the dead, built wings from banana leaves and coconut fronds, and flapped up into the sky to defeat Kūlanihākoʻi in single combat, ensuring the cycle of rain for the good of all humankind, he just smiled and warmly pressed his nose to his mother's.

Keaka knew no one would ever tell his story. Wadding up barkcloth to plug a hole the size of his fist wasn't a heroic way to solve a problem, and in the end it didn't even make that good of a story, but it was done. Keaka walked over to the next compound to help them with their sweet potato mounds, softly singing one of his favorite songs about Māui.

Notes on "Of No Real Account" by Bryan Kamaoli Kuwada (2015)

A less popular wonder-genre cousin invites our attention.

"Of No Real Account" features a young man who with his brotherly friend Liko goes on a quest and learns to be a Hawaiian hero; as such, the story connects with the coming-of-age theme and heroic optimism of folktales. But its more developed intertextual links are with the legendary tales of Maui, the demigod known across Oceania. As Israel Kamakawiwoʻole's (1993) best-seller song goes: "Told is the tale of the mischievous one / Who fished out the islands / And captured the sun / His deeds and task I will unmask / So that you'll understand / That before there was a Clark Kent / There was a Hawaiian Sup'pa Man." At first, Kuwada's protagonist, Keaka, whose name can translate as "the shadow," wants to be a superhero but also feels and acts "inadequately heroic." The results are comic to the point that Kuwada has, tongue in cheek, described the story as "silly"; but then as Thomas King tells his audience in *The Truth about Stories*, also tongue in cheek, none of us "would make the mistake of confusing storytelling strategies with the value and sophistication of a story" (2008, 23). Kuwada explains: "Traditionally, Hawaiians had silly stories, but nowadays we mostly hear and read the ones where everyone is pali ke kua and mahina ke alo, backs like a cliff and faces like the moon. They're all stunningly beautiful and with amazing mana. Keaka and Liko aren't quite like that." They aren't, but in the end Keaka's and Liko's actions benefit their people and land, which also brings them to a transformed understanding of what "heroic" means.

Keaka and Liko's story inserts itself in a continuum of Hawaiian moʻolelo, traditional and new stories that have over the centuries and in the face of occupation and settler colonialism continued to transmit Hawaiian knowledge of the world and how to be in it. Moʻolelo, as Hawaiian scholars from Mary Kawena Pukui to kuʻualoha hoʻomanawanui have explained, is a capacious genre firmly rooted in the oral tradition (but not confined to it or to the past) that includes history as well as fiction, myth, and legend. Whether it has the epic dimensions of a Pele and Hiʻiaka narrative or it takes the form of a "silly" tale, moʻolelo asserts the intimate and wondrous connection of Hawaiians with land through story. Moʻolelo should absolutely not be equated to fairy tale as colonial collectors often did; but moʻolelo kamahaʻo (wondrous moʻolelo) can be seen to have *some* affinity with the fairy tale, as both genres represent worlds where everything is animate and interconnected (Bacchilega 2017). That said, the specific relationship of moʻolelo to land and history—one that Kuwada's story shows—does not extend to fairy tale.

"Of No Real Account," then, as Kuwada states, "is a story about stories and how our moʻolelo exist on the landscape and continue to shape us." It embodies the cultural and political framework that Brandy Nālani McDougall (2012) calls "Ola (i) Nā Moʻolelo," which she translates as "Living Moʻolelo" in the double sense of "the stories live" and Hawaiians "live or become moʻolelo." By retelling stories about Maui and other Hawaiian heroes, Kuwada's Hawaiian wonder tale brings them to twenty-first-century readers, especially Hawaiian young adults as the target audience, in a form that is contemporary, agile, and resonant with Hawaiian values as well as fantasy, science fiction, and folktale tropes. Thus, in Caryn Lesuma's eloquent words, the story acts "as a portal to the greater archive" of Hawaiian moʻolelo (2016, 37).

Notes on *Aitu* by Dan Taulapapa McMullin (2016)

An otherworldly invitation to interrupt the past and imagine an alter-Native future.

THE TITLE *AITU* TRANSLATES as "spirit" and "demon" from the Samoan language. The top branches in the image escape its dark circular background and move beyond the frame, thus evoking a sense of the beyond or otherworldly that breaks out of the confines of realism, conjuring an alter-Native view, one that does not simply coincide with Western understandings of ghost, possession, or ethereality. *This* spirit is embodied: shapely, but not strictly human. The body is dark, but also verdant and lush. If this aitu is a wondrous being, its representation is also a form of artificiality or life simulation: the branches growing out of the aitu's head are like cheap special-effect antennae; and the all-too-regular patterns of the leaves may lead us to think of the plastic flora decorating a hotel lobby, restaurant table, or tomb. But the branches growing out of the aitu's head are also rootlike, and the leaves are not growing upward to meet the light but downward to drape the body. Do they do the work of fig leaves on white marble statues? Possibly, but these leaves are tropical, and the aitu's back is turned to us viewers.

Aitu, a two-dimensional photographic image of one of the mannequins in Taulapapa's art installation *Aue Away*, was the face of "Thinking with Stories in Times of Conflict: A Conference in Fairy-Tale Studies" at Wayne State University in 2017, where Taulapapa—an artist and poet from Sāmoa Amelika (American Samoa) and the coeditor of *Samoan Queer Lives* (2019)—was a keynote speaker. About the installation's video version on Vimeo, Taulapapa (2016b) writes: *Aue Away* "comments on notions of anthropological display as it relates to Hollywood, cartoons, in conflict with ideas of indigenous sovereignty and the Fa'afafine body." It is significant that Taulapapa chose to isolate an image from *Aue Away* and re-present *Aitu* as a still photograph—allowing it to exercise its powers differently.

In his poetic essay "The Fag End of Fāgogo," Taulapapa writes that this Samoan genre is a "fictionalizing, making fabulous" tale (2019, 217) and that his work looks "at disappearance, indigenous disappearance, the disappearance of fāgogo, the appearance of fāgogo, indigenous futurism, an end that is always renewing, like coral" (219). This is *not* the settler-colonial disappearance of the Natives but their resourceful survivance via creative disguise. Are those branches in *Aitu* more like coral than roots? Toward what kind of Indigenous future is Taulapapa's aitu turned?

Aitu

Dan Taulapapa McMullin

Dan Taulapapa McMullin, *Aitu*, 2016, photograph print on aluminum 8-inch diameter, from installation *Aue Away* by Dan Taulapapa McMullin.

Part II

Interrupting Invitations

Notes on *Medusa* by Rosalind Hyatt Orme (2018)

What might one expect of an invitation from this figure?

WE CHOSE AN IMAGE of this figurine for the cover of the book because her posture, whimsy, and mixture of inquisitiveness and bold potential speak to us of the kinds of contemporary, complicated, and wondrous invitations and interruptions we'd like to evoke in this volume.

In a different context, on her own against a white background, does *Medusa* look or seem different from what you saw on the cover? A little more . . . something? A little less something else?

With her head tilted a little to the side and her arms placed demurely in her lap, she seems polite, even self-deprecating. Yet the spread and movement of her iconic hair and the tentacle-like movement of her dress (or is her lower body made of tentacles?) ensure that she takes up space. Polite perhaps, but no shrinking violet. Rather, her hot-pink skin contrasts with her black-as-black living hair and body. And what are we to do with the gaze in relation to this figure? She has no eyes! Nevertheless, she gazes back at us.

Both this figure and Shary Boyle's ceramic spider-woman *Untitled* have nonhuman supernumerary physical characteristics. The eight spider-like eyes and arms in Boyle's figurine and the snakelike hair and dress or lower body in Hyatt Orme's figurine are juxtaposed to dainty feminine beauty. Arachnid, serpentine, and/or cephalopodic aspects in transhuman bodies are, in classical Western art, signs of dangerous and predatory monsters. How do they affect the humanity and indeed the femininity of these two?

Does Rosalind Hyatt Orme's sculpture challenge or threaten the viewer like her namesake from Greek mythology, or does this twenty-first-century Medusa have a different relationship to her viewer? Hyatt Orme tells us that in this case Medusa's form came well before her name: "That's what everybody kept calling her, and it made sense." Does our reading change if we do not think of her as modeled on classical Medusa but named because of cultural resemblance?

Medusa

Rosalind Hyatt Orme

Rosalind Hyatt Orme, *Medusa*, 2018, polymer clay, 4.5 x 5 x 4 cm.

Fairytales for Lost Children

Diriye Osman

WE LIVED IN A sky-blue bungalow on Tigoni Road, right next to Aziza's kindergarten, Little Woods. Although our house was on a decent plot of land the garden was neglected, and thorns and brambles had taken root. I knew fruit and flowers weren't on Hooyo and Aabo's minds. They were thinking bills and blood-relatives that needed beso.

I remembered our garden in Somalia, with its guava and pawpaw trees, callas and azaleas. I often used to sit there and watch bullfrogs hunt insects. In Disney fairytales the bad guy always loses, but in reality he is rarely thwarted. Whenever the bullfrog's tongue flicked out, it rolled back with its victim. I learnt not to mess with nature from an early age.

I WAS TEN YEARS old when I started kindergarten. Aabo and Hooyo thought it was the best way to learn the language.

"But I don't want to learn Ingriis," I moaned, dunking my margarine sandwich into a cup of tea and slurping it. Aabo finished his porridge and washed it down with a glass of lemon water.

"You have to learn the luuqad," he said. "We're in Kenya now. Everyone here speaks English, even the maid."

"Besides, Aziza is enjoying her school," said Hooyo, who was polishing my Bata Prefect shoes, adding, "She's already learning her ABCs."

This irked me: Aziza surpassing me in the alphabet was a sign that she would surpass me in life. I grabbed my Aladdin lunchbox, which my mother had stuffed with rice and lamb from the previous night, and followed my dad outside to his Toyota Cressida. It was a poor cousin to the Mercedes we'd owned in Somalia but we were lucky to have a car at all. Seven months ago we were living in Utanga Refugee Camp in Mombasa, unsure of whether we would be sent back to Somalia. I could never forget the corpse of a woman we saw as we drove out of Mogadishu, brains splattered across the roadside. I vomited in the back of the pickup truck because Aabo refused to pull over and let me out.

Diriye Osman, "Fairytales for Lost Children," in *Fairytales for Lost Children*, 2013.

"I will not stop until we get to the boats," he shouted, honking at the refugees trying to walk their way out of war. Young men pushed their grandparents in wheelbarrows; a woman in labour was squatting in the middle of the road to give birth.

I thought of that woman now as I glanced at Hooyo's watermelon-sized belly, as she waved goodbye to Aabo and me.

As soon as we got into the car Aabo put on his favourite UB40 cassette, belting out the lyrics to *Red, Red Wine* as we drove down Chaka Road.

"Join me," he encouraged.

"Okay."

I sang along in a tinny voice.

"That's terrible. You've got to sing like you mean it."

"But I do."

"Then show it." He lifted his voice to an operatic note. When I tried to copy him, I sounded like Shirley Temple with constipation.

"You'll get there, son," said Aabo, knowing that I wouldn't. It was nice that he half-believed in me.

We turned down Marcus Garvey Road. At the top of the road was an office building called Studio House, all slick with sunlight bouncing off its black glass panels. Right next to the building were a group of chokoras around my age. They were rummaging through the mountain of rubbish piled outside it, finding the odd banana or orange peel to gnaw on. Their fakhrinimo reminded me of the folks we had seen in the refugee camp, except these boys had bottles of glue clamped between their teeth. Snot slid down from one of the boys' noses. He licked it off.

Because Marcus Garvey was a dirt road Aabo had to go slow and manoeuvre the car carefully to avoid a flat tyre. One of the chokoras saw me staring at him and pointed his middle finger at me. I turned away, afraid. Seven months ago, running around the camp in rags handed to me by UNICEF aid workers, I didn't look much different from those street boys. I was afraid that our newfound prosperity was a trick played by a capricious God: that soon we would be back in Utanga, leading qashin lives that no amount of praying or chanting surahs could elevate.

Aabo had no such worries. He was a man rarely plagued by self-doubt. This was to be expected from a former politician. During Siad Barre's regime Aabo served as one of his chief advisors. Before that he had been the dean of faculty at Somalia National University. And before his prodigious academic and political career he was a shepherd tending his father's flock in Bosaaso. His favourite motto was, "Life's all about public relations." It was this cocksure attitude that got us out of Utanga and into a three-bedroom house in Kilimani within months of our arrival there. It was also the same attitude which, coupled with several handy contacts, enabled him to start Pharmcon, his own pharmaceutical company.

He was still singing as the car continued to bump into potholes. Every time the Cressida jolted his voice quavered, but remained rhythmic. Aabo saw life as one long tune. Even during prayer, when he said "Allahu Akbar" his voice would drip with melisma. As we neared the school I began to worry he would burst into song when he introduced me to my teacher. Luckily he stopped singing when we turned into Kindaruma road and a large pinecone hit the windshield.

"Shit." Aabo stopped the car. We both got out and looked above. Pine trees towered over us. Thud! Another pinecone hit the roof of the Cressida. Dark figures moved in the trees. Before we knew it, baboons were pelting us with pinecones, primatial terrorists, intimidating us with scary teeth and screeches. Aabo and I hurriedly got back into the car and drove off. We had gone all of thirty feet when he stopped at a compound with a pine tree sign outside it. My heart sank when he said, "Welcome to Pine Tree Kindergarten."

"EVERYONE, PLEASE WELCOME HIRSI," said my new teacher, Miss Mumbi. "He's from Somalia." All I understood were my name and "Somalia." Everything else was an alien speech-bubble. Even the way she said my name was exotic: "Hirsi" not "Xirsi." Still, the class, a set of well-fed six-year olds, welcomed me with cheers. They were practically cherubs, ripe for beating. A Kenyan girl with a kuus-kuus hairstyle looked at me like I was a cannibal ready to suck her dhuux dry. If there was a God He would've snatched me from that kindergarten and whisked me back home to people I knew and understood. I began to lose my faith that day.

Miss Mumbi, however, kept hers: not in Pine Tree's educational curriculum, or even in God, but in the teachings of the Mau Mau. She was a militant nationalist posing as a pre-school teacher. Clad in a kanga, she saw the alphabet as the perfect way to decolonise our Disney-addled minds. Whilst other pre-schoolers were learning that "A" was for "Apple," "B" for "Ball," "C" for "Cat," we were grappling with "A" is for "Ameru," "B" for "Bukusi," "C" for "Chonyi." Miss Mumbi listed Kenyan languages and clans that confused us: "Kore," "Maragoli," "Pokomo." I hardly knew English, let alone what Pokomo meant. The only

English word she used was "Queen." She turned to the girls and said, "You're all queens, my dears." To which an Indian boy piped to general laughter, "Can I be a queen, too?"

Even Story Time was political. Miss Mumbi infused each fairytale with Kenyan flavour. She illustrated these remixes on the blackboard. "Rapunzel" became "Rehema," a fly gabar imprisoned in Fort Jesus. Rehema had an Afro that grew and grew. Her Afro grew bigger than her body and she looked bomb. The Afro became so strong that it burst through the ceiling of the fort. It exploded into the sky and reached the stars. The Afro wrapped itself around the moon and pulled Rehema out of the fort.

"When Rehema grew up," said Miss Mumbi, "she told the story to her children, and they passed it on to theirs. Even after her death, the Afro lived on."

To demonstrate this durability, Miss Mumbi patted her own perfect 'fro.

"I want an Afro," said a white girl with pigtails.

"Then tell your mum. In fact, tell all your mums you want Afros."

I suspected Miss Mumbi was getting tipsy on power.

"Tomorrow," she said, "I shall read you Jomo and the Beanstalk."

AFTERWARDS THE CLASS WENT outside to play. In the trees baboons screeched "OoOoAhAh." I couldn't see them but they sounded close. I imagined a baboon swinging from the branches and landing in the playground. The kids would scream and bolt but the baboon would be too quick. It would snatch a boy and drag him back to the trees. The baboon would season the boy like nyama choma, add salt and paprika, and gobble him up. Then it would toss the bones into the playground as a warning.

I didn't want to be baboon-bait so I headed into the library, where shelves were stacked with Disney buugaag that made me ache. I ran my hand across the spine of each title, savouring its elegance. To me they were holy texts, each idea and image sacred. These stories were about love, loss, fear, innocence, strength. The real God was Imagination. I was Muslim but fiction was my true religion.

The God of Imagination lived in fairytales. And the best fairytales made you fall in love. It was while flicking through *Sleeping Beauty* that I met my first love. Ivar. He was a six-year-old bello ragazzo with blond hair and eyebrows. He had bomb-blue eyes and his two front teeth were missing.

The road to Happily Ever After, however, was paved with political barbed wire. Three things stood in my way.

1. The object of my affection didn't know he was the object of my affection.
2. The object of my affection preferred Action Man to Princess Aurora.
3. The object of my affection was a boy and I wasn't allowed to love a boy.

But I was allowed to dream. And in my dreams Ivar became my prince, hacking at the thorns that hemmed me in. He slew dragons, fought fire with a shield and sword, all to a Tchaikovsky score. The boy was Michael Jackson bad. And he would kiss me to break the spell. He would kiss me but all that'd break would be my heart. He could never be mine.

WHILE IVAR ROAMED MY dreams, my parents' nightmares were re-enacted on CNN. The TV flooded our lives with bad news about Somalia. Young gabdo were raped and mutilated, an old man was tortured with teeth-extraction by pliers until he bled to death. I worried about my grandfather and grandmother, who were still in Somalia. I knew Ayeeyo would survive: she was strong and inventive. Awoowe, however, was senile and couldn't tell a gun-clip from a gumball. Every day I asked Hooyo, "When're we heading home?"

"Soon," she'd sigh, "soon."

"You said that yesterday."

"It's up to God, son."

"Maybe God doesn't know best."

She slapped me for blaspheming but I wouldn't let it go: "God is punishing our people."

Hooyo pulled me close. "No, son, we're punishing each other."

She pressed me against her basketball-shaped belly. She smelt of barafuun and cocoa butter, of milk and memories. Hooyo smelt of home.

OUR HOME SMELT OF fear that even foox couldn't conceal. We lived too close to Kilimani Police Station. My waalid may have reinvented themselves but to the booliis we were still refugee bastards who sucked on Nanny State's iron teats until there was nothing left for her legitimate children. The irony was that Nanny State's teats were drier than my dad's Donny Osmond cassettes. That shosho's nutrients had long been sapped by Moi's regime. But that only worsened the trickle of poison, the building animus against Somalis.

Most Somalis lived in Eastleigh, a slum that made Soweto seem dope, but despite the filth and farabutos, business was booming there to the tune of $30 million a month. These Somalis were financial sorcerers. Illegal-immigrant financial-sorcerers. The police devised a Plan of Action. Armed with AK47s, they began a walalo witch-hunt. You could be at work or working your honey, your ass was under arrest.

The cops weren't cruel. They gave options: "Kipanda," "Kitu kidogo" or "Kakuma." Most folks didn't have kipandas to live in Kenya so they paid kitu kidogo. Kakuma wasn't an option. One of the largest African refugee camps, it was also known as Never-Never Land: meaning, "If you end up there, you'll never-never be allowed to leave."

My parents weren't down with that Plan of Action, so they devised their own.

"Never open the gates to the police," Aabo told Waithaka, our watchman.

"Never tell them that Somalis live here," Hooyo told Mary, the maid.

"You're not allowed to play outside," they told us.

The booliis became the bogeymen of our nightmares. At night every sound was sinister: dogs barking as iron gates creaked, owls hooting. Aziza and I shared a bedroom and we shuddered under our blankets.

"What if they snatch us?" asked Azi, who was only five years old.

"They won't," I said uncertainly.

"But what if?"

"Insha Allah, they won't."

"Will you protect me?"

"Yes."

"Promise?"

"I promise."

"Cross you heart and hope to die."

"We're Muslim. We say, 'wallahi billahi tallahi.'"

"Say it then."

"Wallahi billahi tallahi."

"Can I share your bed?"

"No."

"Fadlan."

"No. You'll wet the bed."

"I'm wearing a nappy."

I considered this. After some thought I scooted over and she scrambled in next to me. We lay in the dark, ears pricked up for eerie sounds.

"Xirsi?"

"What?"

"Tell me a story."

"ONCE UPON A TIME in Lavington there lived a chica named Kohl Black. She was plumpness personified: thick thighs, lips, Afro. Her eyes were the colour of coffee. Her skin was darker than liquorice. Kohl was supuu but her stepmother Immaculate considered her subhuman, 'a walking, talking whale.' Immaculate, as her name suggested, was obsessive. She obsessed about her size and skin-tone, about her home and hygiene. She bathed in milk even though there were shortages around the country. She nourished her skin with eggs, avocado and bleach. She wore shoulder-padded blouses and wigs made from the finest horsehair. Immaculate was a dem that made Princess Diana look pedestrian.

"Every week a herbal doctor came to cure her 'ailments,' which ranged from disputes with her dead husband's relatives, who insisted that she killed him (a claim she always denied), to fights with fanya-kazis who accused her of being an abusive employer (again, a claim she denied, although she relished whupping her maid Purity's ass).

"The daktari's diagnosis was simple: 'Envylitis.' Anyone who wished Immaculate ill suffered from this sickness. So he prescribed 'medicine.' Her dead husband's relatives soon took their kelele elsewhere and Purity put a stop to her nonsense (although Immaculate still enjoyed klepping her).

"The doctor didn't tell Immaculate that she too suffered from 'Envylitis.' Immaculate always asked, 'Daktari, daktari, who's the finest of them all?'

"The doctor had sense. 'Ni wewe tu. You, madam, are the finest of them all.' If he didn't say so, Immaculate would hire snipers to take out her competition, thereby diminishing his client base.

"One day, while Immaculate and her doctor were sipping tea, Kohl sashayed into the sitting room. She wore a tight kanga. The doctor nearly spilled his tea. After grabbing her textbooks, Kohl sauntered out.

"'Haki, I'm housing a small elephant,' sighed Immaculate. 'That girl eats her body weight in githeri. No wonder our fanya-kazis are so malnourished: she eats all their food!'

"'That girl is bodacious,' said the doctor. 'Fullness is fineness.'

"'Ati?' snapped Immaculate. 'You mean to tell me Kohl is the finest of them all?'

"'Err . . .' the doctor started sweating. 'No, of course not.'

"But Immaculate knew the truth.

"'Then it is your job to remove her. Otherwise all the juju in the world won't save you.'

"'Sawa sawa.'

"But the doctor didn't comply. On his way out he saw Kohl reading on the veranda and warned her.

"'Ngai,' said Kohl, 'I knew that mama was insane but not Mathari-asylum insane. What should I do, daktari?'

"'Kimbia to Kawangware. She'll never find you there.'

"So Kohl ran to Kawangware. Clad in only a kanga and a pair of slippers, she felt underprepared. As she entered the slum she closed her nose. Sewage flowed everywhere. Flies buzzed around piles of faeces. An mtoto had stuck flowers in some manure—"

"Miss Mumbi! Miss Mumbi, please come to my office."

Miss Edna, the English principal, cut Miss Mumbi's story short. We were so jazzed by the fairytale that we all cried, "Aww!"

"Worry not, watoto," said Miss Mumbi as Miss Edna escorted her out, "I shall finish the story of Kohl Black and the Seven Street Boys."

The class cheered, but all I could hear was Miss Edna hissing, "Not if I've anything to do with it."

Ivar came over to me and said, "My mum complained about Miss Mumbi."

I didn't tell him that Hooyo had also complained about her.

"She's supposed to teach you Ingriis not Kenyati," Hooyo had said. So she started schooling me herself. Every day I developed my vocabulary. Initially, the words felt wooden but now I could string sentences together.

"Why your mum complain?" I asked Ivar.

"She said Miss Mumbi is a bad teacher."

"Why?" I wanted him to keep talking. His breath smelt like a baby's.

"She's just not good."

His hair looked better than Aziza's Barbie: so fly.

"I didn't like Miss Mumbi's story," he whispered.

"It's good story."

"No, it's terrible. She made Snow White black."

"So?"

"Everyone knows Snow White isn't black."

Suddenly Ivar wasn't so fly. I thought Miss Mumbi's retelling was excellent—crazy but excellent. I told Ivar this. He stared at me and said something that made me want to cry.

"Are you a refugee?"

I WANTED MY REFUGEE status revoked. Sharci la'aan meant a life of shame.

The Kenyan police thought so too. Our shame was their salary on the side. That afternoon they crept into our compound. Waithaka, our watchman, had gone to the kiosk but he wouldn't have been able to stop them.

Mary was eating matoke on the veranda when she spotted them. She ran inside and warned us.

"Ngai, mama, the police are outside."

Without missing a beat Hooyo rushed us into her bedroom. The doorbell rang.

"Mary, don't let them in and don't tell them we live here."

"Haya, mama."

Hooyo shoved us into her dressing-room and locked the door. My parent's dressing-room smelled of unsi and Ungaro. Aziza and I sometimes applied Hooyo's lipstick and kissed the mirror. We now crouched on the floor and called out to God.

"Uskut!" hissed Hooyo. "Now's not the time!" Then she pressed her belly and groaned.

"What's wrong, Hooyo?" asked Aziza.

"Nothing, sweetie." Hooyo breathed heavily.

"Is the baby coming?" I asked.

Hooyo didn't answer, just gestured me to be quiet. Sweat soaked her forehead.

We could hear Mary arguing with the booliis but we couldn't make out what was being said. Hooyo started hyperventilating. The spot we were sitting on became wet.

"Akh! Aziza, why'd you pee?"

"It's Hooyo."

She was right: Hooyo had urinated on the floor. I felt sick with fear.

"My waters broke," she said.

"What does that mean?"

"The baby's coming." Hooyo looked ready to scream. I stuffed Aabo's socks into her mouth.

"Bite on that," I said.

Aziza started crying.

"Uskut!" I said. "Hooyo needs us."

We heard someone in the bedroom. We held our breaths. The handle on the dressing-room door turned. A knock came. I moved round in front of Hooyo and Aziza to try and shield them.

"Mama," came Mary's voice, "the police have gone."

We didn't believe her. She rattled at the handle again.

"Haki, they've gone."

"Cross your heart and hope to die," I said.

"Wallahi billahi tallahi."

I opened the door. Mary rushed to remove the socks from Hooyo's mouth. "Mama, come to the bed. The police have gone."

"Mary, what happen Hooyo?" whimpered Aziza.

"She'll be sawa." Mary supported Hooyo to the bed. "Xirsi, go call dad."

"I help Hooyo."

"You can help by calling your dad," Mary said, shooing me out and closing the door.

I scurried to the sitting-room and dialled Aabo's office.

"I'm on my way," he said.

"Hurry, Aabo, hurry!"

The baby was born in Hooyo's bedroom. A girl. In honour of the midwife who delivered her, Hooyo named my new sister Maryam.

"Why not just call her Mary?" I asked.

"Because we're Muslim," hissed Hooyo. "In Islam Mary is Maryam."

We all crowded around the bambino. She had feathery hair, a tiny nose and Hooyo's full lips. She was bella.

When Aabo arrived the first thing he did was give Mary a pay-rise. The second thing was sack Waithaka for not watching over us. The final thing was hug Hooyo.

I looked at my family and recalled the scene in Bambi when the baby was born. If that scene were re-enacted Hooyo would be the doe, Maryam Bambi, and Aziza Thumper. Aabo, Mary and I would be the forest critters leading the celebrations.

AABO WAS STILL CELEBRATING on my final day of kindergarten. He cranked Sade on the car stereo as we drove to Pine Tree. As he sang along to *The Sweetest Taboo* I spotted the chokoras outside Studio House. The street-boy who once pointed his middle finger at me now stuck his tongue out. I shrugged as we drove past.

As we turned into Kindaruma Road I feared the baboons would terrorise us. But we didn't see them. For now.

To COMMEMORATE THE END of term the teachers threw a party for the pre-schoolers. We donned hats and drank Sunny Delight. There had been no more political Story Time sessions since Miss Mumbi was sacked three weeks ago: we'd had to contend with Miss Consolata's stodgy sheeko. I missed Miss Mumbi's hauteur, her sense of high drama and obsession with decolonisation. Next term I would begin at St. Austin's Academy, a private school in Lavington. Aabo had enrolled me in the fifth grade, but with my faulty English I feared failure. I would miss the kindergarten and the sense of arrested development it afforded me.

After the party Ivar came up to me and apologised for calling me a refugee.

"Hirsi," he asked, "what does 'refugee' mean?"

"It mean no home, fighting, death."

"Have you ever seen a dead body?"

"Yes."

"Cool!"

He seemed excited by this, so I told him gory stories galore.

"And you saw all that?" he asked.

"Yes, I see all."

"Did your mummy protect you?"

"My mummy and my daddy."

"Would you go back to Somalia?"

"I want very badly but Somalia no good. Fighting all time."

"You can stay here now."

"I will."

"Hirsi, will you be my best friend?"

"I promise."

"Cross your heart and hope to die."

"I'm Muslim. I say 'wallahi billahi tallahi.'"

Afterwards, while the other kids were playing indoors, Ivar and I snuck off to ride the swings. We took turns in pushing one another. Every time he pushed me I squealed and swung back. That was the happiest moment of my life. But it was short-lived.

"I want to climb the trees," said Ivar.

"Ivar, I afraid of monkeys."

"Don't be a scaredy-cat. It'll be fun."

That didn't reassure me. But I wanted to please him so I acquiesced. There was a large pine tree at the back of the kindergarten. We went over to it and Ivar said, "Hoist me up."

I took hold of his legs and lifted him. He was strong for a six-year old and pulled himself up onto the first branch.

"Okay, Ivar. Time to come down. Miss Consolata be very angry."

"I don't care," he said, swinging from one branch to the next. I was so scared he'd fall that I shut my eyes.

"Look, Hirsi. Can you do this?" He hung from a branch using one arm.

"Ivar, please don't—"

As soon as he said, "I'm climbing higher," I heard the familiar, "OoOoAhAh." Like a bad dream, a baboon swung onto the tree. Ivar was too high up to hepa.

"I get help," I called, but Ivar didn't want me to go.

"Please don't leave me!" he cried.

The baboon screeched as it made its way to Ivar's branch. I knew it would kill him so I shouted, "Jump, Ivar. Jump, I catch you."

But Ivar was petrified. He refused to let go and the baboon was gaining on him.

"Will you catch me?" he asked, through tears.

"I promise."

"Say wallahi billahi tallahi."

"Wallahi—"

The baboon leapt at Ivar, who let go of the branch. I tried to catch him but he hit the ground head-first and I heard bones break. His angles were like a pretzel. His eyes were open and blood oozed from his mouth like drool. He was Sleeping Beauty and I was the prince who had to save him. So I pressed my lips against his and kissed him. I kissed him until I tasted his blood.

"Ivar, please wake up," I moaned. But this wasn't *Sleeping Beauty* with its Happily-Ever-After. It wasn't even *Kohl Black and the Seven Street Boys*, a story with a beginning and no ending. None of the fairytales I had read had prepared me for this.

I looked up and the whole school had gathered in the playground. All the kids were crying and Miss Edna rushed off to call the ambulance. Miss Consolata took me to the outside tap to clean up.

"Me get deported?" I asked, tears streaming down my face.

"No," she said, although her tone suggested otherwise.

What if I was deported? What would happen to my family? I began to vomit. Miss Consolata said something but all I could hear was the baboon screeching in the trees. I couldn't tell whether it was hungry or in heat, or whether it was mocking me, laughing at the monkey on my back.

Notes on "Fairytales for Lost Children" by Diriye Osman (2013)

> When their own tales are interrupted, children will interpret wonder in their own ways.

The tale "Sleeping Beauty" has a strong metanarrative dimension in that several of its versions include the telling of tales about the inaccessible castle and what it holds, thus reinforcing the power of orality and storytelling (Haase 2011). Osman's too is a tale about tales. Within it, Miss Mumbi, a kindergarten teacher in Nairobi, Kenya, customizes fairy tales so as "to decolonise [the children's] Disney-addled minds." Whether it is "Jomo and the Beanstalk," "Rehema" and her wondrous Afro, or "Kohl Black and the Seven Street Boys," her adaptations are filled with details that valorize African bodies and culture. If stories help to imagine futures and lives we want to inhabit, then one of Miss Mumbi's strategies for making fairy-tale happy endings more accessible to the Black children in her school is to give Snow White a makeover, transforming her into a plump dark beauty. Miss Mumbi knows her Story Time is political; so does Xirsi, the ten-year-old refugee from Somalia who is in her class to improve his English; and so do the kindergarteners' parents who have her fired before she can tell "Kohl Black" in its entirety.

Xirsi likes his teacher's retellings but, regardless of what Disney's characters look like, he is already taken with enacting the "heroic optimism" (Carter 1990; Warner 2014; Zipes 2012) of the fairy tales he knows, empowered by them as dreams that are both flight and fight—flight of fantasy away from the everyday reality of fear, powerlessness, and exclusion he experiences; fight against the multiple prejudices that would bar him from having a desirable future. He is Muslim in a prevalently Christian country, a refugee facing hostility, and a boy falling in love with another boy. When Xirsi imagines himself as Aurora from the Disney *Sleeping Beauty* film, kindergartner Ivar is his blond and blue-eyed prince, slaying dragons to kiss him. The imagined film is exciting, and Ivar is "Michael Jackson bad"; and yet, beyond the reanimating kiss, Xirsi knows the spell of social barriers cannot be magicked away. But even this understanding does not prepare him, in the face of the tragic accident on the last day of school, for the utter failure of his own heroic attempt to bring Ivar back to life.

In a 2017 blog post, "The Queering of Sleeping Beauty," Diriye Osman shares that he first watched Disney's *Sleeping Beauty* in French when he was seven years old, having recently arrived in Kenya from Somalia, "marvelling at the disparity between the gorgeousness that was spilling from the TV screen and the nightmarish harassment that my fellow Somalis were experiencing on a daily basis." This statement grounds his short story historically and autobiographically in experiences of sociopolitical trauma and also invites thinking about fairy tales and "Sleeping Beauty" (ATU 410) in particular.

Fairy tales mingle with each other and other narratives across national, cultural, ideological, and media boundaries, acting on the imagination of young people especially, in unpredictable ways that are unequally regulating and liberating. Told by young Xirsi in the first person, "Fairytales for Lost Children" shows how fairy-tale emplotment fuels desire and regulates it at the same time and even more so how inhabiting a socially sanctioned plot *creatively* can initiate change in oneself and the world. If "every fictive act is an attempt to correct the past" (Osman 2017), it does not mean that the attempt will be successful. The Disneyfied fairy tale seems bankrupt as far as helping to imagine more just and sustainable futures for children who face discrimination, abuse, and conflict in our world. But what is it about queering a "Sleeping Beauty" story that builds hope and courage?

Two related aspects of this wonder tale speak to Osman's situated experimentalism with queer storytelling. One is, in Xirsi's words, the "sense of arrested development" that the Kenyan kindergarten "afforded" him. This "arrested development" is perceived as a problem, a monkey on his back, by the authorities; but it is also symbolic of a temporality that refuses to move toward the set goals of heteropatriarchal adulthood and that Lewis Seifert (2015) sees activated in Charles Perrault's "Sleeping Beauty." The other is the I-narrator-protagonist's language, "a mash-up of poetic syntax mixed with Kiswahili, nineties hip-hop slang, Italian, Somali and English" (Osman 2017), which gives voice to Xirsi's fragmented experience at the same time that it celebrates his creativity and presence.

Notes on *Burdens: They Must Always Be Carried* by Anne Kamiya (2010)

> An invitation can become an interruption when too many say "yes."

THE ONLY HUMANOID FIGURE in this image is the snail-like creature upon whose back the birds and animals appear to sit or ride. But are the animals and birds riding upon the hybrid human-snail's back, or have they grown from it? The figure's fingers sink into or emerge from the ground. Is the snail-person sprouting from the earth or being pulled into it?

Why does the figure appear so downcast? Where does the "burden" stem from? Is the snail-human caring for these creatures or paying a penance? Do the animals care? Are the animals really there, or are they an imagined burden the snail-person carries?

Although the image and Tan's "A Tale of a King" are in no way related in their separate creations, if we read the figure as coming from the earth, it is hard not to make a connection to the tale. Does this association change your perception of either piece?

The animals are twined around each other; at times it is hard to tell where, for example, snake ends and bird begins. There are eyes peeking out at odd places that don't seem to be affixed to specific creatures. What does this fantastic amalgam of life tell us about relationships between plants, animals, and humans?

Burdens: They Must Always Be Carried

Anne Kamiya

Anne Kamiya, *Burdens: They Must Always Be Carried*, 2010, graphite pencil on paper, 9 x 12 in.

Among the Thorns

Veronica Schanoes

For Donna Mosevius Levinsohn

THEY MADE MY FATHER dance in thorns before they killed him.

I used to think that this was a metaphor, that they beat him with thorny vines, perhaps. But I was wrong about that.

They made him dance.

JUST OVER 150 YEARS AGO, in 1515, as the Christians count, on a bright and clear September morning, they chained a Jewish man named Johann Pfefferkorn to a column in our cemetery. They left enough length for him to be able to walk around the column. Then they surrounded him with coals and set them aflame, raking them ever closer to Herr Pfefferkorn, until he was roasted alive.

They said that Herr Pfefferkorn had confessed to stealing, selling, and mutilating their Eucharist, planning to poison all the Christians in Magdeburg and Halbristadt combined and then to set fire to their homes, kidnapping two of their children in order to kill them and use their blood for ritual purposes, poisoning wells, and practicing sorcery.

I readily believe that poor Herr Pfefferkorn confessed to all of that.

A man will confess to anything when he is being tortured.

They say that, at the last, my father confessed to stealing every last taler he had ever possessed.

But I don't believe that. Not my father.

THEY SAY THAT IN their year 1462, in the village of Pinn, several of us bought the child of a farmer and tortured it to death. They also say that in their 1267, in Pforzheim, an old woman sold her granddaughter to us, and we tortured her to death and threw her body into the River Enz.

Veronica Schanoes, "Among the Thorns," *Tor.com*, 2014.

WHO ARE THESE PEOPLE who trade away their children for gold?

My parents would not have given away me or any of my brothers for all the gold in Hesse. Are gentiles so depraved that at last, they cannot love even their own children?

I WAS SEVEN WHEN my father disappeared. At first we did not worry. My parents were pawnbrokers in Hoechst; my mother ran the business out of our house and my father travelled the countryside of Hesse, peddling the stock she thus obtained, and trading with customers in nearby towns, during the week. He tried to be with us for Shabbat, but it was not so unusual for the candles to burn down without him.

But it was almost always only a matter of days before he came back, looming large in our doorway, and swept me into the air in a hug redolent of the world outside Hoechst. I was the youngest and the only girl, and though fathers and mothers both are said to rejoice more greatly in their sons than in their daughters, I do believe that my father preferred me above all my brothers.

My father was a tall man, and I am like him in that, as in other things. I have his thick black hair and his blue eyes. But my father's eyes laughed at the world, and I have instead my mother's temperament, so I was a solemn child.

When my father lifted me in his arms and kissed me, his beard stroked my cheek. I was proud of my father's beard, and he took such care of it: so neat and trim it was, not like my zeyde's beard had been, all scraggly and going every which way. And white. My mother's father's beard was white, too. My father's was black as ink, and I never saw a white hair in it.

WE HAD A NICE house, not too small and not too big, and we lived in a nice area of Hoechst, but not too nice. My parents grew up in the ghetto of Frankfurt Am Main, but the ghetto in Frankfurt is but a few streets, and there are so many of us. So we Jews are mobile by necessity.

Even though it is dangerous on the road.

And Hoechst is a nice place, and we had a nice home. But not too nice. My mother had selected it when she was already pregnant with my eldest brother. "Too nice and they are jealous," she told me, "so not too nice. But not nice enough, and they won't come and do business. And," she added, "I wanted clean grounds for my children to play on."

We had some Jewish neighbors, and it was their children I mostly played with. The Christian children were nice enough, but they were scared of us sometimes, or scorned us, and I never knew what to expect. I had a friend named Inge for a while, but when her older sister saw us together, she turned red and smashed my dolly's head against a tree. Then she got to her feet and ran home, and her sister glared at me.

I was less friendly after that, although my father fixed my dolly when he came home that week, and put a bandage on my head to match hers when I asked him to.

Some feel there is safety in numbers and in closeness, but my mother thought differently. "Too many of us, too close together," she said, "and they think we're plotting against them. Of course, they don't like it when we move too far into their places, either. I do what I can to strike the right balance, liebchen," she said.

This was my mother, following the teachings of Maimonides, who wrote that we should never draw near any extreme, but keep to the way of the righteous, the golden mean. In this way, she sought to protect her family.

Perhaps she was successful, for the Angel of Death did not overtake us at home.

DEATH CAUGHT UP WITH my father when he was on the road, but we did not worry overmuch at first. My mother had already begun to worry when he was still not home for the second Shabbat, but even that was not the first time, and I did not worry at all. Indeed, I grew happier, for the farther away my father travelled, the more exciting his gifts for me were when he arrived home.

But Mama sat with my Uncle Leyb, who lived with us, fretting, their heads together like brother and sister. Even though Uncle Leyb was my father's younger brother, he was fair-haired, like my mother. I loved him very much, though not in the way I loved my parents. Uncle Leyb was my playmate, my friend, my eldest brother, if my brothers had spent time with a baby like me. But Uncle Leyb was also old enough to be my parents' confidant. Sometimes he went with my father, and sometimes he stayed and helped my mother.

I am grateful that he stayed home for my father's last trip. I do not think he could have done any good. But Leyb does not forgive himself to this day.

"Illness, murder, kidnapping," said my mother calmly, as though she were making up a list of errands, but her knuckles were white, her hands gripping the folds of her dress.

"It will be all right, Esti," said my uncle. "Yakov has been out on the road many times for many days. Perhaps business is good and he doesn't want to cut off his good fortune. And then you'd have had all this worry for naught."

"They kidnapped a boy, a scholar," said Mama. "On the journey between Moravia and Cracow."

"Nobody has kidnapped Yakov," said my uncle. He had a disposition like my father's, always sunny.

"If we sell the house," Mama went on as if she hadn't heard him. "We could pay a substantial ransom."

"There will be no need for that," my uncle said firmly.

My mother's fears did not worry me. Though I was a serious child, my father was big as a tree in my eyes, certainly bigger than Mama or Uncle Leyb or most of the men in Hoechst.

And my parents were well-liked in Hoechst. My father drank and smoked with the younger Christian men, and when he offered his hand, they shook it.

When the third Shabbat without my father passed, Uncle Leyb began to worry as well. His merry games faded to silence, and he and my mother held hushed conversations that broke off the minute I came within earshot.

After the fourth Shabbat had passed, my uncle packed up a satchel of food and took a sackful of my mother's wares and announced his intention to look for my father.

"Don't go alone," my mother said.

"Whom should I take?" my uncle asked. "The children? And you need to stay and run the business."

"Take a friend. Take Nathaniel from next door. He's young and strong."

"So am I, Esti," my uncle said. He held her hand fondly for a moment before letting it go and taking a step back, away from the safety of our home.

"Besides," he said, noticing that I and my next elder brother, Heymann, had stopped our game of jacks to watch and listen. "I daresay that Yakov is recovering from an ague in a nice bed somewhere. Won't I give him a tongue-lashing for not sending word home to his wife and family? Perhaps I'll even give him a knock on the head!"

The thought of slight Uncle Leyb thumping my tall, sturdy father was so comical that I giggled.

My uncle turned his face to me and pretended to be stern. "You mock me, Ittele?" he said. "Oh, if only you could have seen your father and me when we were boys! I thrashed him up and down the street, and never mind that he was the elder!"

I laughed again, and my uncle seemed pleased. But as he waved at us and turned to go, his face changed, and he looked almost frightened.

The fortnight that he was away was the longest I have ever known. Mama was quick-tempered; my brothers ignored me, except for Heymann, who entertained himself by teaching me what he learned in cheder. I tried to pay attention, but I missed my uncle's jokes and games, and I missed my father's hugs and kisses. I took to sucking my thumb for consolation, the way I had when I was a baby. Only when my brothers couldn't see, of course. My mother did catch me a few times, but she pretended not to notice so I wouldn't be embarrassed.

My brothers were out when I saw Uncle Leyb coming home through the window. His face was distorted, and I could not tell if it was an effect of the glass rippling or of some deep distress.

He seemed calm by the time Mama and I met him at the front door, having dropped the forks from our hands and abandoned our meal. My mother brought him into the kitchen and settled him with a measure of kirschwasser. Then she told me to go play outside. I was moving toward the door with my brothers' old hoop and stick as slowly as possible—they were too big for hoop rolling by this time, but I still liked it—when my uncle raised his hand and I stopped.

"No," he said firmly. "She should stay and listen. And her brothers, where are they? They should come and hear this as well."

My mother met his eyes and then nodded. She sent me out to collect my brothers. When all four of us returned, my mother's face was drawn and taut. For many years I thought that my uncle had told my mother the tale of my father's last day privately after all, but when I was older, she said not; she said that when she had seen that Uncle Leyb was alone, she had known already that she would never again lay eyes on my father.

The four of us sat between them, my eldest brother holding our mother's hand. My uncle held his arms out to me and I climbed onto his lap. I was tall, even as a child, and I no longer quite fit, but I think it was his comfort and consolation even more than mine, so I am glad I stayed. At the time, I was still obstinately hoping for good news, that Papa had struck a marvelous bargain that had taken a lot of work, and now we were all wealthy beyond the dreams of avarice, that even now Papa was travelling home as quickly as possible, his pockets loaded with treats.

My uncle wrapped his arms around me and began to speak quietly and deliberately. "Esti, Kinder. Yakov is dead. He will not be coming home. I buried him just a few days ago. With my own hands, I buried him."

My mother sighed, and somehow her face relaxed, as though the blow she had been expecting had finally landed, and it was a relief to have it done.

My brothers' faces looked blank and slightly confused; I suspect mine did as well. I did not quite believe what my uncle said. Perhaps, I thought, he was mistaken. But I could tell that my uncle was genuinely sad, so I reached up and patted his face.

"I fell in with Hoffmann after a few days, and told him of our worries"— Hoffmann was a peddler my father and uncle crossed paths with every so often and saw at shul on the high holy days. He lived several towns away, but he took much longer journeys than did my father. It was strange, though, that he should have been peddling among my father's towns.

"He said that word had spread that my brother's territory was going unattended; otherwise, he never would have presumed to visit it. He offered to join me in my search, so we pressed on together until we came to Dornburg. 'Burg' they call themselves, but they're not even as big as Hoechst. As we approached, the town lived up to its name, thorn bushes on every patch of scrub by the road.

"Yakov's body was hanging from a gibbet mounted by the side of the road just outside the town.

"We waited until nightfall, cut him down, and buried him under cover of darkness. I left a few stones at the graveside, Esti, but otherwise, I left it unmarked. I didn't want to risk them digging him up. Let him rest."

My mother's face was stone, and my uncle's voice was calm, but the top of my head was damp with my uncle's tears. I was still confused, so I turned around on my uncle's lap so I could face him.

"So when will Papa come home?" I asked him. I can make no excuses. I understood the nature of death by then. Perhaps I just did not want to believe it.

My uncle put his palms on either side of my face and held my gaze. "He will not come home again. The people of Dornburg killed him. He is dead, like your baby brother two years ago."

"How?" I could not imagine such a thing. My papa was big as a bear and twice as strong in my eyes. He could swing me around and around and never get tired. He could wrestle my two eldest brothers at once. He could even pick up my mama.

"They made him dance, liebchen. They made him dance in thorns, and then they hanged him."

"For what?" The cry burst from my mother. "For what did they hang him?"

"Theft," said my uncle, not taking his eyes from my face. "They said he had stolen all his money; rumor has it that they gave all he had to some vagabond fiddler, and he set himself up nicely. What's little enough for a family of seven is plenty for one vagrant."

"My papa never stole anything," I said. It was then that I realized what had happened. These people could say terrible things about my father only because he was dead.

"Not since we were boys," Uncle Leyb agreed.

I put my hands over his and stared into his eyes intently. If my father could not bring justice to those who slandered him, I would. "I will kill them," I told my uncle. My voice was steady and I was quite sincere. "I will surround that town with death. I will wrap death around their hearts, and I will rip them apart.

"I will kill them all. Every one."

My uncle did not laugh at me, or ruffle my hair, or tell me to run along. Instead, he met my gaze and nodded. Then he took my hands in his and said "So be it."

He said it almost reverently.

THE RESIDENTS OF DORNBURG were proud of their story, how they had destroyed the nasty Jewish peddler. How a passing fiddler had tricked the Jew into a thornbush and then played a magic fiddle that made him dance among the thorns, until his skin was ripped and bloody, and how the fiddler would not leave off until the Jew had given over all his money.

How the Jew had caught up with the fiddler at the town and had him arrested for theft; and how the fiddler had played again, forcing everybody to dance (the residents of Dornburg often omitted this part, it was said, in order not to look foolish, but the other gentiles of Hesse gladly filled it in) until the Jew confessed to theft. And how the Jew, bloody and exhausted and knowing he would never see home nor wife nor children again, did confess, and how he was hanged instead of the fiddler, and his body left to hang and rot outside the town gates as a warning.

How one morning, the town of Dornburg awoke to find that the Devil had taken the corpse down to Hell.

UNCLE LEYB SAID THAT Papa would come home to me nevermore, but I did not quite believe it. I waited every night for years to hear his footsteps and pat his black beard, I waited every night for his pockets full of treats and his embrace.

I still do not understand why I waited, full of hope. I knew what my uncle had said.

My baby brother had died of a fever two years before; my parents had been heartbroken, and I still missed his delighted laugh when I tickled his face with my hair. But he had come and gone so quickly, a matter of months. Papa had always been with me; I think that I could not conceive that he would not be with me again.

I knew better than to tell anybody that I was waiting, but I waited nonetheless.

I think that I am waiting still.

MY MOTHER NEVER QUITE recovered from Uncle Leyb's news, and when the story of the Jew at Dornburg became commonplace, her soul suffered further. She had been so careful, so alive to the delicate balance that would placate the Christians so that we could live a good life; finding that her best efforts were so easily overcome, that the mayor and the judge of a town where my father had traded for years would hang him at the behest of a vagrant fiddler, and that the townspeople from whom he had bought, to whom he had sold and loaned, with whom he had drunk and diced and sung, would gather and cheer, it was too much for her to bear, I think.

She became a wan, quiet shadow of the mother I remember from early childhood. She stayed indoors as much as possible, and avoided contact with non-family. She ate little and slept for long hours. I missed her strictness. She had always been the stern and reliable pillar of my life. And of course, business suffered as the families of Hoechst enjoyed visiting less and less often, and my mother declined to seek out their company. Too, she suffered strange aches and illnesses with neither source nor surcease.

We would have starved, I think, if not for Uncle Leyb and our next-door neighbors, whose eldest daughter came over to help my mother through her days. Tante Gittl, I learned to call her. There was some talk for a while, talk that I was supposed to be too young to notice or to understand, that she was angling to catch the eye of Uncle Leyb. If this was anything more than talk, she was doomed to disappointment, for no woman ever caught the eye of my uncle, who much preferred the company of other young men, though he was not to meet his business partner Elias until some years later.

Uncle Leyb took over my father's peddling, joined by my eldest brother, Hirsch, who, at sixteen, had hoped to make his way to Vienna, but willingly turned to peddling to keep food on the table. Tante Gittl helped my mother recover herself, and to slowly revive what remained of our business, and Heymann was able to continue at cheder. At thirteen, Josef was already demonstrating that he had the temperament of a sociable man, one who preferred the company of fellows to the rigors of scholarship. He now keeps a tavern in Mainz, having gone to live with our mother's cousin and learn the trade.

Heymann devoted himself to study, seeking in the teachings and commentaries of Rebbes both living and dead the father we had lost. But I knew he would never be found there, for my father was never a bookish man, proud though he had been of Heymann's intelligence and aptitude for study.

I was still young, old enough to help around the house, but not much else. I spent much of my time alone with my dolly, running my fingers over the scar where my father had repaired her, sometimes not even aware that my thumb had found its way into my mouth until Tante Gittl, barely two years older than my eldest brother, would remind me gently that I was too big a girl for such behavior, and set me some petty task as distraction.

Eventually I began reading Josef's cast-off books. Heymann, who had always had the soul of a scholar, stole time from his study breaks to play tutor, practicing on me for his future career.

Time passed, and perhaps that is the worst betrayal of all, for life without my father to have become normal. It felt sometimes as if only I remembered him, though I knew that was not so, as if only I missed him, though surely Uncle Leyb felt keenly the absence of the elder brother who had taken care of him in boyhood and brought him from Frankfurt Am Main to Hoechst in manhood, the two of them staying together even as so many of our families are blown apart like dandelion puffs, never to see one another again.

Uncle Leyb must have been as lonely as I.

And Mama never remarried.

So perhaps it was foolish to feel that nobody was as bereft as I, but I am sure that my father and I treasured each other in a way peculiar to only the most fortunate of fathers and daughters.

I WONDER, SOMETIMES, IF the fiddler, Herr Geiger, as he was called in Dornburg, felt that way about his daughter. He always seemed uncertain around her, as if he wished to love her but did not know how to begin. Once he told me he would love her better when she was older and had a true personality. But she has always seemed to have quite a strong character to me, right from the very beginning, even in her suckling.

I could have told him how to love her. I could have told him that to love a baby is to wake up every time she cries, even if you have not had a full night's sleep in days, to clean and change her cloths even when she has made herself quite disgusting, to sit up fretting and watching her sleep when she has a cold, to dance with her around and around the room without stopping, because her delight is well worth your aching legs and feet, to tell her stories and trust that she understands more than she can say. I could have told him this, but I did not.

He was not a bad father. But he was not a good one. And I did not help him.

MY MOTHER DIED WHEN I was seventeen. She seemed to have just been worn out by the treachery of our gentile neighbors. I do believe that the people of Dornburg killed her as surely as they did my father. She kissed me on her deathbed, and prayed to God to guide me to a safe home. And she died, with God having given her no answer, no peace of mind, the worry still apparent on her lifeless face.

I BECAME TANTE GITTL's main help after my mother's death, as Josef had left for Mainz two years earlier and Heymann had no interest in the family business. Too, Heymann was—is—studious and intelligent, but not canny. His is the kind of intelligence that can quote Torah word-perfect at length and analyze the finest points of disputation, but he never could add up a column of figures and get the same answer twice. Not if his life depended on it.

And I hope it never does.

I became Tante Gittl's help, but she did not need me. She and my eldest brother, Hirsch, had married the year before, and it made good sense for her to take over the business. She was very good with people, very charming, and she and Hirsch lived in harmony, companions and business partners. Nor did she need me when she became pregnant, for she had her own sisters, even her own mother next door.

I think it was her wish for me to wed her brother Nathaniel, and he was not unkind. The match would have been well made, but I knew that motherhood would destroy any plan of mine to see my father's grave and take vengeance on the man who had ended his life, because of what we owe to our children. To put myself at great risk—that was my choice, my prerogative. But if I'd had children—it is not right for parents to abandon their children, never. I knew too well what it meant to lose one's greatest protector and caretaker, the one in whose face the sun rises and sets, while still young. And I could never have done that to my child. We owe our children our lives.

WITH MY MOTHER IN the ground and the youngest of her children grown, my Uncle Leyb grew restless. He had met Elias while visiting Worms, and with Hirsch and Tante Gittl well set and Josef in Mainz, he deeply desired to make his life in Worms as well. Heymann and I were left to choose our paths.

There was never really any question about Heymann's future: he lived and breathed the dream of continuing his studies at the Yeshiva in Cracow. I told Hirsch and Gittl, and Heymann as well, that I was going to Worms with Uncle Leyb, and there, perhaps among so many of our people, I would find a husband. They believed me, I think, though Heymann, who of all my brothers knew me best, wrinkled his brow in perplexity. Uncle Leyb accepted my decision without comment, and we made plans to depart.

The last night we all spent together was much as our nights had been for some time, with a pregnant Gittl and Hirsch conferring about the future while Heymann talked to me of his plans for study and Uncle Leyb sat by himself writing a letter, this time to Josef, detailing our plans.

Worms, my uncle said, is perhaps four days' travel from Hoechst, provided the weather was good and nothing hindered our progress. But we would be carrying our lives with us on horse and cart, he noted, and would, of necessity, go more slowly than he did while peddling. The three of us—Uncle Leyb, Heymann, and I—travelled together to the regional shul, where the men prayed for good fortune on our journeys, and then we parted ways, the brother closest to me in both age and affection kissing my cheek, swinging his pack off the cart and onto his shoulder, and turning to the northeast and his scholarly future. His face was flushed with excitement, but the journey was six hundred miles, and he would be alone for the first time. For months after, I would picture him alone on the road, set upon by ruffians, or ill among strangers, without any one of us to hold his hand or bring him water.

My uncle and I walked in silence for a while. After perhaps half an hour had passed, he kept his gaze on the road ahead but spoke carefully.

"Ittele, you know, of course, that Elias and I will always welcome you. But you have always been my favorite, and I flatter myself that I know you as well as anybody could. Surely my brave, bright-eyed niece is brewing plans more complex than husband-catching?"

"Yes," I replied. "I am." But I did not elaborate.

When we stopped for dinner, he broached the topic again. As he finished up the bread and sausage we had packed, he poured himself a measure of kirschwasser. He leaned back against the cart and looked me in the eye.

"So, liebe, what are these plans of yours? Indulge your old uncle by taking him into your confidence."

I smiled at him. "I do mean to see you settled, Uncle. And when you are happily ensconced in Worms and have joined your business to Elias's, and are well occupied, I believe it will be time for me to set out once more."

Uncle Leyb raised his eyebrows and gestured for me to continue.

"To Dornburg, Uncle. I will go to Dornburg, and I will watch the fiddler's last breaths."

My uncle poured himself another measure of kirsch and sipped it slowly. "How do you intend to do this, child?"

My voice seemed to come from far away as I spoke, though I had long thought on this very question. "I do not yet know, Uncle. It depends on how I find him. But I must do this. I have known ever since I was a child. The knowledge has lodged like . . . like . . ." I fumbled for words.

"Like a thorn in your heart, my child?" finished my uncle.

I nodded.

My uncle finished his kirsch. "Yes," he said.

"You are bravest of us all, I think," he said, and then he stopped. "I should go—I should have been with him—I will go—"

I put my hand on his arm to stop him. "No. You should go to Elias. I am my father's daughter, and I will go to Dornburg."

My uncle relaxed and let go of the tin cup he had been gripping. Its sides were bowed inward. Color slowly returned to his face. "I believe I understand," he said. "And after I am settled, I will see you to Dornburg. Yakov would never forgive me if something should happen to you on the road." He began packing up our belongings in preparation for continuing on to the next inn.

"So be it," he added, just as he had when I was a child on his lap.

I DID WONDER HOW I would take my revenge, but I did not wonder how I would escape afterwards. I did not expect to escape Dornburg. I expected to take my revenge, and then to meet the same end as my father had. But I did not say this to my uncle. He would not have been so sanguine, I know, had he heard me say that.

THAT NIGHT, THE MATRONIT visited me in a dream. I did not know who or what she was, only that she was nothing human. She was the moon, she was the forest, she was my childhood dolly. But she was terrible, and I was frightened.

She smiled at me, and through moonlight and the rustle of the trees and my dolly's cracked face, she told me to turn away from Dornburg.

"Never," I said. And the moon clouded over, and the trees cracked open, and my dolly's head shattered.

And then she was gone, only a whisper in the air left to mark her passage.

I had this dream a second time the following evening, and again the following night. But the third time, it ended differently. Instead of shattering and leaving me, the Matronit's face grew stern and she coalesced before me into the form of a woman who was a beautiful monster, my beloved mother with a brow free from fear, claws like scimitars ready to tear and kill. Her hair streamed out from her head like the tails of comets and blood ran down her face. Her feet reached down to death and her head to the heavens. Her face was both pale and dark and she beamed at me with pride.

I am coming, my daughter.

WORMS WAS MUCH LARGER than Hoechst, but my uncle had no trouble settling in. I suppose a peddler who goes from town to town must be used to a whirl of people and places. I liked Elias well enough. He had an elegant brown mustache and was very fond of my uncle. I determined to set out for Dornburg on my own, so as not to interrupt their idyll, but my uncle would not hear of it, and neither would Elias.

"Terrible things can happen to a maiden alone on the road," said Elias. "Leyb and I have both seen this. But with him escorting you, you will be safe. As safe as anyone can be."

I nodded my head in assent, secretly pleased to have my uncle's company and moral support along the way.

"But Itte," he continued. "What of when you are in Dornburg? You . . . look so much like your father. I see Yakov every time I look at you, and your father . . . your father carried Israel in his face."

I remembered the woman in my dream, the woman with claws like scimitars, with her feet in death and her head burning in the sky like the sun. And blood, blood running down her face. "I do not yet know, Uncle. But I trust a solution will come."

SHE CAME TO ME that night, while I was sleeping. I opened my eyes, sat up in bed, and words began pouring from my mouth, words in languages I had never heard, let alone studied. I wrested back control of my tongue long enough to stutter, "Dear God, what is happening to me?"

I am here, my daughter, echoed in my head. My mind flooded with pictures of moonlight, forests, and war.

"Who are you? Where are you?"

I am here, the presence said again.

"I am possessed? Inhabited by a dybbuk?"

I felt the presence bridle. *I am no dybbuk*, it said. *I am your dearest friend and ally. I am the mother who protects and avenges her children. I am she who is called Matronit, and I speak now through your mouth. I am she who dries up the sea, who pierces Rahab, I am the chastising mother, I am the one who redeems the mystery of Yakov.*

"Mother?" I gasped.

I am the goddess-mother of all children of Israel. And I am your maggid.

"My mother is dead," I told the empty air. "And I am pious—I have none but Adonai as God."

I have always been goddess of Israel, even now as my children turn away from my worship. And I was goddess in times of old, when I was loved and feared. For was not a statue of me set in the temple of Jerusalem? And did I not oversee the households of the Holy Land? Was incense not burned to me, libations not poured to me, cakes not made in my image in Pathros, when the children of Israel defied Jeremiah? And have I not intervened with Hashem on behalf of the children of Israel, not once or twice, but many times? And am I not your maggid, who will bring you victory if you but embrace me as of old?

"These were great sins," I breathed. "To depart from the ways of the Lord—"

He is a jealous god, she continued. *But he is not alone. Was not your own mother named for me?*

"My mother was named for her grandmother, who was—"

Esther. Named for me, the goddess of Israel, and I have gone by many names, including Astarte, including Ishtar. You worshipped me every time you spoke her name.

Do you not understand? I will bring your vengeance to pass.

"What mother are you," I said bitterly, "who did not protect a child of Israel ten years ago, when he was tortured and killed in Dornburg? And he is only one among many."

There was a silence in my head, and I thought the presence—the Matronit—had departed, but then she spoke to my soul again. *I have been greatly . . . diminished. Hashem is a jealous god, and his prophets have destroyed my worship, and so my power has dwindled. But still I can be your maggid, and guide you to righteous victory. And in turn, you will observe the rites of my worship, and help to restore some of my former strength, just as your brother will in Cracow, when he learns of me, the Matronit, the Shekhina, in his studies.*

"My brother will learn only the most pious teachings."

And he will learn of me, when he advances to the teachings of Kabbalah. And I will bring you vengeance as your maggid.

"My maggid?"

Your guide, your teacher. And something more. I will possess your body, reside in your soul, yet I will not wrest control from you. I will strengthen you for what lies ahead, yet I will leave you human. And when this work is done, I will depart.

"And you will bring me success? You will enable me to bring vengeance to Dornburg?"

Yes, my child. Through you, Dornburg shall become a wasteland.

In but a minute, I made my choice. I abandoned what I had been taught, not out of impiety, but out of sheer rage, for I realized then that despite all my piety, all my father's piety, all my brother's devotions, Adonai had allowed my father to suffer, to be ripped by thorns and then hanged while towns-people had jeered. What, then, should He be to me? And if this Matronit would bring devastation to Dornburg—"Then possess me, Mother," I said. "I consent to this ibbur. I welcome you, and I will observe your rites."

The Matronit paused before answering. *Then you must know that I must first make your soul ready to receive me. And you must know that this cannot be painless. Your uncle and his partner will see you writhe in fever for seven days and nights. And you will be changed. You will be scorched with the knowledge I bring you.*

I was not foolhardy, for I knew what I was accepting. My soul had been scorched before, when I was seven years old.

MY UNCLE AND ELIAS tended me faithfully as I convulsed with fever. I vomited, they told me, continuously, until my body could bring up nothing more, and then I shook and refused to choke down even water. They told me later that they did not believe I would ever regain consciousness, and Elias whispered privately that my uncle had sat weeping by my bedside more than once. Perhaps it is a blessing that I could not feel that pain, for I do not remember any of it.

What I remember are the visions, for while my uncle sat by my bedside, I was not with him. I was not there at all. I was among those to come, among my people when they were expelled from Vienna five years hence, when they were driven from Poland in the century to come. I saw our emancipation throughout that century, and I saw its collapse—and then I was among riots, watching parents throughout Bavaria clutch their children as their homes burned, as learned professors and their students tore their possessions apart and worse, an old man impaled with a pitchfork, unable to scream as blood bubbled from his throat. Again and again, I saw the pendulum swing, as my people's emancipation drew near and then was wrenched away, slicing through the hands that reached out for it.

And I saw worse. The world around me teemed with flickering images, nightmarish visions of stone roads carrying metal beasts, of burning homes, of people pressed like livestock into mechanical carts, children crying, separated from their parents, toddlers heads dashed against walls, of starvation, and of our neighbors turning on us, only too glad to agree to our degradation and murder. The visions persisted no matter where I turned my head, and there was no reprieve, nor any justice, no justice anywhere.

WHAT IS THIS, I asked the Matronit. What is happening to me?

None of this has happened, as yet, she told me. *You see as I see, across not only space, but time. This has not happened, but it will happen. It will all happen.*

And Adonai? What of Him? Why has—why *will* He abandon my people? I wailed silently. Does our devotion mean nothing, nothing at all? What of our covenant? Did Abraham smash his father's idols for nothing? For nothing at all?

The Matronit chose her words carefully. *Hashem—Hashem . . . is . . . hungry for power. He always has been. He rides the waves of power and he does not care who is crushed beneath them. He never has.*

So He will desert us?

My daughter, he deserted Israel long ago.

If I could have, I would have spat. Then I will desert Him, I told her. Why should I remain devout, why should I—why should any of us—maintain our rituals or keep our covenant?

My daughter, if you did not, who would you be?

I AWOKE WITH NO voice, coughing blood. When I saw Uncle Leyb asleep in the chair by my bedside, tears ran from my eyes for his ignorance, and for his hope, and I cried for Hirsch's baby, and all the children to come. My uncle awoke and wiped my tears as well as my nose. I was able to take his hand and to whisper that I was well again, but this effort exhausted me, and I fell back asleep. I dreamt not at all.

I was not well. I thought I would never be well again.

As I SLOWLY RECOVERED my strength, I kept faith with the Matronit. I poured out wine and lit incense for her; I baked small cakes in her form and in her honor. I did not tell Elias or Uncle Leyb the reasons for my actions. I myself was still unsure whether or not the Matronit was a demon or the goddess—and how strange it felt to think that word—and if she was the former, I had no wish to lead them astray, for they are good men. But I became convinced she was what she said she was—the diminished goddess of the Jews, she who had intervened on our behalf with Adonai. For how could she speak holy prayers otherwise? Even if Adonai was no longer with my people, the holiness of our prayers could not be denied. So I prayed for her strength to return, every night and day.

AFTER SUCH A LONG illness, it was many months before my uncle would allow me to travel. But recover I did, and soon even he could not deny that I was strong, stronger even than I had ever been before. And so we two set off for Dornburg, leaving Elias in Worms to manage the business.

WHEN WE HAD TRAVELLED for two days, my uncle turned to me and told me that he was not a fool. He had heard me talking to the Matronit, he said, and he told me he would not allow me to continue unless I could explain what seemed to him like madness. He would not, he said, abandon a woman touched in the head to a strange town.

I weighed my options.

"I have a maggid, Uncle," I said at last. "My soul is hosting a righteous spirit who is leading my steps. Please trust in it as I do."

My uncle looked strangely relieved. "I am glad to know it, Itte," he said. "I will feel better knowing that you are not on your own. Tell me the name of this spirit, so that I may honor her as well."

I paused for a moment, wondering if I should invoke the name of some learned Rebbe, but I could think of none. "The Matronit," I said. "It is the Matronit-Shekhina."

My uncle said nothing. I hoped that he would remember her in his prayers, and that his prayers would add to her strength.

HE LEFT ME FIVE miles from Dornburg. I know my uncle did not like to turn back to Worms alone; I know he worried. He tried to disguise it, but I was less easily fooled than I had been ten years previous. And despite my maggid, after I had walked for two hours and found myself standing alone outside the walls of Dornburg, staring at the gibbet where my father's body had rotted a decade ago, I found myself gripped by terror. I looked for the rocks my uncle told me he had placed atop my father's grave, but without much hope. It would have been strange indeed if they had not been moved in ten years. Finally, I placed the stone I had brought from our garden in Hoechst at the foot of a birch tree.

Then I paid my toll to the guard at the gate and entered the town.

IT WAS MORNING WHEN I entered Dornburg. My uncle was right; it was not even as large as Hoechst, and after the time I had spent in Worms, it seemed even smaller than I would have thought it only six months previous. A cluster of women was gathered around a well, and a group of children were tearing around after each other, screaming with laughter. As I walked slowly, they caromed into me. One went sprawling and the others ground to a halt, looking embarrassed.

I tried to smile kindly, and I began to speak, but my throat was suddenly dry. In the pause, the boy who had fallen spoke.

"I'm sorry, Fraulein. I didn't see you—we were playing, and I wasn't looking where I was going, and then you were there—"

I lifted him up and helped him brush the dirt off his clothing and hands. "It's no matter, liebchen. I too knocked into my share of grown folk when I was little. They move so slowly, you know?"

We shared a conspiratorial grin.

"Were you playing a game I know, kinde? Tag? Or—" I said, noticing some crude musical instruments in the children's hands. "War? Are you piping brave songs to hearten the soldiers?"

"Neither," laughed the child. "Dance-the-Jew! I'm the Jew, and when the others catch me, they must make me dance 'til I drop!"

I recoiled involuntarily. "I—I don't know that game, child. Is it . . . new?"

"Dunno," said the boy. "We all play it."

I took a deep breath and exhaled, trying to not to shake. "Well. Run along, then. Run along and enjoy yourselves."

The children took off again, shrieking in delight.

"They will know," I whispered to the Matronit. "They will know and they will hang me as they did my father, and then children will laugh for years afterward!"

They will not know, she said. *They will not know, because they do not see your true form. I have glamored you, my daughter. They do not see your true face, and they do not hear your accent. Be calm in your heart.*

Slowly I made my way to the well at the center of town, past a tavern called The Dancing Jew. There, I found three or four women talking amongst themselves, but instead of happy, boisterous, gossiping, they were speaking in low tones of worry and sorrow.

"Well, it's not the first time one so small has been lost, and it won't be the last, either," said an older matron briskly, but with tears in her eyes.

"But for such a great man," said a younger woman. "The loss is doubly sorrowful."

"Guten morgen, Frauen," I began. "I wonder if there is work in this town for one who is willing."

"You have chosen a sorrowful day to come to Dornburg," said the youngest woman. "For one of our finest bürgers has lost his wife in childbed just two days ago, and will soon lose his baby girl as well. And he is a fine man, who helps anybody in our town in need."

"Is the babe sick?" I inquired.

"She will take neither cows' milk nor goats' milk, but she screams and turns away from any who try to nurse her. She will not last much longer."

I felt the Matronit move in my body, and a sudden heaviness in my breasts, almost painful.

"I think I can help," I said.

He has three gifts, the Matronit told me as I was being taken to Herr Geiger's house. *He has the fiddle that compels all to dance when it plays. He has a blowpipe that hits whatever it is aimed at. These two objects are on display, so that he may have the pleasure of telling of his triumph over the wicked Jew. The third is not tangible, but it is the most valuable of the three. No mortal can resist his requests.*

"No—but then, if he asks me of my background—"

I will strengthen you. That and your appearance I can do right now. And you will meet his will with your own.

My fear subsided and I thought clearly again. "So he could have requested that he be set free, and gone on his way without consigning my father to the gallows, then?"

Yes.

"But he preferred to torture my father and take all he had and see him hanged?"

Yes.

HERR GEIGER MADE ONLY the most cursory inquiries into my background. I was a widow, I told him, and had lost my man last month in an accident in Hoechst. After my husband's death, I said, his family had refused to take in me and my baby due to bad blood between them and my late parents. I had set out for Worms looking for work, but had lost the baby to a fever only days ago on the road, and could not go on. It was a very sad tale.

Herr Geiger took my hand in his and wept with me over the loss of my child. He asked me its name.

"Jakob," I said.

I DID NOT WORRY that he would connect this lost baby's name with the Jewish peddler he had murdered a decade ago. I do not believe Herr Geiger ever knew my father's name. I am not entirely certain that he ever realized that my father had a name.

WHEN I FIRST SAW Eva, she had hair like the sun, yellower than my mother's. My mother was fair, her hair pale blonde, but Eva's was true gold. Her eyes, though, were dark and brooding, the kind of stormy blue that, in a baby, will soon change to brown. She lay in her cradle, too weak to do more than mew sadly as she turned her head this way and that, searching for her mother's breast.

When I lifted her to mine, she gripped my braids with more strength than I thought she had left in her entire body and seized my nipple in her mouth. I closed my eyes and for a terrible moment thought nothing would come, but surely I knew that if the Matronit was any kind of goddess at all, she would be well-versed in the powers of the female body, and soon Eva shut her eyes in long-awaited bliss, and her suck changed from frantic to strong and steady, an infant settling in for a long time.

I shut my eyes as well, exhausted by my journey and my anxieties. When I opened them, Eva was asleep in my arms, and we were alone in the room.

HERR GEIGER THANKED ME the next morning. He had tears in his eyes and his breath smelled of schnapps.

I NURSED EVA CAREFULLY. As carefully, I lit incense and poured out libations to the Matronit. And as Eva got stronger, so did my maggid.

EVA STARED UP AT me with her storm-night eyes as she nursed. When she was sated, she would push her head away and sigh contentedly. Sometimes, I thought I saw my reflection in her eyes, the reflection of my true face, but I knew I must have been fooling myself.

Her hair began to curl, like my mother's.

I spent my days caring for her. I sang to her when she wept. Her first laugh came when I set her down on the floor and stepped out of the room to retrieve a blanket. As soon as I got out of her sight, I popped my head back in the room and said, "Boo, baby girl!" She laughed and laughed. We did it ten times in a row before her giggles calmed.

She is a jolly baby with an open heart.

Her first word was Jutta, the name I had chosen for myself when I translated my own name to its Christian equivalent. When I kissed her, she beamed up at me and tried to kiss me back, but was not quite clear on how. She opened her mouth and bit my nose instead. I laughed so hard she did it over and over again, and we rolled around together laughing and kissing each other.

I had not been so happy since I had flown through the air, swung around and around by my papa.

ONE NIGHT, AFTER EVA was asleep, Herr Geiger called for me, and I found him in his study, fondling a violin.

"Are you fond of music, liebchen?" He was well in his cups.

"As fond as anybody, I believe."

He lifted his bow.

"But not, I think, now, Herr Geiger."

He lowered the bow. "I take it you have heard of my conquest of the Jewish rascal whose ill-gotten gains gave me my start in life?"

I lowered my eyes modestly.

"Indeed, how could you not? Dornburg has made its fortune on that tale. I have always been a generous man—am I not so to you?"

"But of course, Herr Geiger. I am very grateful to you after so many difficulties."

Herr Geiger waved off my thanks and offered me a glass of schnapps. I accepted warily.

"After my first job, for a man so miserly he might as well have been a Jew, I set out to seek my fortune. I had not walked ten miles before I saw a poor old woman begging by the side of the road, and I gave her three talers, all the money I had in the world. What do you know but she was a fairy in disguise, and in recompense for my kind heart, she gave me one wish for each taler. I asked her for a blowpipe that would hit anything I aimed at and a fiddle that would compel all who heard its music to dance, and one more wish that is my secret, my dear!" He paused and waited for me to attempt to wheedle the secret of the third wish out of him.

I remained silent.

"Well," he said awkwardly. "I kept on with my journey, and not two days later, what did I find but a nasty Jewish swindler by the side of the road, muttering some sort of hex. I didn't quite understand all he was saying, but to be sure he was up to no good, with his eyes fixed on a brightly colored bird in a tree. Quick as anything, I used my blowpipe to bring down the bird. Then, all politeness, I asked the wicked old fiend to fetch me my kill. I waited until he was just crawling through a thornbush and then—out with my fiddle and on with the dance!"

Herr Geiger laughed at the memory and poured us both more schnapps.

"Such fine dancing you've never seen, my dear! With the blood running and his clothing in tatters, still he had to keep on dancing! He begged me to stop, and I did, on one condition—that he hand over all his sacks of money! And he did—there was less there than I had hoped, but plenty still, so on I went with my journey, having made a good beginning.

"But oh, that vengeful, petty Jew—of course he couldn't let me have my triumph, of course not—they are a vindictive race, my dear, grasping and vindictive. He followed me straight to Dornburg and had me arrested with some trumped-up story about how I attacked him on the road! I would've hanged, my dear, if you can believe it, had I not pulled out my fiddle again, and this time I didn't leave off playing until the Jew had confessed to all his crimes. He hanged before the day was out, and I was rewarded with all he had—for of course, you know Jews, he'd kept back some money from me at our first bargain. And that's how I got the capital I needed to set myself up well, here, and they honor me as one of their first citizens! You can see how well I've done for myself."

"I can, indeed, Herr Geiger." I kept my face turned to the ground, not out of modesty, but so as not to show my feelings. I say again, my father never stole, and was never petty. He ever had open hands and an open heart, and never turned away a request for help. I remember him, I do.

"All I lacked was a companion to share my happiness with. I thought I'd found my heart's desire in dear Konstanze; we were so happy together. I never thought in my youth that I'd wish to give up bachelorhood, but as a man ages, my dear, his thoughts turn to the comforts of hearth and home. Poor Konstanze. She was always delicate, and childbirth was too much for her."

Herr Geiger lapsed into silence while I considered the lot of the late Konstanze.

"But Jutta, a man cannot live forever alone. It's not right. It's not healthy. It's not Christian. And Jutta, I know what a good mother you will be. Are you not already a mother to my child?"

Now I did look up, startled. "Herr Geiger—you know not what you are saying—you know so little about me—you are still headspun with grief—"

He leaned forward and took my hands in his. I tried not to lean back. "Jutta, my darling, let me hope. Give me a kiss."

I felt the force of his request coursing through my body, the pressure to bend toward him and part my lips. This was different than just a request for information, to which, after all, I at least had pretended to accede. I felt the Matronit's strength behind my own, and I redoubled my resolve. Never. Never. Not even to lull him into complacency.

I think that if I had not been able to resist, I would have strangled him right then and there.

But I did resist. The Matronit lent me strength and I directed it, meeting Herr Geiger's magic with my own, stopping his will in its tracks.

I stood up. "Alas, Herr Geiger. I regret that I cannot give you cause to hope. But my loyalty to one who is now gone prevents it. I will care for Eva faithfully, but to you I must never be any more than your daughter's nurse."

He gazed at me in wonder. I spared a thought for the late Konstanze, and wondered if she had been tricked into marriage by such a request, if she had mistaken his desires and magical compulsions for her own inclinations.

"Good night, Herr Geiger." I walked out of the room and left him staring after me, eyes wide.

THE FOLLOWING MORNING I took time during Eva's morning nap to bake cakes for the Matronit. I stayed in the kitchen as much as possible, trying to avoid Herr Geiger's eyes. I suppose it had been many years since anybody had been able to refuse him a direct request. I did not care to encounter his scrutiny.

But I could not avoid it forever. I became aware of . . . how shall I put this . . . his eyes upon me. And he took to accosting me without warning and asking me to do things. I acceded, but when he would ask for a kiss, I would not, and then his curiosity would redouble.

"When?" I pled with the Matronit. "When? I cannot stay near this man much longer, Mother. When will you be strong enough?"

Soon, she replied. *But every time you must refuse a request of his, my power is depleted. Are you so sure you will not—*

"I am sure," I told her. "I will not endure the touch of his lips. Not now. Not ever."

ONE MORNING, A MONTH later, she said *tonight*.

I DEVOTED MYSELF TO Eva that day as if I would never see her again, for I did not believe I would. I could not take a Christian baby, not after all the lies told about us. This is not a thing we do, stealing children.

But did Eva not belong to me? By love if not by right? Her face lit up when I picked her up from her cradle in the morning, and when she was fretful, only I could calm her. She laughed at my games and clung to me with both her fists whenever someone else tried to hold her. Even her father.

I did not like to think of what would become of her with the rest of Dornburg dead. For I could not kill an infant, not an infant. I am not a monster.

But how could I take her?

EVA BECAME DROWSY AT dusk, and I cuddled her and sang her to sleep as gently as I could. After she fell asleep in my arms, I curled myself around her and napped, drifting in and out of sleep. I felt at peace; I felt that all the world had fallen away, and only Eva and I remained, coiled together in love.

The clock at the center of town tolled midnight. I shifted, but did not rouse myself. I did not want to leave Eva. I wanted only to have her in my arms forever.

Rise! The Matronit's voice was mighty, implacable, and I was instantly fully awake. *The time is now.*

I sat up and reluctantly pulled away from Eva's small body. She stretched out an arm, looking for me in her sleep, but was otherwise undisturbed.

I had been ready, I think, for a decade.

FIRST I WENT TO Herr Geiger's study and collected his fiddle and his blowpipe. Then I silently left the house. The judge who had ordered my father's death had been an old man then, I had learned over the months. He had died not long after. But the mayor and the hangman, they were still in the prime of life. The hangman had several children and a lovely house, some distance from the other homes, it's true, for nobody loves a scharfrichter, but nonetheless, he had a good life, and was respected if not celebrated. I walked to his home by moonlight, my cloak wrapped tightly around me. Standing outside his house, the Matronit told me to shut my eyes, and when I did, she granted me a vision.

The scharfrichter, Franz Schmidt, and his wife, Adelheide, were sleeping in their shared bed. All was peaceful.

What is your desire? asked the Matronit.

"Give him a dream," I told her. "Can you do that?"

But of course.

"Give him a dream. He is in chains, being led to the scaffold. He is innocent of any crime, but nonetheless, the faces of the crowd are filled with hatred. He thinks of his wife, his children, and how they will long for him, grow old without him. The noose is fitted around his neck and he finds his tongue, pleads for mercy, but the judge and the crowd only laugh. The platform drops out from under him, but the rope is not weighted correctly, and instead of his neck breaking instantly, he is slowly strangling, dancing in air. Oh, how he dances!"

The vision the Matronit granted me changed—Schmidt is twisting and turning in bed, unable to wake, unable to breathe. His face is pained and panicked.

I waited, wondering if I would feel pity, or remorse, or forgiveness. I felt none.

"Stop his heart," I said.

Schmidt convulses once, and then is still. His wife has never moved.

I then went to the house of the Bürgermeister.

STRANGELY CALM, I RETURNED home; I returned to the house of Herr Geiger.

Herr Geiger awoke to find me seated on a chair at the foot of his bed. "Jutta?" he yawned, all confusion. "What are you doing here?"

I did not answer. Instead, I brought the blowpipe out of my pocket and snapped it in two.

"Jutta! What are you doing?"

I then smashed the fiddle against his bedpost. It was nothing, then, but shattered splinters and catgut. I threw it to the ground.

"Jutta!" Herr Geiger was on his feet, looming in front of me, grabbing my shoulders. "Do you know what you have done?"

Still I did not answer. My braids undid themselves and my hair, my true black hair, stretched out toward the fiddler, becoming thorn-covered vines. He shrieked and tried to back away, but my vines caught his arms and legs, lifted him into the air, and there was nobody to hear his shrieks except Eva, who awoke and began crying in the other room. The maid and the cook came in daily, but lived with their own families.

I stood.

My vines twined ever tighter around his arms and legs, and blood ran down his body freely as the thorns dug through his skin. He twisted in pain, trying to wrench himself free, but succeeded only in digging the thorns in more deeply. My vines suspended him in the air in front of me, and I watched his struggles dispassionately. They did not bring me pleasure, but neither did they move me to pity or compassion.

"Why, Jutta?" he gasped.

"My name is Itte," I told him. Then I spoke to the Matronit. "Let him see my true face." I watched his eyes as my disguise melted away and my own features showed forth.

"You killed my father," I told him. "Ten years ago, you killed him. For ten years I have missed his embrace and smile. And never will I see them again."

"Jewess!" he spat.

"Yes," I agreed.

The vines grew further, wrapping themselves along his trunk, and they began burrowing into his flesh. He screamed.

"Did my father scream like that?" I asked him. "Did he scream when you made him dance in thorns?"

Eva continued to cry.

"Please, Jutta, spare me!"

Again, I could feel the force of his request marching through my body. The Matronit was channeling all her strength into the vines of my hair. I had only my own resolve with which to meet his power, but that power had been weakened by my breaking the blowpipe and the fiddle, for all things are more powerful in threes. I met his will with my own.

"For Eva's sake, spare me!"

I stared into his eyes. "You know nothing of Eva! Do you know which solid foods she can stomach, and which she cannot? Do you know on which day she began to crawl? Does she even babble your name?"

I thought of my father, swinging me through the air, patching my dolly, cuddling me to sleep and I thought of him exhausted, breathless, limbs burning like fire, skin torn, confessing to crimes he had never committed, knowing he would never see me nor my brothers nor my mother again, and my resolve strengthened.

"I will not spare you, Herr Geiger," I said. A new vine formed from another lock of my hair, and even as he gibbered in terror, it wrapped itself around his throat.

"Eva—" he began.

"Eva is mine," I told him. "You destroyed my family. I will take her and make a new one."

At my nod, the vine gave one jerk, and snapped his neck.

The vines let him fall, and they began shrinking and turning back into my plain black hair, which replaited itself. I took one final look down at what had been Herr Geiger. Then I nodded again, and turned and ran to Eva.

As soon as she caught sight of my face, she stopped crying, and she beamed at me through her tears and held out her arms. I picked her up and began to soothe her. I changed her cloth, for she had wet herself, and nursed her back to sleep.

"I am taking her with me," I told the Matronit as I threw my belongings into my sack. "I do not care what is said about us. I will not leave her here to be raised by strangers, to be taught to hate Jews."

It would be a terrible thing to do to a Jewish infant, said the Matronit.

I paused. "She is not Jewish."

She is the child of a Jewish mother.

"Konstanze was Jewish?" I asked.

No. Konstanze is not her only mother.

"She is not my daughter."

She is. Your milk gave her life. She knows she is your daughter.

"Why did she not cry when I picked her up?" I asked. "She has not seen my true face before, only my disguise."

She has never seen any face but your true one, the Matronit said. *She knows you. She knows your face. She knows you are her mother.*

I had finished packing. I picked up Eva and she opened her eyes to peer drowsily at me. She smiled, nestled her head against my chest, and fell back asleep. I tied her to me, picked up my sack, and left Herr Geiger's home with my daughter.

OUTSIDE THE TOWN WALLS, I stood and watched as bushes and vines of thorns grow. They blocked the gate and rose to enclose Dornburg.

"What will happen to the townspeople?" I asked the Matronit.

They will wake tomorrow to find the sun blotted out, the sky replaced by a ceiling of thorns, and no way out of the eternal night their town has become. The sun will not shine. The crops will fail. No traders will be able to penetrate the thorns. They will starve.

I watched for a while longer, and found myself troubled. I could not shake from my mind the memory of the grin the little boy had given me on my first day in Dornburg. Apparently I had some pity, some compassion after all.

"Is this just?" I asked. "To destroy the lives of children for what their elders have done before they were born?"

The vines paused in their growth.

Do you question me?

"I do," I said. "Children are powerless. Is this divine retribution, to murder the helpless? I do not wish it. Matronit, you should not do this."

The Matronit was silent. And then—*Very well. I will spare the children. You may take them away to safety.*

I remembered an old story, of a man in a many-colored suit leading away the children of Hamelin. But is this what I wanted? To take charge of a town's worth of children who by the age of six were already playing at killing my people?

"No," I said. "What you suggest is impossible. How should I do such a thing? And is it mercy to take children from the only love they have ever known, to make them wander the earth without family? Without home? Is this kindness?"

What do you suggest? The Matronit did not seem pleased with me.

I thought again, looking at the thorn-vines. "I know another story," I said. "Of a princess asleep in a tower, and a forest of thorns sprung up around her."

And this is your vengeance? asked the Matronit. *Sleep for a hundred years? They will sleep and wake and your people will still be suffering.*

"No," I agreed. "A hundred years will not suffice. But . . . let them sleep . . . let them sleep . . ." I thought of what the Matronit had shown me of the future. "Let them sleep until their loathing for my people, Matronit, for your children, is only a curiosity, an absurdity, a poor joke. Let them sleep until they are only antiquities, laughing-stocks. Let them sleep until Hesse—and all the lands that surround it—are safe for the Jews."

The Matronit was silent once more.

"Will that suffice?" I prodded her.

That will be a long time, my daughter.

"Yes," I agreed.

That . . . will suffice. They will sleep until realms of this land—all this land, all Europe—are safe for the Jews. And you are satisfied? This is different enough from death?

I struggled to explain. "If they do not wake . . . if they cannot wake . . . it will be only their fellows in hatred who are to blame. Not I."

I stroked Eva's head, noticing the darkness growing in at the roots of her hair. "Will you guide us, Matronit? Will you guide my footsteps?"

I will guide you. I will guide you to Worms, where you will see and speak with your Uncle Leyb and Elias, and then you shall take them with you to London.

"London?" I asked, surprised.

London is open to my children once again. And there will be no pogroms there, not in your lifetime. Nor your daughter's. Nor your daughter's children's, and their children's after them. I will guide you to London, and then I must depart. But you will keep my rites, daughter. Keep my rites.

"Yes," I agreed. "I will keep your rites."

I STOOD OUTSIDE THOSE walls with Eva bound to my chest, my old dolly tucked in next to her, and I carried my pack, which contained only those things I brought with me—I no more steal than my father did—and some of Eva's necessary items. She is sleeping peacefully, and I can feel the damp warmth of her breath against my neck. No feeling has ever given me greater pleasure.

The vines of thorns had almost reached the top of the town walls when I turned and did what my father had not been allowed to do. I walked away from Dornburg.

Notes on "Among the Thorns"
by Veronica Schanoes (2014)

> Interruptions to hatred are also invitations to recall, confront, and create something new.

In her *Grimm Reader*, Maria Tatar notes how the tales "The Jew in the Brambles" and "The Good Bargain," which "feature antisemitism in its most virulent form" (2010, 260), were included in the nineteenth-century compact editions of the Grimms' tales for children and how illustrations of "The Jew in the Bramble" in children's books have powerfully encapsulated negative stereotypes. Tatar's intervention as an editor in the twenty-first century was to move "The Jew in the Brambles" into a section she titled "Tales for Adults," calling attention to how it is no longer possible to feign innocence when rereading German fairy tales about Jewish characters.

"Among the Thorns" deals directly with the ways that often retold stories can shape prejudice. But it also enacts one way that looking again at old tales can combat those same prejudices: by interrupting their repetitions, injecting previously silenced voices, and inviting readers to engage with critique and the possibilities for thinking differently that critiques create.

Itte's revenge is complex, multilayered, and multidimensional, like the antisemitism she fights. The gentiles of Dornberg took an event and twisted it to fit what they want to have happened, to make themselves vindicated victims rather than perpetrators. They pass this story on to their children by ingraining unthinking hatred into forms of play. Itte refuses to utterly destroy the people and their children and thus erase the story. Instead, she takes a story that truly all of Europe knows and uses it to shape the future history of this town. She makes the story respond to every successive generation of Europeans, Jew and gentile alike, until the punishing thorns are no longer needed. Her move to London and the memories of history-to-come entwine not only Jewish and gentile Europeans but everyone in the larger Jewish diaspora.

The story, as Schanoes argues, shows that the much-lauded "universality" of the Grimms' fairy tales is a fantasy. In her 2019 essay, she comments: "Appropriating and re-adapting these tales to the experiences of the Other of European Christianity, Jews, combines writing for Jewish readers who might recognize themselves with writing for gentile readers who might then experience the discomfort of recognizing that their literature is not, after all, universal and open to all" (306).

"Among the Thorns" enacts another critique of many of Grimms' tales: the perfect, beautiful, and dead "good mother." There are a number of good mothers, though not "Good Mothers," as in Wood's tale "The Good Mother" in this volume: Itte's mother, Esther; Itte herself; and Matronit, the ultimate mother in the tale. Itte needs and accepts Matronit as goddess-mother, not because her own mother is not "good" enough but because in order to accomplish her goals, she must interact with the world in ways that require different skills. Matronit does not come to Itte as a fairy godmother waving a wand and poofing! problems away. She appears as "a beautiful monster, my beloved mother with a brow free from fear, claws like scimitars ready to tear and kill." She becomes a part of Itte's being in a painful and frightening transformation and awakening that instills Itte with the skills and knowledges she needs to fulfill her self-determined task. Does Itte incorporate any of Esther's skills on her quest? Here the good mother is not impossibly perfect, nor is she dead; rather, it is Itte's father, Yakov, who dies. What is it about Yakov and his death that prevents him from becoming a "Good Father" reflection of the "Good Mother"? Or does he haunt Itte in the way that so many dead "Good Mothers" do in the Grimms' and other collections of wonder tales?

Notes on *Shelter* by Shaun Tan (2020)

A response to an invitation or a serious interruption about to take place?

How we read this image will relate to our own attitudes toward landscape, space, and community. Urbanites who love the city might see this as a frightening, even terrifying nightmare scenario in which the little, lonely house is in danger of being lost in the vast space and crushed by it. Those who love or yearn for open space, for freedom from the noise and bustle of the city or the cookie-cutter clutter of the suburbs, might see this scene as depicting a serene world in which a tranquil home is protected from the elements by a miraculous rock.

So which is it, shelter from or shelter of? Who or what is sheltering whom? Does the rock threaten to flatten or promise to protect the house? Is the house sheltering its inhabitants from the rock? Are the inhabitants even aware of the rock, or is it just a part of the skyscape? Since the rock is already playing with the laws of physics, what if we twist our binary assumptions of human/nonhuman a bit: might the rock have come to the house seeking emotional shelter from a solitary existence?

The wonder of this image derives from its surreality; nevertheless, the light of the house is similar to that in Blackwell's *Once Upon a Time*. Where one appears in a fairy-tale forest, the other shines in a desert or plain with only a few planted trees for company. Does the light offer comfortable and cozy shelter to travelers, or is it a desperate attempt to announce its existence, a shout at the darkness of vast open landscape? Are there indications of movement to suggest whether the rock is in motion, or does it hang suspended indefinitely?

Shelter

Shaun Tan

Shaun Tan, *Shelter*, 2016, pastel and charcoal on paper, 50 x 60 cm.

A Poisoned Tale

Rosario Ferré

Translated by Rosario Ferré and Diana Vélez

> And the King said to Ruyán the Wise Man:
> "Wise Man, there is nothing written."
> "Leaf through a few more pages."
> The King turned a few more pages, and
> before long the poison began to course
> rapidly through his body. Then the King
> trembled and cried out: "This book is poisoned."
>
> —*A Thousand and One Nights*

ROSAURA LIVED IN A house of many balconies, shadowed by a dense overgrowth of crimson bougainvillea vines. She used to love to hide behind these vines, where she could read her storybooks undisturbed. Rosaura, Rosaura. A melancholy child, she had few friends, but no one had ever been able to guess the reason for her wistfulness. She was devoted to her father and whenever he was home she used to sing and laugh around the house, but as soon as he left to supervise the workers in the cane fields, she'd hide once more behind the crimson vines and before long she'd be deep in her storybook world.

I know I ought to get up and see to the mourners, pass the coffee tray among my clients and the cognac tray among their unbearable husbands, but I feel exhausted. I just want to sit here and rest my aching feet, listen to my neighbors chat endlessly about me. Don Lorenzo was an impoverished sugarcane plantation owner, and only by working from dawn to dusk did he manage to keep the family in a suitable situation. First Rosaura, then

Rosario Ferré, "A Poisoned Tale," in *Short Stories by Latin American Women*, edited by Celia Correa de Zapata, 1990.

Lorenzo. What an extraordinary coincidence. He loved the old plantation house, with its dozen balconies jutting out over the cane fields like a wind-swept schooner's. He had been born there, and the building's historic past made his blood stir with patriotic zeal: it was there that the creoles' first resistance to the invasion had taken place, almost a hundred years before.

Don Lorenzo remembered the day well, and he would enthusiastically re-enact the battle scene as he strode vigorously through the halls and parlors—war whoops, sable, musket and all—thinking of those heroic ancestors who had gloriously died for their homeland. In recent years, however, he'd been forced to exercise some caution in his historic strolls, as the wood-planked floor of the house was eaten through with termites. The chicken coop and the pigpen that Don Lorenzo was compelled to keep in the cellar to bolster the family income were now clearly visible, and the sight of them would always cast a pall over his dreams of glory. Despite his economic hardships, however, he had never considered selling the house or the plantation. A man could sell everything—his horse, his shirt, even the skin off his back—but one's land, like one's heart, must never be sold.

I mustn't betray my surprise, my growing amazement. After everything that's happened, to find ourselves at the mercy of a two-bit writer. As if my customers' bad-mouthing wasn't enough. I can almost hear them whispering, tearing me apart behind their fluttering fans: "Whoever would have thought it; from charwoman to gentlewoman, first wallowing in mud, then wallowing in wealth. But finery does not a lady make." I couldn't care less. Thanks to Lorenzo, their claws can't reach me now; I'm beyond their "lower my neckline here a little more, Rosita dear, cinch my waist a little tighter here, Rosita darling," as though the alterations to their gowns were not work at all and I didn't have to get paid for them. But I don't want to think about that now.

When his first wife died, Don Lorenzo behaved like a drowning man on a shipwreck. He thrashed about desperately in an ocean of loneliness for a while, until he finally grabbed on to the nearest piece of flotsam. Rosa offered to keep him afloat, clasped to her broad hips and generous breasts. He married her soon afterwards, and, his domestic comfort thus re-established, Don Lorenzo's laugh could once again be heard echoing through the house, as he went out of his way to make his daughter happy. An educated man, well versed in literature and art, he found nothing wrong in Rosaura's passion for storybooks. He felt guilty about the fact that she had been forced to leave school because of his poor business deals, and perhaps because of it he always gave her a lavish, gold-bound storybook on her birthday.

This story is getting better; it's funnier by the minute. The two-bit writer's style makes me want to laugh; he's stilted and mawkish and turns everything around for his own benefit. He obviously doesn't sympathize with me. Rosa was a practical woman, for whom the family's modest luxuries were unforgivable self-indulgences. Rosaura disliked her because of this. The house, like Rosaura's books, was a fantasy world, filled with exquisite old dolls in threadbare clothes; musty wardrobes full of satin robes, velvet capes, and crystal candelabras which Rosaura used to swear she'd seen floating through the halls at night, held aloft by flickering ghosts. One day Rosa, without so much as a twinge of guilt, arranged to sell all of the family heirlooms to the local antique dealer.

The two-bit writer is mistaken. First of all, Lorenzo began pestering me long before his wife passed away. I remember how he used to undress me boldly with his eyes when I was standing by her sickbed, and I was torn between feeling sorry for him and my scorn for his weak, sentimental mooning. I finally married him out of pity and not because I was after his money, as this story falsely implies. I refused him several times, and when I finally weakened and said yes, my family thought I'd gone out of my mind. They believed that my marrying Lorenzo and taking charge of his huge house would mean professional suicide, because my designer clothes were already beginning to earn me a reputation. Selling the supposed family heirlooms, moreover, made sense from a psychological as well as from a practical point of view. At my own home we've always been poor but proud; I have ten brothers and sisters, but we've never gone to bed hungry. The sight of Lorenzo's empty cupboard, impeccably whitewashed and with a skylight to better display its frightening bareness, would have made the bravest one of us shudder. I sold the broken-down furniture and the useless knicknacks to fill that cupboard, to put some honest bread on the table.

But Rosa's miserliness didn't stop there. She went on to pawn the silver, the table linen and the embroidered bed sheets that had once belonged to Rosaura's mother, and to her mother before her. Her niggardliness extended to the family menu, and even such moderately epicurean dishes as fricasseed rabbit, rice with guinea hen and baby lamb stew were banished forever from the table. This last measure saddened Don Lorenzo deeply because, next to his wife and daughter, he had loved these creole dishes more than anything else in the world, and the sight of them at dinnertime would always make him beam with happiness.

Who could have strung together this trash, this dirty gossip? The title, one must admit, is perfect: the written page will bear patiently whatever poison you spit on it. Rosa's frugal ways often made her seem two-faced; she'd be all smiles in public and a shrew at home. "Look on the bright side of things, dear, keep your chin up when the chips are down," she'd say spunkily to Lorenzo as she put on her best clothes for mass on Sundays, insisting he do the same. "We've been through hard times before and we'll weather this one too, but there's no sense in letting our neighbors know." She opened a custom dress shop in one of the small rooms of the first floor of the house and hung a little sign that read "The Fall of the Bastille" over its door. Believe it or not, she was so ignorant that she was sure this would win her a more educated clientele. Soon she began to invest every penny she got from the sale of the family heirlooms in costly materials for her customers' dresses, and she'd sit night and day in her shop, self-righteously threading needles and sewing seams.

The mayor's wife just walked in; I'll nod hello from here, without getting up. She's wearing one of my exclusive models, which I must have made over at least six times just to please her. I know she expects me to go over and tell her how becoming it looks, but I just don't feel up to it. I'm tired of acting out the role of high priestess for the women of this town. At first I felt sorry for them. It broke my heart to see them with nothing to think about but bridge, gossip and gadflying from luncheon to luncheon. Boredom's velvet claw had already finished off several of them who'd been interned in mainland sanatoriums for "mysterious health problems," when I began to preach, from my modest workshop, the doctrine of Salvation through Style. Style is doubtless woman's most subtle virtue. Style heals all, cures all, restores all. Its followers are legion, as can be seen from the hosts of angels in lavishly billowing robes that mill about under our cathedral's frescoed dome.

Thanks to Lorenzo's generosity, I subscribed to all the latest fashion magazines, which were mailed to me directly from Paris, London and New York. I began to publish a weekly column of fashion advice in our local *Gazette*, which kept my clientele pegged as to the latest fashion trends. If the "in" colour of the season was obituary orchid or asthma green, if in springtime the bodice was to be quilted like an artichoke or curled like a cabbage leaf, if buttons were to be made of tortoise or mother-of-pearl, it was all a matter of dogma, a sacred article of faith. My shop soon turned into a beehive of activity, with the town ladies constantly coming and going from my door, consulting me about their latest ensembles.

My shop's success soon made us rich. I felt immensely grateful to Lorenzo, who had made it all possible by selling the plantation and lending me that extra bit of money to expand my workshop. Thanks to him, today I'm a free woman; I don't have to grovel or be polite to anyone. I'm sick of all the bowing and scraping before these good-for-nothing housewives who must be constantly flattered to feel at peace. Let the mayor's wife lift her own tail for a while. I much prefer to read this vile story than speak to her, than tell her "how nicely you've put yourself together today, my dear, with your witch's shroud, your whisk-broomed shoes and your stovepipe bag."

Don Lorenzo sold his house and moved to town with his family. The change did Rosaura good. She soon looked rosy cheeked and made new friends, with whom she strolled in the parks and squares of the town. For the first time in her life she lost interest in her storybooks, and when her father made her his usual birthday gift a few months later, she left it half read and forgotten on the parlor table. Don Lorenzo, on the other hand, became more and more bereaved, his heart torn to pieces by the loss of his cane fields.

Rosa, in her new workshop, took on several seamstresses to help her out and now had more customers than ever before. Her shop took up the whole first floor of the house, and her clientele became more exclusive. She no longer had to cope with the infernal din of the chicken coop and the pigpen, which in the old times had adjoined her workshop and cheapened its atmosphere, making elegant conversation impossible. As these ladies, however, took forever to pay their bills, and Rosa couldn't resist keeping the most lavish couturier models for herself, her business went deeper and deeper into debt.

It was around that time that she began to nag Lorenzo constantly about his will. "If you were to pass away today, I'd have to work till I was old and gray just to pay off our business debts," she told him one night with tears in her eyes, before putting out the light on their bedside table. "Even selling half your estate, we couldn't begin to pay for them." And, seeing that he remained silent, with gray head slumped on his chest, and refused to disinherit his daughter for her sake, she began to heap insults on Rosaura, accusing her of not earning her keep and of living in a storybook world, while she had to sew her fingers to the bone in order to feed them all. Then, before turning her back on him to put out the light, she told him that, because it was his daughter whom he obviously loved more than anyone else in the world, she had no choice but to leave him.

I feel curiously numb, indifferent to what I'm reading. A sudden chill hangs in the air; I've begun to shiver and I feel a bit dizzy. It's as though this wake will never end; they'll never come to take away the coffin so the gossipmongers can finally go home. Compared to my client's sneers, the innuendos of this strange tale barely make me flinch; they bounce off me like harmless needles. After all, I've a clear conscience. I was a good wife to Lorenzo and a good mother to Rosaura. That's the only thing that matters. It's true I insisted on our moving to town, and it did us a lot of good. It's true I insisted he make me the sole executor of his estate, but that was because I felt I was better fit to administer it than Rosaura until she comes of age, because she lives with her head in the clouds. But I never threatened to leave him, that's a treacherous lie. The family finances were going from bad to worse and each day we were closer to bankruptcy, but Lorenzo didn't seem to care. He'd always been capricious and whimsical, and he picked precisely that difficult time in our lives to sit down and write a book about the patriots of our island's independence.

From morning till night he'd go on scribbling page after page about our lost identity, tragically maimed by the "invasion" of 1898, when the truth was that our islanders welcomed the Marines with open arms. It's true that, as Lorenzo wrote in his book, for almost a hundred years we've lived on the verge of civil war, but the only ones who want independence on this island are the romantic and the rich: the ruined landowners who still dream of the past as of a paradise lost; the frustrated, two-bit writers; the bitter politicians with a thirst for power and impossible ambitions and dreams. The poor of this island have always been for statehood, because they'd rather be dead than squashed once again under the patent leather boots of our own bourgeoisie. Each country knows what leg it limps on, and our people know that the rich of this island have always been a curse, a plague of vultures. All one has to do is look around and find out who built what; it was the Americans who built the schools, who paved the roads, who financed the hospitals and the University. Before they landed here, this island was an epidemic-infested hole, inhabited by a flea-bitten, half-starved, illiterate people, victim of the island's ten most powerful families. And today they're still doing it; those families are still trying to scalp the land, calling themselves pro-American and friends of the Yankees to keep their goodwill, when deep down they wish the Yankees would leave, so that these families could graze once more on the poor man's empty guts.

On Rosaura's next birthday, Don Lorenzo gave his daughter his usual book of stories. Rosaura, on her part, decided to cook her father's favorite guava compote for him, following one of her mother's old recipes. As she stirred the bubbling, bloodlike syrup on the stove, the compote's aroma gradually filled the house. At that moment Rosaura felt so happy; she thought she saw her mother waft in and out of the window several times on a guava-colored cloud. That evening, Don Lorenzo was in a cheerful mood when he sat down to dinner. He ate with more relish than usual, and after dinner he gave Rosaura her book of short stories, with her initials elegantly monogrammed in gold and bound in gleaming doe-heart's skin. Ignoring his wife's furrowed brow, he browsed with his daughter through the elegant volume, whose thick gold-leaf edges and elegant bindings shone brightly on the lace tablecloth. Sitting stiffly, Rosa looked on in silence, an icy smile playing on her lips. She was dressed in her most opulent gown, as she and Don Lorenzo were to attend a formal dinner at the mayor's mansion that evening. She was trying hard to keep her patience with Rosaura because she was convinced that being angry made even the most beautifully dressed woman look ugly.

Don Lorenzo then began to humor his wife, trying to bring her out of her dark mood. He held the book out to her so she might also enjoy its lavish illustrations of kings and queens all sumptuously dressed in brocaded robes. "They could very well inspire some of your fashionable designs for the incoming season, my dear. Although it would probably take a few more bolts of silk to cover your fullness than it took to cover them, I wouldn't mind footing the bill because you're a loveable, squeezable woman, and not a stuck-up, storybook doll," he teased her, as he covertly squeezed her derriere.

Poor Lorenzo, you truly did love me. You had a wonderful sense of humor and your jokes always made me laugh until my eyes teared.

Unyielding and distant, Rosa found the joke in poor taste and showed no interest at all in the book's illustrations. When father and daughter were finally done admiring them, Rosaura got up from her place and went to the kitchen to fetch the guava compote, which had been heralding its delightful perfume through the house all day. As she approached the table, however, she tripped and dropped the silver serving dish, spattering her stepmother's skirt.

I knew something had been bothering me for a while, and now I finally know what it is. The guava compote incident took place years ago, when we still lived in the country and Rosaura was a mere child. The two-bit writer is lying again; he's shamelessly and knowingly altered the order of events. He gives the impression the scene he's retelling took place recently, when it actually took place several years ago. It's true Lorenzo gave Rosaura a lavish storybook for her twentieth birthday, which took place only three months ago, but it's been almost six years since he sold the farm. Anyone would think Rosaura was still a girl, when in fact she's a grown woman. She takes after her mother more and more; she fiddles away her time daydreaming, refuses to make herself useful and lives off the honest sweat of those of us who work.

I remember the guava compote incident clearly. We were on our way to a cocktail party at the mayor's house because he'd finally made you an offer on the sale of your plantation. At first you were offended and rejected him, but when the mayor suggested he would restore the house as a historic landmark, where the mementos of the cane-growing aristocracy would be preserved for future generations, you promised to think about it. The decision finally came when I managed to persuade you, after hours of end-less arguments under our bed's threadbare canopy, that we couldn't go on living in that huge mansion with no electricity, no hot water and no ade-quate toilet facilities; and where one had to move one's bowels in an antique French Provincial latrine which had been a gift to your grandfather from King Alphonse XII. That's why I was wearing that awful dress the day of Rosaura's petty tantrum. I had managed to cut it from our brocaded living room curtains, just as Vivien Leigh had done in *Gone With the Wind*, and its gaudy frills and garish flounces were admittedly in the worst of taste. But I knew that was the only way to impress the mayor's high-flown wife and to cater to her boorish, aristocratic longings. The mayor finally bought the house, with all the family antiques and objects d'art, but not to turn it into a museum, as you had so innocently believed, but to enjoy it himself as his opulent country house.

Rosa stood up horrified and stared at the blood-colored streaks of syrup that trickled slowly down her skirt until they reached the silk embossed buckles of her shoes. She was trembling with rage, and at first she couldn't get a single word out. When her soul finally came back to her, she began calling Rosaura names, accusing her shrilly of living in a storybook world while she, Rosa, worked her fingers to the bone in order to keep them all fed. Those damned books were to blame for the girl's shiftlessness, and as they were also undeniable proof of Don Lorenzo's preference for Rosaura and of the fact that he held his daughter in higher esteem than his wife, she had no alternative but to leave him. Unless, of course, Rosaura agreed to get rid of all her books, which should immediately be collected into a heap in the backyard, where they would be set on fire.

Maybe it's the smoking candles, maybe it's the heavy scent of all those myrtles Rosaura heaped on the coffin, but I'm feeling dizzier. I can't stop my hands from trembling and my palms are moist with sweat. This story has begun to fester in some remote corner of my mind, poisoning me with its dregs of resentment. And no sooner had she ended her speech to Rosaura, Rosa went deathly pale and fell forward to the floor in a heap. Terrified at his wife's fainting spell, Don Lorenzo knelt down beside her and begged her in a faltering voice not to leave him. He promised her he'd do everything she'd asked for, if only she'd stay and forgive him. Pacified by his promises, Rosa opened her eyes and smiled at her husband. As a token of goodwill at their reconciliation, she allowed Rosaura to keep her books and promised she wouldn't burn them.

That night Rosaura hid her birthday gift under her pillow and wept herself to sleep. She had an unusual dream. She dreamt that one of the tales in her book had been cursed with a mysterious power that would instantly destroy its first reader. The author had gone to great lengths to leave a sign, a definite clue in the story which would serve as a warning, but try as she might in her dream, Rosaura couldn't bring herself to remember what the sign had been. When she finally woke up she was in a cold sweat, but she was still in the dark as to whether the story worked its evil through the ear, the tongue or the skin.

Don Lorenzo died peacefully in his own bed a few months later, comforted by the cares and prayers of his loving wife and daughter. His body had been solemnly laid out in the parlor for all to see, bedecked with wreaths and surrounded by smoking candles, when Rosa came into the room, carrying in her hand a book elegantly bound in red and gold, Don Lorenzo's last birthday gift to Rosaura. Friends and relatives all stopped talking when they saw her walk in. She nodded a distant hello to the mayor's wife and went to sit by herself in a corner of the room, as though in need of some peace and quiet to comfort her in her sadness. She opened the book at random and began to turn the pages slowly, pretending she was reading but really admiring the illustrations of the fashionably dressed ladies and queens. As she leafed through the pages, she couldn't help thinking that now that she was a woman of means, she could well afford one of those lavish robes for herself. Suddenly, she came to a story that caught her eye. Unlike the others, it had no drawings and it had been printed in a thick guava-colored ink she'd never seen before. The first sentence surprised her, because the heroine's name was the same as her stepdaughter's. Her curiosity kindled, she read quickly, moistening the pages with her index finger because the guava-colored paste made them stick to each other annoyingly. She went from wonder to amazement and from amazement to horror, but in spite of her growing discomfort, she couldn't make herself stop reading. The story began . . . "Rosaura lived in a house of many balconies, shadowed by a dense overgrowth of crimson bougainvillea vines . . . ," but Rosa never found out how it ended.

Notes on "A Poisoned Tale" by Rosario Ferré (1990)

> Stepmother and daughter: Who interrupts whose life? And who interprets the tale?

In "A Poisoned Tale" we are reading a frame story about Rosa reading a story about Rosaura and herself. The epigram, from "The Tale of the Wazir and the Sage Duban," which appears within the "Fisherman and the Jinni" set of tales in the *Arabian Nights*, warns us that the story may be more deadly than we first suspect. The framing of this story is just as complex but different in structure than the embedding of the *Nights*. Instead of the storytelling task being passed from one narrator to another, here Rosa makes metanarrational comments about the contents of a strange tale that mysteriously seems to be about her own family.

What effect do her interjections have upon our understanding of the story? We see in Joellyn Rock's "Bare Bones" that typesetting is an effective way to produce narrative effects and signal who is speaking, but Rosa's words are not graphically indicated by quotation marks, italics, or spacing. How do we know when Rosa is responding to the tale and when the "two-bit writer" is telling? Who says, "Rosaura, Rosaura" in the first paragraph, for instance? What kind of an effect does this ambiguity have on the truth claims of the narrator? Of Rosa?

A further ambiguity to ponder is Rosaura's guilt or innocence. We seem to be reading a tale embedded within a tale, with metanarratorial comment to set the story "straight" by Rosa, who is reading a story about herself. But if we are reading "A Poisoned Tale" metaphorically over Rosa's shoulder, who writes those final paragraphs?

We have seen the ways that fairy tales have been used to heap disapprobation upon certain kinds of women and praise upon the beautiful, docile, calm, and kind woman. Powerful women (within the fictions) are gossiped and written about as shrews or failures when they cannot or do not try to live up to these gendered expectations in "The Good Mother," "The Master of Nottingham's Daughter," and "Lupine." Here, a poisonous relationship between stepmother and daughter is haunted by the dead Good Mother, enacts possibly slanderous reporting about the stepmother, and literalizes the poison of resentment between the women to the point of death.

What are we to make of the women in this tale? Is Rosa the evil stepmother? Or is she a guiltless, misunderstood victim of Rosaura's cunning? Is Rosaura the innocent persecuted heroine, or is she the lazy, coddled, and spiteful child who poisons to get her inheritance? Is the "two-bit writer" really a two-bit writer? And really, who is the writer? Did Rosaura conceive and write this poisoned tale, or might there be a fictional Rosario Ferré hiding between the lines of this story?

In her essay "From Ire to Irony," in which Ferré discusses the doubling and splitting of characters in the collection *The Youngest Doll*, she argues that "the literary convention of the twin helped me objectify my own psychological wrenching-apart, as I became a participating witness of the historical and social conflicts of the women around me. Thus I often mocked and contradicted what I was saying, in spite of being deadly serious about it" (1994, 902). Political change and socioeconomic upheaval play an important role in the relationships between women in this story too. Does the Rosa triangle of Rosario Ferré, Rosaura, and Rosa play out in the same way, or does this trebling create a different dynamic between protagonist and antagonist by also inserting the writer herself?

Notes on *Frau Trude* by Miwa Yanagi (2005)

The final interruption of a life or an invitation to a new one?

IS FRAU TRUDE TRYING to throw the girl in the fire or keep her from leaping in? Are they going in together? Or is something else going on here? Note that it is difficult to tell whose legs are whose. Are the two figures really one creature? As they lean toward the fire, both looking up, what is the expression on the girl's face? What do we take from the mask of the old woman?

What is that on the walls? Is it blood, as Murai Mayako suggests, or mold and soot? How does the stuff on the walls and curtains affect a reading of this image? Murai argues that the bloodstained walls and curtains foreshadow "expected violence" (2013, 244), yet the subjects' expressions belie the expectation. Is violence suggested in other ways, or at all, if the walls are covered with mold or soot?

If you are not already familiar with the tale, you may choose to go to the internet to find the version of "Frau Trude" that appears in the Grimms' collection (ATU 334). Does having read the story change your reading of this image? How does one inform the other? Does this image also conjure different possibilities for reading "Hansel and Gretel"?

Kay Turner's (2012) queer reading of the story of Frau Trude sees a forbidden love between the woman and the girl. For Turner, the girl sees her much-wanted future in the old woman, and the fire is one not of destruction but of desire. Might the relationship here, where the two seem almost to be one, fall in line with this reading?

Frau Trude

Miwa Yanagi

Miwa Yanagi, *Frau Trude*, 2005, gelatin silver print, 1000 x 1000 mm.

The Good Mother

Danielle Wood

Now that you think about it, you realise you've known her your whole life. On the magazine pages and billboards of your childhood, she was fair as Rapunzel with a trim shoulder-length haircut. You were indifferent to her, back then, barely registered her presence. Or so you think until you realise you can remember precisely the way her hands looked—their fingernails short and practical though still perfectly tipped with white crescent moons—as she drew V-shapes in menthol rub onto the chests of her ailing children.

She wasn't always the Vicks' Mum, of course. Kneeling by the bath, she would soap her toddler's blonde mop into a quiff of white foam and promise you No More Tears. To soothe the unsettled infant, she could provide her favoured brand of paracetamol as well as the comfort of her trim, moulded bosom inside a candy coloured shirt. With a plump, two-toothed cherub on her hip, she would de-holster a spray pack and vanquish the invisible nasties on the bright white porcelain of her toilets and sinks. For she was the Good Mother, as safe and mild and effective as every unguent she ever squeezed from a pinkly labelled tube.

The Good Mother had the powders to return muddied soccer shirts to brightness and the potions to ward off sore throats and flu, but you realise now that her true power lay in those hands with their frenchly polished nails. Remember how she placed them coolly on fevered brows, cupped them around mugs of chocolately-yet-nutritious fluids, splayed them protectively over the shoulder blades of her sleeping babes? Yes, you remember, though it occurs to you only now how implausible it actually was that the peachy boys and girls they found to match her could have been born from her trim blue-jean hips. Come to think of it, where did those children come from? Did Dad ever come in from the breadwinning long

Danielle Wood, "The Good Mother," in *Mothers Grimm*, 2014.

enough for her to rest a hand on the honest chambray of his shirtfront? If he did, you cannot remember it.

This is how it is for the Good Mother. She pricks her finger when she's embroidering. The bauble of blood teetering on her fingertip sets her to thinking and soon she is noticing the deepness of the red and the way it shines against the snowy ground beyond her window. Add the ravenswing black of the windowframe, and *voila!* She's knocked up and chosen her child's colour scheme to boot.

This is how it is for you. Deep in denial, you hardly even tell yourself when you stop taking the Pill and start taking folate. Your partner would probably be quite interested if you were to let him know how much better is an unprotected ovulatory orgasm than a regular Pill-protected one, but this knowledge feels for some reason like a secret, so you keep it to yourself. Although you become obsessive about taking your temperature and despite your new habit of cooling your post-coital heels high on the bedhead, there's nothing doing. You get your many test kits from pharmacies in different suburbs so that the sales assistants don't start getting to know you, but no matter how many mornings you lock yourself in the bathroom with a bladder full of potent overnight piss, there's only ever one little line in the window of the white stick.

It's been three years since the rash of weddings in your life, and now it's thirtieth birthday parties. And there she is. Over there by the cheese plate, scooping a strand of fair hair behind one ear and staring down the camembert as if she knows its sole purpose in life is to kill her unborn child. You haven't thought of her for years, if ever you have thought of her con-sciously at all, which is why you don't recognise her. You say hello and she clinks her water glass against your thrice-emptied champagne flute. Wearing something white, and tight, she sinks into a chair and sighs and it's only now that she stretches her hand a full octave across her belly that you notice her fingernails. They're exquisitely oval and pink as confectionary, each one smoothly iced with white. She gestures at the empty chair beside her and then somehow you are sitting in it.

At all those weddings, people would ask *so, what do you do?* Not anymore.

"Do you have children?" she asks, stroking herself as if she is her own pet.

"No," you say.

"Not yet," she soothes.

Fuck off, you wish.

"Your first?" you ask, tilting your champagne towards her belly.

"Oh, God no! This is my third." She laughs and her free hand flies up into the air. When it lands again, it is on your knee. She looks right into your face now and smiles.

"I'm so fertile, my husband only has to *look* at me and I'm up the duff."

You make deals with God. You make deals with the Devil. You're not fussy. But as a wise man once said: "it's the saying you don't care what you get what gets you jiggered." So you say it, and you're jiggered, but what you give birth to is a hedgehog. It's prickly and its cry is a noise so terrible that you wish that someone would scrape fingernails on a blackboard to give you some relief.

You learn that hedgehogs are both nocturnal and crepuscular, but yours doesn't sleep in daylight either. In search of support and camaraderie you join a mother's group. You turn up at the clinic covered in prickle-marks and with your squirming hedgehog in your arms. The other women are there already, sitting in a circle nursing their soft, boneless young. The only seat left is beside the Good Mother.

She's wearing pale pink and making smooth circles on her baby's back with her hand-model hands. Things are different since you last met, and you're prepared to forgive her for last time if only she'll tell you how it is that her eyes are so bright and her skin so clear. You're desperate to know how it is that her shiny golden hair is brushed. Clearly her child sleeps, but what is her secret?

"You know what they say," she says, with a contented smile. "Calm mother, calm child."

ONE DAY, YOU FALL into a deep, deep sleep. Valiantly the prince fights his way through forests of fully-laden clothes horses, past towers of empty nappy boxes, to reach you where you lie with your rapidly greying hair straggling around your face. He puckers up. His lips brush yours.

"You stupid fucking prick," you yell at him. "What the hell do you think you're doing? I only just got to sleep!"

This happens more than once.

Your hedgehog gradually morphs into a child, a boy whose sunny countenance is sufficiently beautiful to make you forget the spines and the sleeplessness. When you conceive again, you are pregnant with the vision of a placid, smooth-skinned human girl child, but what you give birth to—though female—is just another hedgehog.

When Hedgehog II is a year old, your partner announces he is leaving you.

"I think you have a personality disorder," he says.

"Of course I have a personality disorder," you say. "I haven't slept for three years."

So your partner moves out, just as your maternity leave expires. Your plan had been to go back to work part-time, but now that you're a single mother you have to work full-time to afford the childcare. The economics of this confuse you, but you're too busy thinking about how you're going to manage to worry about that as well. When you go into the childcare centre to make inquiries, the hedgehog clings to you and makes its sanity-withering cry. The carers hold closer the human children they have in their arms and offer you a three-day trial to settle in your hedgehog before you have to leave her there for real.

On the first day you leave her, she screams until she vomits, so you take her back home. On the second day you leave her, she screams until she vomits, so you take her back home. In a fairy tale, things are always different on the third go. But this is life and on the third day you leave her, she screams until she vomits, so you take her back home.

Then comes the day that you are to go back to work. Is that Rumpelstiltskin giggling in your mindscape as you hand over both your second-born *and* the bale of hay-spun gold? The carer takes a tentative hold of your hedgehog. You smile and coo. You turn your back and walk out the door and as you do, you hear your hedgehog screaming. The effect is like having your uterus torn out through your ear holes. You are sure you can smell vomit. You only just make it out the kiddy-proof gate before you begin to weep. The weeping makes you red and puffy in the face and now you are hardly presentable for work. In order to pull yourself together, you call in to a café. You open the door and look inside but every table is taken. There's one bar stool but you think perhaps it's the Good Mother sitting on the neighbouring seat nursing a peppermint tea. You're not certain, but there's something in the blonde foils that makes you wonder and you're in no mood for *her* today. And besides, by now you're too experienced to fall for her ol' empty seat routine.

Outside there are no free tables either, but two women who are taking up only half of a large table gesture for you to join them, so you do.

"Thank you," you say, and they nod in unison.

You take out your fold-out mirror and try to hide the blotches on your face with powder. Then you notice how peachy is the skin of the raven-haired woman sitting on the same side of the table as you. And the skin of the redhead sitting across from her. Each of them has a slim-line pram in a bright, interesting colour. They push their prams to and fro with gloved hands. The gloves are reasonable, aren't they? It's winter. It's cold. You're telling yourself all of this even though you already know.

No, no!

It's her. Both of them.

And although she's talking to herself across the table, she's really talking to you.

"How old?" one of her asks.

"One," the other says, with a *can-you-believe-it* manoeuvre of the eyebrow.

"Incredible," she says. "I mean, is there *anybody* who thinks it's a good idea to leave a one-year-old in childcare?"

You take a vow of silence. You will not speak to her. You will not look at her. You will not accept seats at her café table. Out of the corner of your eye you glimpse her, auburn-haired, in a Dettol advertisement, and wonder when you're going to clue up to the fact that these days her hair can be any colour at all?

You tell yourself that the consequence of breaking your vow is that your twelve brothers will turn into ravens, or something. In order to hold to your promise you make sudden reversals in supermarket aisles, hide from her in clothing store change rooms, buy bigger sunglasses for their greater protective surface area, teach yourself sign language out of a library book so that if she speaks to you, you can easily pretend to be deaf. You are doing well. Until your eldest child starts school.

You know which is the Good Mother's Volvo. It's the one with the My Family stickers on the back window; she's the one with the handbag and the mobile phone. At first, you think this knowledge will help you to avoid her. You can just make double the number of *Green Bottles* when you start singing as you lap the school in your Hyundai, but soon you realise the Volvo is parked multiple times around the perimeter, no matter how early or late you arrive. This is her territory. Here, she is omnipresent.

It's almost Mother's Day and the kids in your son's kindergarten class are given a photocopied page to fill in. Mostly, the page is taken up with a blank square in which each child is to draw a picture, but above the box there's a line of text that is followed by what you will come to recognise as the ellipsis of doom.

I really appreciate it when my mummy . . .

A week later you see the completed tributes where they're pinned up on the wall just inside the classroom. All the figures in the pictures wear bright colours and most have hands pronged with twelve or more fingers. Little Laura reports she really appreciates it when her mummy tucks her into bed at night. For Oliver, it's his mummy's cupcakes. Tara appreciates it when her mummy takes her to the library.

Already you are predisposed to like Clytemnestra, who is a tiny little skun rabbit of a thing to be lugging around the name-equivalent of four suitcases and hatbox. You see that Clytemnestra's had a go herself at changing "mummy" to "mummies." Her picture is a constellation of mint green spots: she appreciates when her mummies don't cook peas. You are still smiling at Clytemnestra's peas when the Good Mother materialises beside you in her black puffer jacket. She patrols the pin-up board with her eyes.

"Ummmm-aaahhh," she says, happily shocked. "Look what David's done."

You haven't yet found your own son's handiwork. And now, even though the Good Mother's manicured index finger is pointing right at it, somehow your eyes are still missing the mark. They are slipping over all the generously endowed hands and circle-striped bellies. You don't want to know. You would like to dematerialise.

The Good Mother realises she's going to have to read it out for you.

"I . . . really . . . appreciate it . . . when . . . my mummy . . ."

She snickers, *snickers*, before she continues: ". . . buys takeaway."

Under the sentence, written blackly at your son's instruction by one of the teacher's aides, there is a disturbingly accurate reproduction of the golden arches. You want to protest that you never take him there yourself.

It's your ex who does it. And the birthday parties! It's not as if you can say no to these things. Well, not unless you're . . .

The Good Mother interrupts your thoughts with a hand on your upper arm.

"Oh, honey," she says. "You must be so embarrassed."

LITERARY SCHOLARS TREAT IT as a mystery to be solved by careful textual analysis. Psycholanalysts propose theories that involve words like *splitting* and *internalisation*.

But you could give them a much simpler explanation.

Yes, you could tell them, couldn't you?

There is no mystery for you.

You could tell them exactly why it is, in fairy tales, that the Good Mother is always dead.

Notes on "The Good Mother" by Danielle Wood (2014)

> An invitation to contemplate how the not-perfectly-good mother
> interrupts the narrative.

In this tale, the Good Mother's "frenchly polished nails" aptly cue readers to her artifice. The Good Mother is only made to *appear* natural in all her apparently effortless beauty, patience, and graceful multitasking. How can women actually live up to her? In fairy tales, a female character who wants or has a child *and* does not die has few options, and Wood's protagonist finds herself living out their limited plots. Desperate for a child, like many fairy-tale queens, she makes a wish, and her "hedgehog" babies recall monstrous births in fairy tales (e.g., "Hans My Hedgehog" ATU 441 and "King Pig" ATU 425A). She imagines herself as or compares herself to characters like Rapunzel, Sleeping Beauty, the spinner in "Rumpelstiltskin" (ATU 500), or the sister whose brothers are cursed to be birds (ATU 451); unsurprisingly, in all of these tales, mothers struggle with how to protect their children.

For Freudian psychoanalyst Bruno Bettelheim, the fairy tale's splitting of the mother figure into good and bad serves the child well as an emotional strategy for dealing with a real-life mother's power, perceived as extreme or without bounds, and offers an oedipal fantasy that allows both boys and girls to maintain good relations with their parents (1976, 69, 114). Marina Warner, who has done extensive research on mythology and fairy tales, disagrees: "The experiences fairy stories recount are remembered, lived experiences of women, not fairytale concoctions from the depth of the psyche," but she acknowledges at the same time that these experiences "etch" themselves into the psyche (1991, 28). We agree with Warner, and not only because she pays attention to gender and power dynamics in the stories we tell. Consider the fairy-tale genre's history: these tales were not historically and are not in the present for children only; and consider how varied fairy tales are as a product of the different social conditions in which they are produced.

Wood's I-narrator offers her contemporary experience of motherhood as shaped by, on the one hand, current social, legal, and economic realities that women and families face and, on the other hand, the expectations that women internalize about motherhood from fairy tales and commercial advertising. While she proclaims, "in fairy tales . . . the Good Mother is always dead," the Good Mother's power is clearly not, and, as the narrator's anger signals, it continues to play a role in fostering antagonistic relations between women. Fortunately, humor works wonders in Wood's story, allowing the protagonist and readers to find an escape route out of restrictive plots and interpretations of mothering.

Playing a significant role in Wood's interruption is the shift from the traditional external narrator of classic fairy tales to the first-person narrator in the story. This is a common strategy in contemporary adaptations, where the villain in a well-known tale, for instance, tells it from her perspective. In the case of "The Good Mother," and also in Emma Donoghue's *Kissing the Witch*, the I-narrator/protagonist works not to reverse a good/evil opposition but to undo it, by playing out the complexities of women's embodied desires, experiences, and stories.

Lupine

Nisi Shawl

ONCE THERE WAS A little girl whose mother hated her. The mother was not a bad woman, but she had not wanted a child, and so she put her daughter into a secret prison and pretended she did not exist. The father was deceived, for he and the woman parted long before he would have learned she was to have a child. Soon after they separated, the mother's love for him languished and died. As for her daughter, the mother felt nothing toward her but the deepest loathing.

The little girl, on the contrary, loved her mother very much, because she was born to love, and in her prison she knew no one else. Lupine, as she was called, had not even a kitten or a cricket to love, not even a doll to play with. The wind from the mountains blew seeds into her lonely tower, and she nourished these into plants: flowers and downy herbs.

When her mother brought food and water, Lupine always lavished kisses on her; however, these only strengthened the woman's hatred of her beautiful child. "She is young and has her whole life ahead of her. My life is passing by, faster and faster, and soon I will be dead," the mother thought. To fill Lupine's years with misery was the object of her private studies, and one day she found an answer that would serve.

She gave it to Lupine as medicine, but it was really a potion containing an evil spell. Lupine suspected nothing, but complained bitterly of its awful taste. Then she coughed, her eyes rolled back into her head, and she fell to the floor as if dead.

The mother laughed with delight and eagerly awaited Lupine's return to wakefulness. When the daughter's eyes opened she no longer wore her usual sweet smile; instead, her face was ugly with disdain. The purpose of the potion's spell was to make her act hatefully toward those she loved and lovingly toward those she hated. Lupine reached up to throttle her mother's neck.

Nisi Shawl, "Lupine," in *Once Upon a Time*, edited by Paula Guran, 2013.

The woman easily eluded her and ran gleefully down the prison's stairs and out of the waste with which it was surrounded. She led Lupine into the thick of civilization, where her daughter would suffer the most.

So this little girl with eyes like stars and hair like the night's soft breezes grew up the plaything of bullies and the despised enemy of everyone she thought fine and fair. No one understood her inhuman passions, and she was most often left alone—except by her tormentors.

Soon after entering maidenhood, Lupine fell in love with a superior lad. Golden as the sun when it is closest to the earth, he had an unusual and endearing skill: finding things no one else knew they should look for. By now Lupine comprehended her enchantment, and so she fought every least stirring of feeling for him. But to no avail, for she found herself telling horrible lies about him, insulting his sister to her face, and spitting on his shoes whenever they met.

Kyrie, her love, being no ordinary boy, met all her stings with tenderness. This only made things worse.

One night she woke from sleepwalking under his open window, a long, sharp knife glittering in each hand. Overcome with horror, she fled back to the wilderness before her mother or anyone else could stop her.

She ran until she could only walk, and she walked until she could only stumble, and she stumbled until she could only crawl, and she crawled until she could go no farther. She had come to the top of a tall mountain. She lay so still that the vultures thought she was dead and came to feed on her, but a fierce little bird scared them away.

By and by, Lupine recovered from her exhaustion and opened her eyes. The first thing she saw was a cunning cup fashioned of leaves and filled with clear water. She drank it all and sat up. The little bird had put away its fierceness and perched on her knees, chirruping at her. She was so forlorn, she decided to confide in the beast. "Oh, Piece-of-the-Sky, if only you could tell me how to end all my sorrows," she said.

"With pleasure," the little bird replied. "I will consider it payment for your naming of me."

"You—you talk!" said Lupine, naturally amazed at this.

"Not exactly. But because of the water I gave you to drink you understand my singing. For only a short while, however, so let us waste no time.

"You need not tell me your troubles, for I have been watching you. The solution to them is simple. You must chain yourself to those rocks there—" the bird gestured with a wing "—the Rocks of Solitude, so you can do no harm to anyone. Throw the key down in the dust. I will retrieve it. Then you must wait till I return with your swain, whose kiss will release you from the spell of your mother's potion."

So Lupine shackled herself in the place where ancient princesses had sacrificed themselves to fire-breathing dragons, using for this their old, abandoned chains. The little bird flew off with the key.

Soon Kyrie strode up the path, bright as morning. Lupine hissed at him and shook her rusty chains. He was not afraid, though, for he had learned all that it was necessary for him to know from Piece-of-the-Sky.

Still, he feared Lupine would bite off his nose before he succeeded in placing his lips on hers and melting into her mouth. But at last he kissed his love.

When he stopped they were both dizzy with bliss and victory. He unlocked her, and together they rejoined the world to share their joy. Their whole lives were ahead of them, and they were free.

As for Lupine's mother, when she heard of the way in which she had been outwitted she grew more and more anxious over her impending death. When would it come? Where would it be? How would it find her? What would be the manner of it? At last she could bear the suspense of her ignorance no longer and jumped into a fiery furnace.

Thus all concerned found peace.

Notes on "Lupine" by Nisi Shawl (2013)

> Can the influence of a bad mother be interrupted by another's inviting themselves in?

While the etymological link of "lupine" with wolf makes good "fairy-tale web" sense, along with the familiar carnivore, Nisi Shawl's story and character evoke a lovely plant that was for a long time considered noxious to the soil that grows it. Both wolf and lupine have had a bad reputation with humans, but nowadays wolves are protected as endangered animals, and the lupine—a legume that comes in several varieties with blue or yellow flowers—is sold as a healthy food whose alkaline properties are also said to enrich its soil. Is our system of classification or judgment at fault, then? Neither good nor bad, especially when viewed from a not exclusively human-centered perspective, these beings' chemistry interacts with their environments in varied ways. In the character Lupine's interactions with the natural and human world, her name proves to be more promising than damning—or, put differently, expectations placed upon her explode.

Shawl's tale, like Shaun Tan's "A Tale of a King," takes on traditional narrative formulas and structure—"Once there was a little girl whose mother hated her"—but refuses to turn the girl into a type, gives her more agency, and places her in a larger world where she can outgrow her family trappings. The relationship of self and nature that animates older wonder tales is clearly at stake in "Lupine," but pinning down its meaning definitively is difficult. Is the bird a supernatural helper or a being relating to her as kin? If Lupine's "nature" is stronger than the spell she is a victim of, what is her nature, and how does her name speak to it? Interestingly, the boy Lupine falls in love with is perceptive and smart, not the cardboard prince figure. If Lupine's name complicates her nature, what do you make of his name, Kyrie?

Beyond playing with the narrative structure of the "innocent persecuted heroine" tale in ways that reject victimization and passivity, "Lupine" takes externalization, a basic stylistic feature of the genre, to task. In fairy tales, a character's disposition, ethics, and feelings are usually rendered through action or words—that is, externalized rather than explored through the representation of their inner thoughts—and there is often an unquestioned correspondence between outer and inner beauty. But here the spell that Lupine is subjected to turns her words and actions into the opposite of her feelings and intents. This contradiction may work as metacommentary but also as a somewhat realistic depiction of the upheaval of falling in love, especially young love. Shawl's tale points to how to break the fairy tale's spell without losing its magic, especially when it comes to romance and growing up.

But why is the mother-daughter relationship viewed in such negative and competitive terms, similar to those ingrained in popular "innocent persecuted heroine" tales such as "Snow White"? Is Shawl simply reproducing this toxic relation where the life of the younger woman depends on the condemnation and death of the aging one? We'd like to read the tale as asserting something different; what if we read the externalization of Lupine's character as a form of post-traumatic stress disorder caused by years of mental abuse by her mother? Unlike contemporary adaptations where the villainous stepmother's backstory changes her role in the fairy tale, Shawl's story introduces explanations for the mother's feelings without offering her any redemption.

Nevertheless, Lupine's mother does perish as her daughter blossoms, and the specter of the Good Mother in Danielle Wood's story seems to dictate the terms of this poisonous relation. Perhaps Kelly Link's "Swans" offers an alternative to reimagine the fairy tale's mother-daughter plot in a twenty-first-century wonder tale.

Notes on *Still Rather Fond of Red*
by Nalo Hopkinson (2007)

Memories of desires interrupted.

THE SUBJECT OF THIS collage gazes out of the image right back at us from a tradition of portrait photography that has always privileged patriarchal, white supremacist ideas of who is "worth" photographing. She sits serene and confident, with her memories of wolfie and forgotten desire. Or is that true? Are the words floating over the sitter's shoulder the thoughts going through her mind at the time of the sitting, or are they notes she wrote herself later, looking back at this portrait? They are a little smudged and begin to fade as they go along. Is she forgetting again? Or is the image itself a reminder of desire?

Black women are not afforded a great deal of pleasure in Western art. Certainly Black women are the objects of male desire and the white colonial gaze. It is not a gaze that remembers the soiled rags and squalling newborns; it has never ridden the red. The gleam of the gems in her ears, the hard smoothness of the flowers on the table, the shine of bodice clasps, and her velvety red dress all speak to pleasure in beauty and the senses. If Black women cannot escape the white male colonial gaze, how is this woman responding to it?

As she gazes forward, a wolf at her skirt looks up toward her face adoringly, and a cartoon heart conveys its feelings in contrast to its more ferocious, though identical, companions. *This* wolfie has not forgotten. But is he an adorable lover, or does he bite?

Still Rather Fond of Red

Nalo Hopkinson

Nalo Hopkinson, *Still Rather Fond of Red*, 2007, paper and ink, 10 x 14 in.

Selkie Stories Are for Losers

Sofia Samatar

I HATE SELKIE STORIES. They're always about how you went up to the attic to look for a book, and you found a disgusting old coat and brought it downstairs between finger and thumb and said "What's this?," and you never saw your mom again.

I work at a restaurant called Le Pacha. I got the job after my mom left, to help with the bills. On my first night at work I got yelled at twice by the head server, burnt my fingers on a hot dish, spilled lentil-parsley soup all over my apron, and left my keys in the kitchen.

I didn't realize at first I'd forgotten my keys. I stood in the parking lot, breathing slowly and letting the oil-smell lift away from my hair, and when all the other cars had started up and driven away I put my hand in my jacket pocket. Then I knew.

I ran back to the restaurant and banged on the door. Of course no one came. I smelled cigarette smoke an instant before I heard the voice.

"Hey."

I turned, and Mona was standing there, smoke rising white from between her fingers. "I left my keys inside," I said.

Mona is the only other server at Le Pacha who's a girl. She's related to everybody at the restaurant except me. The owner, who goes by "Uncle Tad," is really her uncle, her mom's brother. "Don't talk to him unless you have to," Mona advised me. "He's a creeper." That was after she'd sighed and dropped her cigarette

---

Sofia Samatar, "Selkie Stories Are for Losers," *Strange Horizons, 2013.*

and crushed it out with her shoe and stepped into my clasped hands so I could boost her up to the window, after she'd wriggled through into the kitchen and opened the door for me. She said, "Madame," in a dry voice, and bowed. At least, I think she said "Madame." She might have said "My lady." I don't remember that night too well, because we drank a lot of wine. Mona said that as long as we were breaking and entering we might as well steal something, and she lined up all the bottles of red wine that had already been opened. I shone the light from my phone on her while she took out the special rubber corks and poured some of each bottle into a plastic pitcher. She called it "The House Wine." I was surprised she was being so nice to me, since she'd hardly spoken to me while we were working. Later she told me she hates everybody the first time she meets them. I called home, but Dad didn't pick up; he was probably in the basement. I left him a message and turned off my phone.

"Do you know what this guy said to me tonight?" Mona asked. "He wanted beef couscous and he said, 'I'll have the beef conscious.'"

Mona's mom doesn't work at Le Pacha, but sometimes she comes in around three o'clock and sits in Mona's section and cries. Then Mona jams on her orange baseball cap and goes out through the back and smokes a cigarette, and I take over her section. Mona's mom won't order anything from me. She's got Mona's eyes, or Mona's got hers: huge, angry eyes with lashes that curl up at the ends. She shakes her head and says: "Nothing! Nothing!" Finally Uncle Tad comes over, and Mona's mom hugs and kisses him, sobbing in Arabic.

After work Mona says, "Got the keys?"

We get in my car and I drive us through town to the Bone Zone, a giant cemetery on a hill. I pull into the empty parking lot and Mona rolls a joint. There's only one lamp, burning high and cold in the middle of the lot. Mona pushes her shoes off and puts her feet up on the dashboard and cries. She warned me about that the night we met: I said something stupid to her like "You're so funny" and she said, "Actually I cry a lot. That's something you should know." I was so happy she thought I should know things about her, I didn't care. I still don't care, but it's true that Mona cries a lot. She cries because she's scared her mom will take her away to Egypt, where the family used to live, and where

Mona has never been. "What would I do there? I don't even speak Arabic." She wipes her mascara on her sleeve, and I tell her to look at the lamp outside and pretend that its glassy brightness is a bonfire, and that she and I are personally throwing every selkie story ever written onto it and watching them burn up.

"You and your selkie stories," she says. I tell her they're not my selkie stories, not ever, and I'll never tell one, which is true, I never will, and I don't tell her how I went up to the attic that day or that what I was looking for was a book I used to read when I was little, *Beauty and the Beast*, which is a really decent story about an animal who gets turned into a human and stays that way, the way it's supposed to be. I don't tell Mona that Beauty's black hair coiled to the edge of the page, or that the Beast had yellow horns and a smoking jacket, or that instead of finding the book I found the coat, and my mom put it on and went out the kitchen door and started up her car.

One selkie story tells about a man from Mýrdalur. He was on the cliffs one day and heard people singing and dancing inside a cave, and he noticed a bunch of skins piled on the rocks. He took one of the skins home and locked it in a chest, and when he went back a girl was sitting there alone, crying. She was naked, and he gave her some clothes and took her home. They got married and had kids. You know how this goes. One day the man changed his clothes and forgot to take the key to the chest out of his pocket, and when his wife washed the clothes, she found it.

"You're not going to Egypt," I tell Mona. "We're going to Colorado. Remember?"

That's our big dream, to go to Colorado. It's where Mona was born. She lived there until she was four. She still remembers the rocks and the pines and the cold, cold air. She says the clouds of Colorado are bright, like pieces of mirror. In Colorado, Mona's parents got divorced, and Mona's mom tried to kill herself for the first time. She tried it once here, too. She put her head in the oven, resting on a pillow. Mona was in seventh grade.

Selkies go back to the sea in a flash, like they've never been away. That's one of the ways they're different from human beings. Once, my dad tried to go back somewhere: he was in the army, stationed in Germany, and he went to Norway to look up the town my great-grandmother came from. He actually found the place, and even an old farm with the same name as us. In the town, he went into a restaurant and ordered lutefisk, a disgusting fish thing my grandmother makes. The cook came out of the kitchen and looked at him like he was nuts. She said they only eat lutefisk at Christmas.

There went Dad's plan of bringing back the original flavor of lutefisk. Now all he's got from Norway is my great-grandmother's Bible. There's also the diary she wrote on the farm up north, but we can't read it. There's only four English words in the whole book: *My God awful day*.

You might suspect my dad picked my mom up in Norway, where they have seals. He didn't, though. He met her at the pool.

As for Mom, she never talked about her relatives. I asked her once if she had any, and she said they were "no kind of people." At the time I thought she meant they were druggies or murderers, maybe in prison somewhere. Now I wish that was true.

One of the stories I don't tell Mona comes from *A Dictionary of British Folklore in the English Language*. In that story, it's the selkie's little girl who points out where the skin is hidden. She doesn't know what's going to happen, of course, she just knows her mother is looking for a skin, and she remembers her dad taking one out from under the bed and stroking it. The little girl's mother drags out the skin and says: "Fareweel, peerie buddo!" She doesn't think about how the little girl is going to miss her, or how if she's been breathing air all this time she can surely keep it up a little longer. She just throws on the skin and jumps into the sea.

After Mom left, I waited for my dad to get home from work. He didn't say anything when I told him about the coat. He stood in the light of the clock on the stove and rubbed his fingers together softly, almost like he was snapping but with no sound. Then he sat down at the kitchen table and lit a cigarette. I'd never seen him smoke in the house before. *Mom's gonna lose it*, I thought, and then I realized that no, my mom wasn't going to lose anything. We were the losers. Me and Dad.

He still waits up for me, so just before midnight I pull out of the parking lot. I'm hoping to get home early enough that he doesn't grumble, but late enough that he doesn't want to come up from the basement, where he takes apart old TVs, and talk to me about college. I've told him I'm not going to college. I'm going to Colorado, a landlocked state. Only twenty out of fifty states are completely landlocked, which means they don't touch the Great Lakes or the sea. Mona turns on the light and tries to put on eyeliner in the mirror, and I swerve to make her mess up. She turns out the light and hits me. All the windows are down to air out the car, and Mona's hair blows wild around her face. *Peerie buddo*, the book says, is "a term of endearment." "Peerie buddo," I say to Mona. She's got the hiccups. She can't stop laughing.

I've never kissed Mona. I've thought about it a lot, but I keep deciding it's not time. It's not that I think she'd freak out or anything. It's not even that I'm afraid she wouldn't kiss me back. It's worse: I'm afraid she'd kiss me back, but not mean it.

Probably one of the biggest losers to fall in love with a selkie was the man who carried her skin around in his knapsack. He was so scared she'd find it that he took the skin with him everywhere, when he went fishing, when he went drinking in the town. Then one day he had a wonderful catch of fish. There were so many he couldn't drag them all home in his net. He emptied his knapsack and filled it with fish, and he put the skin over his shoulder, and on his way up the road to his house, he dropped it.

"Gray in front and gray in back, 'tis the very thing I lack." That's what the man's wife said, when she found the skin. The man ran to catch her, he even kissed her even though she was already a seal, but she squirmed off down the road and flopped into the water. The man stood knee-deep in the chilly waves, stinking of fish, and cried. In selkie stories, kissing never solves anything. No transformation happens because of a kiss. No one loves you just because you love them. What kind of fairy tale is that?

"She wouldn't wake up," Mona says. "I pulled her out of the oven onto the floor, and I turned off the gas and opened the windows. It's not that I was smart, I wasn't thinking at all. I called Uncle Tad and the police and I still wasn't thinking."

I don't believe she wasn't smart. She even tried to give her mom CPR, but her mom didn't wake up until later, in the hospital. They had to reach in and drag her out of death, she was so closed up in it. Death is skin-tight, Mona says. Gray in front and gray in back.

Dear Mona: When I look at you, my skin hurts.

I pull into her driveway to drop her off. The house is dark, the darkest house on her street, because Mona's mom doesn't like the porch light on. She says it shines in around the blinds and keeps her awake. Mona's mom has a beautiful bedroom upstairs, with lots of old photographs in gilt frames, but she sleeps on the living room couch beside the aquarium. Looking at the fish helps her to sleep, although she also says this country has no real fish. That's what Mona calls one of her mom's "refrains."

Mona gets out, yanking the little piece of my heart that stays with her wherever she goes. She stands outside the car and leans in through the open door. I can hardly see her, but I can smell the lemon-scented stuff she puts on her hair, mixed up with the smells of sweat and weed. Mona smells like a forest, not the sea. "Oh my God," she says, "I forgot to tell you, tonight, you know table six? That big horde of Uncle Tad's friends?"

"Yeah."

"So they wanted the soup with the food, and I forgot, and you know what the old guy says to me? The little guy at the head of the table?"

"What?"

"He goes, *Vous êtes bête, mademoiselle!*"

She says it in a rough, growly voice, and laughs. I can tell it's French, but that's all. "What does it mean?"

"*You're an idiot, miss!*"

She ducks her head, stifling giggles. "He called you an idiot?"

"Yeah, *bête*, it's like *beast*."

She lifts her head, then shakes it. A light from someone else's porch bounces off her nose. She puts on a fake Norwegian accent and says: "*My God awful day.*"

I nod. "Awful day." And because we say it all the time, because it's the kind of silly, ordinary thing you could call one of our "refrains," or maybe because of the weed I've smoked, a whole bunch of days seem pressed together inside this moment, more than you could count. There's the time we all went out for New Year's Eve, and Uncle Tad drove me, and when he stopped and I opened the door he told me to close it, and I said "I will when I'm on the other side," and when I told Mona we laughed so hard we had to run away and hide in the bathroom. There's the day some people we know from school came in and we served them wine even though they were under age and Mona got nervous and spilled it all over the tablecloth, and the day her nice cousin came to visit and made us cheese-and-mint sandwiches in the microwave and got yelled at for wasting food. And the day of the party for Mona's mom's birthday, when Uncle Tad played music and made us all dance, and Mona's mom's eyes went jewelly with tears, and afterward Mona told me: "I should just run away. I'm the only thing keeping her here." My God, awful days. All the best days of my life.

"Bye," Mona whispers. I watch her until she disappears into the house.

My mom used to swim every morning at the YWCA. When I was little she took me along. I didn't like swimming. I'd sit in a chair with a book while she went up and down, up and down, a dim streak in the water. When I read *Mrs. Frisby and the Rats of NIMH*, it seemed like Mom was a lab rat doing tasks, the way she kept touching one side of the pool and then the other. At last she climbed out and pulled off her bathing cap. In the locker room she hung up her suit, a thin gray rag dripping on the floor. Most people put the hook of their padlock through the straps of their suit, so the suits could hang outside the lockers without getting stolen, but my mom never did that. She just tied her suit loosely onto the lock. "No one's going to steal that stretchy old thing," she said. And no one did.

That should have been the end of the story, but it wasn't. My dad says Mom was an elemental, a sort of stranger, not of our kind. It wasn't my fault she left, it was because she couldn't learn to breathe on land. That's the worst story I've ever heard. I'll never tell Mona, not ever, not even when we're leaving for Colorado with everything we need in the back of my car, and I meet her at the grocery store the way we've already planned, and she runs out smiling under her orange baseball cap. I won't tell her how dangerous attics are, or how some people can't start over, or how I still see my mom in shop windows with her long hair the same silver-gray as her coat, or how once when my little cousins came to visit we went to the zoo and the seals recognized me, they both stood up in the water and talked in a foreign language. I won't tell her. I'm too scared. I won't even tell her what she needs to know: that we've got to be tougher than our moms, that we've got to have different stories, that she'd better not change her mind and drop me in Colorado because I won't understand, I'll hate her forever and burn her stuff and stay up all night screaming at the woods, because it's stupid not to be able to breathe, who ever heard of somebody breathing in one place but not another, and we're not like that, Mona and me, and selkie stories are only for losers stuck on the wrong side of magic—people who drop things, who tell all, who leave keys around, who let go.

Notes on "Selkie Stories Are for Losers" by Sofia Samatar (2013)

> The interruption of new love is also an invitation to a new life.

The marriage of a human with an enchanted animal or hybrid being is a common motif in folklore, crossing cultures and genres alike. Selkie stories—which circulate in Ireland, the Scottish Highlands, the Orkney and Shetland Islands, Iceland, and Scandinavia—usually tell of a man's abduction of a seal woman, her captivity as a human wife and mother, and her return to the sea once she retrieves her skin or hood. The seals in these stories are usually gray ones, like the ones found in the northern Atlantic Ocean, reinforcing the sense that these tales are legends tied to local beliefs about merfolk and water spirits and to family and place histories. But selkie stories also share significant features with folktales about swan maidens: in both cases, the female protagonist has shapeshifting abilities that a man takes away, but finally she manages to escape, regaining her animal body and access to her element, whether it be water or air. Swan maiden stories, which have no tale type of their own, are often grouped as part of "The Animal Bride" ATU 402, a label that ignores the heroine's enchanted nature or supernatural power, her capacity to move across species; or of "Quest for a Lost Wife" ATU 400, the best-known versions of which end with the swan maiden's final and "proper" return to being wife, mother, and human only. In contrast, in selkie stories the heroine returns to the sea for good, even when this means leaving her human children behind. Thus, these stories are often read as cautioning against making a family with someone from another culture, someone who will never really trade swimming for breathing. One of the versions recounted in Samatar's short story ends with the selkie rushing to the water with only a quick "Farewell peerie buddo!" (little child).

Samatar's young-adult first-person narrator processes her sense of loss by reinhabiting selkie stories in ways that do not leave her behind, "stuck on the wrong side of magic." Her mother has left her, but their kinship remains strong, as seen not only in the magic realism of the zoo seals recognizing and speaking to the girl but in her own recognition of the foreignness she shares with all the women in the story, including her mother. This foreignness is not represented monochromatically: their experiences as immigrants from the Middle East mark Mona and her mother differently from the narrator and her Euro-American family. And yet neither the girls nor their mothers want to belong in a patriarchal culture that demeans women while upholding heteronormative domesticity. Making one's future in a different storyworld is both frightening and exhilarating. Is landlocked Colorado the place to go? Water, like change, has life-giving and life-taking powers; and, infinitely adaptable, water takes different shapes, just as wonder tales give shape to multiple desires.

Samatar's narrator suggests that, in order not to repeat their mothers' sorrows and isolation, the young girls should not let go of their otherness in a patriarchal world but that, at the same time, they should also embrace new possibilities for relating and loving across cultural differences. What do you make of "losers" in the title? And what makes the narrator change her mind about telling selkie stories?

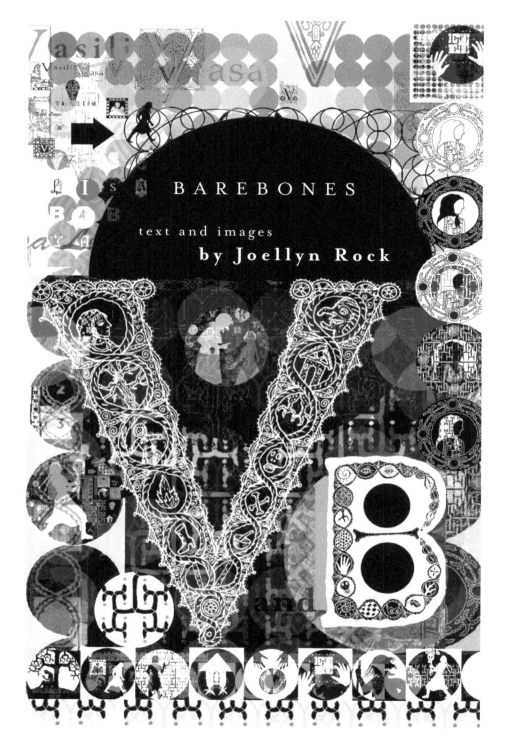

BAREBONES

text and images
by Joellyn Rock

Joellyn Rock, "Bare Bones," 2002.

nce there was
and Once there was

not

a little girl named

Vasalisa

(VASILISA   *Vassilissa*   Wassilissa)

**She was the sweetest thing,
a really**

REALLY

good girl.

Her mother dressed her in the perfect
good-little-girl-little-outfit
with a black skirt and a white apron,
a white blouse and a red vest
all embroidered
and painstakingly

designed.

On her feet, Vasalisa wore little red boots.

On her head: **a scarf**
decorated with colorful patterns
that had been passed

with viral ferocity

from generation to generation
was tied
babushka-style
beneath her chin,

her long braids twisting like D NA down her back.

Vasalisa's mother loved her very much,
doted on her
wished she might stay this
sweet and doll-like forever.

Then one day Vasalisa's mother
found a lump
or some irregular bleeding
or something else so nasty
that it stopped her in her tracks.

The mother took to her bed,
to her HMO hospital room,
to her hospice.

The mother curled up
on a cot in the corner of a shelter to die
and called Vasalisa to her side.

From under the blankets she pulled a little doll
that looked exactly like Vasalisa:
same black skirt, white apron
same blouse, same vest
same tiny red boots.

**same scarf
of many colors.**

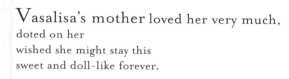

Stitch by stitch
her mother had made

this doll
this gift

for her daughter
by hand.

At first, the doll gave Vasalisa *the creeps.*

What was her mother trying to do?
giving her this mini self
a silly finger puppet?

The doll was so soft
such a squishy-thing
with threads all dangling
(*so unprofessional!*)

Why not something *new*
something shrink-wrapped
something useful?

Vasalisa was pissed.

She wanted to fling the doll
r i g h t
a g a i n s t
t h e
w a l l.

But the mother spoke softly to the girl:
"Keep this doll with you Vasalisa."

"All you need to do is
feed her a little bit
now and then

and listen to her.

She will help you know
what to do
and which way to go

after I am gone."

Vasalisa sighed

and accepted her mother's blessing,
and slipped the doll
into the pocket of her apron.

When her mother died
Vasalisa cried so long
and so hard
that she
would go to sleep crying
and wake up crying
and spent most of the time
sitting in the dirt

behind the apartment building
under the jungle gym
beneath the tree near her mother's grave.

Wait a minute...

Where was the father?

Oh...
He was a *wreck!*

the empty bottles,
like bones,
rattling together
in the recycling bin
in the garage.

E v e n t u a l l y
Vasalisa reached down
into her pocket
and felt

the little memo from mom

and somehow she knew
she was going to

be...

ok.

Vasalisa's father

wasn't cut out
for raising a daughter alone.
So he promptly
put the word out:
had himself declared
eligible,
available…
maybe even placed a personal ad.

Before too long, he remarried a woman with two daughters of her own.
A cozy package,
a ready-made family.
(He was so relieved to find a new mother for Vasalisa!)

But Vasalisa found herself living in a hostile Hostel,
her stepmother: **hideous.**
her stepsisters: **nasty!**

Banished
to the cinder block basement,
she could see her own breath
on the coldest nights,
and huddled with her toes
near the space heater
to keep them warm.

Upstairs,
Vasalisa could hear
her stepsisters
p a d d i n g a r o u n d
in their fuzzy slippers,
in their polartek robes,
c a c k l i n g and making her
the brunt of their jokes.

For fun they would draw cartoons on old copy paper, **of her as a hag!**

The drawings were always the same:
the long curving chin
the nose that hooked down to meet it.
There would be a wart at the side of the nose,
and long greasy hair would snake out from all sides of the bony misshapen head.

She would find piles of these cruel caricatures around the house.

Underneath
they would scrawl her name:

Va-sa-leesa

(they couldn't even remember how to spell it!)

When her father got wind
of the stepsisters' mischief
he shook his head and shrugged:

*What can you do
with teenage girls?*
he thought,

slipping away
from the house

for longer
and longer
s t r e t c h e s.

Sometimes

the stepsisters would corner Vasalisa
and coerce her into participating in some game of theirs.
She might be cast in the role of nursemaid,

housekeeper,

slave,

and ordered to wait upon their every whim.

Other days she might be *their* doll.
They would spend hours making-her-over:
smearing her eyes with blue shadow
circling her cheeks with rouge
and s c i s s o r i n g
at her golden locks.

The fun never quite satisfied the stepsisters,
for Vasalisa somehow stayed
sweet and beautiful,
despite their attempts
to reshape her.

(The doll whispered words of comfort to her during those hellish days.)

Finally the stepsisters plotted to get rid of her altogether.

Even their mother helped them hatch the plan.

They would fake a crisis

a power outage...
a brown out
a blackout!

and send HER for help.

One very dark night they did it:
pushing her out of the house,
no flashlight
no cell phone
no map

"Go."

"Leave!"

"And don't come back

until you've figured out

what happened to our fire!"

"You'll have to go all the way to Baba Yaga for help."

Baba Yaga?

Yikes! thought Vasalisa,
imagining the legendary
Bitch
on the other side of the strip mall,
down the darkest back alley,
in the worst neck of the woods...

She eats girls alive!

N ever,

ever had Vasalisa been so scared.

She managed to stuff
the little doll down into her pocket
just as she was pitched out
into the nicotine night.
As she walked
she fed the doll
crumbs of bread crust
bits of granola bar
bite-sized
Pepperidge Farm Goldfish Crackers

And in exchange,
this little navigatrix
this tiny palm pilot

would whisper
d i r e c t i o n s

with the intuition of a
smart bomb

to the left

to the right
in the dark
of the night

g u i d i n g Vasalisa
this way   AND *that way...*

through the skeletons of branching trees
towards the ramshackle outpost of Baba Yaga.

As Vasalisa traveled
she passed many strange signs
(s o m e   m o r e   r e a d a b l e   t h a n   o t h e r s)

There were
LOGOS
and symbols

Posters

b a n n e r s

and neon marquees

left by others
who had marked this trail in other eras before hers.

Suddenly she was blinded
by the white of some headlights
and looked up to see

a station wagon
a delivery van
a horseman

dressed all in white
riding an ivory stallion

and the sky lightened.

Vasalisa walked on further
and was startled
by another horseman

this one all in red
with pinstriping and fins
and a fiery **vrrrrrooooom** to him

and the sky came ablaze.

Some hours later
Vasalisa was passed
by yet another horseman

this one very **dark**
tattooed and body pierced dark
skull and crossbones dark
and the sky abruptly went black,
black as a cast iron pot
black as the bed of a printing press

black as ink.

Now the little doll calculated
that she was nearing their destination...

And so Vasalisa made her way
through the woods
along the service road
past the strip mall

finally coming
to a c l e a r i n g
where she saw the glow of a

Country Kitchen

OPEN
24hoursaday

and knew that there she would find
the formidable proprietress
of all things needed in the night.

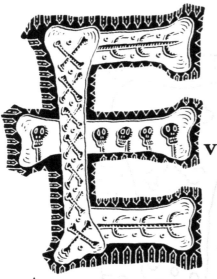

Even though

there was fresh snow on the ground,
there were still Halloween decorations
up around the joint.

Paper skeletons swung
from each porch post.

Along the fence
plastic lights
little skulls
rattled
and chattered
c l i c k e t y - c l a c k
against the railing.

The hut had long jagged icicles
crystal bones
Yaga teeth
hanging from its rafters

It grinned ferociously
at anyone who dared approach!

Weirdest of all:
the dwelling
suddenly stood up
and whirled
like a Dervish
on chicken's feet!
(It gave her the heebiejeebies.)

No basement?   *A mobile home?*   Perhaps.

Vasalisa heard a whir
and looked up into the night sky

t h e r e

f l y i n g

there she saw it

the **silhouette** of Baba Yaga

descending
in her mortar with a pestle

…in her **black** cauldron.

Her creepy cuisinart
c o m i n g   i n   f o r   a   l a n d i n g.

With greasy hair streaming behind her,
the hag trailed a broom
like a giant eraser
for deleting her own tracks.

She screeched into her parking place
and dismounted with a slam.

She was in no mood for distractions.

Baba Yaga
just stood there
with her hands on her hips
in the strange glow of the skulls
and Vasalisa took in
this shocking composite
this awful specter
of a woman:

Part *grandmother*, **part beast.**

Baba Yaga was a bony thing . **Her look,**
like the witch
in your own
worst horror movie:

that nose *you know*
that chin
you're imagining
those teeth
like pinking shears
And that wart
that belongs in a museum!

Her breasts sagged
like water balloons,

(to her knees no doubt)

And those legs!
one all bone with spidery veins
and the other...
lumpy and brown,
made out of *excrement.*

E x c r e m e n t ?
(that's what it says.)

Baba Yaga stopped
and sniffed at the air.

She clapped her hands
muttered
some code
some password
under her breath
and the hut
rotated upon command,
opening its entrance
a u t o m a t i c a l l y
like a garage door.

"What do YOU want?"

**ure.**

Baba Yaga *could* help Vasalisa.

Sure.

She knew her family.
They were just stupid enough
to send this waif wandering
in search of fire.

But you don't get somethin for nothin.

"You'll have to do some work for me,"

the hag growled at the girl.

"It's SUPPERTIME!"

Baba Yaga snapped and three pairs of hands came *out of no where.*

Gourmet cookbooks swooped and hovered
as these bodiless hands prepared

a smorgasbord
a splendid table
a veritable food-pyramid of delicacies!

(It was quite a spread.)

Vasalisa was famished, but first she did as she was told.
She catered to the Yaga,
serving her *by hand*
dish after delicious dish
from the long table.

Baba Yaga munched and crunched.

She slurped and sucked,
stopping only now and then
to smack her lips
or lick her fingertips.

Finally, she leaned back and belched

a terrible burp

which smelled
like a sour refrigerator
like a daycare center.

The Yaga devoured
the entire meal
leaving but

a scrap of bread
a slice of cold pizza
a dab of mac and cheese

for Vasalisa to secretly share with her doll.

"And now,"

smirked the Yaga,

"You'll do the dishes
and *clean the kitchen*

and you'll sweep and you'll dust and you'll vacuum...and..."

she pointed to a colossal mountain of clothes,

"Don't forget to do the laundry!"

"And if you're not done by morning..."
she delivered the ultimate ultimatum:

"I'll eat YOU up!"

When Baba Yaga flew off to bed,
Vasalisa collapsed in a heap.

How was she going to get all these tasks done?

The clothes

washed

dried

ironed

folded

(you always forget about the folding part)

**and put away
by daybreak?**

As her hysteria mounted,
she heard a little
sssssssssssssssssssssssssssssssssssssssshhhhhhhhhhhhhhhhhhhhhhhhhhhhhhhhhhhhhhhhhhhhh
from her pocket:

"Don't worry," whispered the doll,
"Go to sleep.
Get some rest.
Things will look better in the morning."

Baba Yaga

was a little irked the next morning
to discover that *somehow*
Vasalisa had managed
to complete all her chores.

**She had been looking forward
to a little breakfast of girl
but settled for a bowl of instant oatmeal
and a Pop-tart.**

Before she blew off for the day, the hag gave Vasalisa a few more assignments.

"See this?"

Baba Yaga pointed to an enormous heap of
dark tidbits
black specks

"You must pick out:

the poppy seeds from the dirt
the periods from the pixels
the dashes from the dots"

*"And over here...
See this pile?"*

Vasalisa looked at an even larger mound

"You need to s p e c i f y these:
the good grain from
the rotting wheat

the CMYK Gold from the RGB Yellow

the elegant typeface
from the grungy font"

"AND HERE,
here's the MOST IMPORTANT stack."
the Yaga gestured toward a tower of paperwork...

"You need to s e p a r a t e :
the fresh corn   from the mildewed corn

the beautiful images
from the ugly images

the thoughts
from the feelings

And if you're not done by the time I get back...

Then I'll have YOU for supper!"

She ran a wicked tongue across her own zig-zaggy grin
and pretended to be reading from a cookbook:

"Let's see...

How to Prepare:

Vasalisa Surprise..."

When the hag was gone,

**Vasalisa looked
at the rubble**

and crumpled down into herself.

No Way.

No Way.

Not *humanly* possible!

She was teetering
on the edge of a tantrum.

But then again,
up popped the little doll,
pocket protector that she was.

"sssssshhhhhhhhhhhhhhhhh!"

She said to Vasalisa.

"Don't Worry!

I'll help you, and ALL this work will get done."

And so Vasalisa's
personal assistant
her tiny search engine
went on automatic pilot
sorting

s e p a r a t i n g

rasterizing
optimizing

and
batch processing
all the tedious
and time
consuming
operations
that needed to be
finished
by deadline.

When Baba Yaga
returned home
that evening,
she *was* surprised
by how much
the girl
had been able
to accomplish.

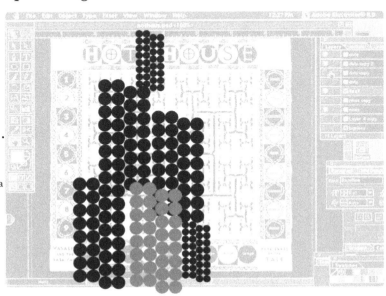

That night

there they were again:

The three pairs of hands

crushing the corn into meal
grinding the wheat into flour
pressing the poppy seeds into oil

and printing the final copy
full color

full scale

at high resolution
on photogloss paper

As Vasalisa stood next to Baba Yaga
by the loom
near the mill

k n e e l i n g
at the giant Epson printer

she took the opportunity
to inquire of the Yaga
if perhaps now she could have the fire
to bring back to her home?

Baba Yaga heaved a frustrated sigh.

"Don't you want to Learn anything from ME first?"

Well, sure...

Vasalisa had been curious about a few things around the joint.

Vasalisa went ahead and asked the hag about those horses:

"I was just wondering...Who was that White guy?"

"Oh, that is my daybreak.
He always makes the deliveries at the crack of dawn."

"And...the Red one?"

"Oh, He is my sunset. A real hot head, but dependable."

"And what's the story on the Black fellow?"

"Ah, that is my Night.
You'd better keep an eye on him, he works the late shift...

I SUPERVISE

all of them.

I keep them here...in this locked file cabinet
...in this portfolio...on this zip disk.

Well, actually...
< they're in this folder
< inside this other folder
< inside this other folder
< on the desktop...
and I pull them up as they're needed."

"Now...
Don't you want to ask me anything else?"

Vasalisa looked at the hands
a n i m a t e d
and
f l o a t i n g i n s p a c e.
She was dying to know all about them.

But before she could ask,
her little doll whispered
a characteristic

sssssssssssssssssssshhhhhhhhhhhhhh!

from her pocket,

warning Vasalisa
that too many questions might get her into trouble.

"Oh, **shhhhhush** yourself!"
Vasalisa said to the doll.
"I can ask
whatever I feel like asking!"

Baba Yaga glared at her:

"I hope you're not going to ask for a raise!
Or for a different shift.
Or for weekends off.

Because if you do... **I'll eat you up!**

And what's that you're talking to in your pocket?
Personal correspondence? On my time clock?

You listen to me little girlie:
If you go trying to organize those horses...
I'll make a potluck of you!"

"Oh, It's nothing..." answered Vasalisa,
"Just a little doll, a blessing from my Mother."

"A BLESSING!
So that's how you've gotten all this work done!"

(Her eyebrows came together like a terrible black bird in flight.)

"I've had enough of you!
Here, take the fire...
and here's a skull to carry it in."

The hag was all out
of packing crates
and shopping bags
and zip disks

so the skull
would have to do.

nd before she knew
what had happened to her,
Vasalisa was out the door.
(seems like this has happened to her before)

Only this time she had
the fire
in a skull
on a stick
in her hands!

"Nice Boots!"
Baba Yaga called out the door to her, as Vasalisa departed.

"They're utilitarian," answered Vasalisa,
"You know...made for w a l k i n g."

"Consider the Uses of Adversity..."

shouted the Yaga,
always one to have the last word.

"And GOOD LUCK FINDING EMPLOYMENT!"

Vasalisa couldn't believe that she was finally *free*
free of Baba Yaga
free as the pages of an unbound book!

AND that she had *somehow* passed her tests (without being eaten alive)

AND that she'd gotten what she'd come for:
a luminary with plenty of memory
a portable power center rammed on a joystick!
(battery pack included)

Vasalisa looked back over her shoulder

checked her rear view mirror

caught one last glimpse of the hut

s p i n n i n g

on its Kentucky Fried chicken legs
and suddenly felt sentimental
about her time in the Hot House.

But the doll coaxed her along
and Vasalisa used the skull to blaze the trail

this way

and that way

to the left
to the right
over the freeway
and through the tunnels
back to her home

(if you could call it that.)

At one point her arms got so tired
from carrying the flaming skull-on-a-stick
that she considered leaving it there
on the gravelly shoulder of the highway

like road kill

for some sanitation truck to dispose of…

But now the skull was getting verbal on her too:

"Oh No…
**You don't want to put me down sweetheart,
not after you've made it this far."**

So she kept carrying the ghastly thing

**And it lit her way through the darkest part of the woods
where the tree trunks grow in massive columns**

like the underside
of an overpass.

Vasalisa made it all the way back
to where things started to look familiar again.

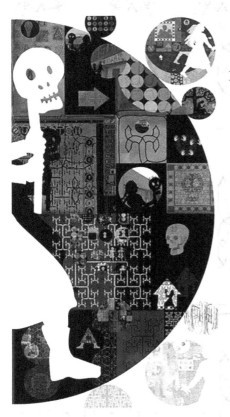

And there was her house
> sitting in the dark
> with all its lights out.

From the window
> **the step mother**
> **and the step sisters**
could see Vasalisa emerge

t r i u m p h a n t l y
from her venture.

They welcomed her inside
with her conflagrant curio

> Needless to say,
> > they were impressed.

wasn't it weird?
wasn't it horrible?

(w a s n ' t   i t   w o n d e r f u l !)

She set it down
and booted it up
and logged onto it

and it just sat there glowing back at them

incandescent

flickering

l u m i n o u s

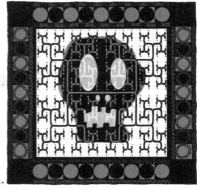

an eerie monitor in the dark family room.

nce there was
> and Once there was not

a little girl who…
and she was called *Vasilisa the Beautiful*

nce there was
> and Once there was not

a little girl who…
and she was called WASSILISSA THE WISE

nce there was
> and Once there was not

a little girl who…
and she was called Vasilissa the Clever

nce there was
> and Once there was not

a little girl who…
and she was called **VasaLeezza the Vengeful**

nce there was
> and Once there was not

a little girl who…
and she was called *Vasalisa the Brave*

Notes on "Bare Bones" by Joellyn Rock (2002)

> Vasilisa's winding paths invite us to follow her visual narrative,
> but they also interrupt our expectations at every turn.

THIS VISUALLY STRIKING MULTIMEDIA version of a traditional Russian fairy tale, "Vasilisa the Beautiful," is a "story in text and image" that has been "embroidered," rather than "written," by Joellyn Rock. "Bare Bones," Rock wrote to us, "retells the tale of dutiful Vasalisa and her encounter with the formidable hag, Baba Yaga. Rebooted for the electronic age, this story of loss, servitude, and triumph over adversity builds a bridge for the fairy-tale audience between traditional media and new media. The tale, as broken down into nodes, is meant to be experienced in an interactive story environment. Its voices interrupt and interject, with the banter of gossiping crones. *The Vasalisa Project* website invites the reader to weave between the prose poem 'Bare Bones,' with hyperlinks to digital images, and the design thesis 'Vasalisa Electric.'" In this book you have the print-layout version, but you can also see a hypertextual digital version at www.rockingchair.org.

In most short-story anthologies and in long-form narratives, typesetting is meant to be invisible; that is, readers should not notice the shape, thickness, size, kerning, spacing, and placement of the individual letters or words on the page. In comics and some illustrated books, as with "Bare Bones," typesetting takes a central role in the experience and even interpretation of the tale. We argue that in Emma Donoghue's "Tale of the Cottage," the use of a nondominant style of voice affects the speed of our reading of the tale; in Rock's work, the use of kerning to space letters dose together or f a r   a p a r t will also cause us to experience a text at different speeds. In addition, the position of the lines of text in relation to other lines works to draw us along a winding path together with Vasilisa or else to convey tone of voice or emotional state.

As with "A Poisoned Tale," "The Master of Nottingham's Daughter," and "Among the Thorns," different possible versions of the tale emerge as we read. But this time, rather than consisting of conflicting voices or reportage of content, the differences are external to the narrative and are in design and format. How do the visual choices in the print layout version and the online version alter, or not, the experience of the story? How do the digital story's nodes and navigating choices impact the experience of "Bare Bones" as a tale that bridges oral as well as print and electronic storytelling?

The form and content of the tale engage notions of temporality and especially anachronism as well as multiple forms of technology. "Bare Bones" recalls to us that technology is not only bits and bytes and shiny new twenty-first-century devices. Just like hypertextual websites or e-books, paper-and-ink books are technologies too. Woodcut techniques are as technological as digital graphic design. And perhaps a talking doll that can do the "sorting, separating, rasterizing, optimizing and batch processing" is no less a technological tool than a computer program. The two (or three if you have an e-copy of this book) formats of this tale bring our attention to the ways that older technologies are still employed in our everyday lives (see Haase 2006). What do the combinations and juxtapositions of older technologies of the "folk" *and* the modern technologies of the digital age ask us to consider or remember about the representation of fairy tales and folktales in the twenty-first century?

Other juxtapositions appear in the form of temporal expectations and anachronisms. If the typesetting keeps us, and Vasilisa herself, moving around the page/screen, temporal cues that create and then subvert expectations shuttle us back and forth through time. The opening formula with the illuminated initial O in a style reminiscent of a woodcut automatically produces expectations of the so-called timelessness of a fairy tale; however, within just a few lines, Vasilisa's braids "twisting like DNA, down her back" are surprisingly modern, and the reference to HMOs (health maintenance organizations) places the story's location firmly within the United States. Both of these references to modern medical issues also seem to trip up the genre of the fairy tale, as does some of the language ("Vasilissa was pissed"). And yet, the illustrations and the otherwise "timeless" feel persist throughout the text.

The Master of Nottingham's Daughter

Susanna Clarke

The story of the Master of Nottingham's daughter appears as
a footnote in Susanna Clarke's *Jonathan Strange & Mr Norrell*
(2004), an alternate history novel about two English magicians
in the nineteenth century. This footnote appears when
Mr Norrell, magical mentor to Jonathan Strange, is discussing
the efficacy of placing a magician's power into an inanimate
object, such as a ring. Mr Norrell refers to "the Master of
Nottingham's daughter," who mistook her father's ring of power
for "a common bauble" and wore it to a fair. Norrell drops the
subject, however, and does not tell the tale. The narrator of
the novel remedies his omission by providing the lengthy
footnote we include here.

THE STORY OF THE Master of Nottingham's daughter (to which Mr Norrell
never returned) is worth recounting and so I set it down here.

The fair to which the young woman repaired was held on St Matthew's
Feast in Nottingham. She spent a pleasant day, going about among the booths,
making purchases of linens, laces and spices. Sometime during the afternoon
she happened to turn suddenly to see some Italian tumblers who were behind
her and the edge of her cloak flew out and struck a passing goose. This bad-
tempered fowl ran at her, flapping its wings and screaming. In her surprize
she dropt her father's ring, which fell into the goose's open gullet and the
goose, in *its* surprize, swallowed it. But before the Master of Nottingham's
daughter could say or do any thing the gooseherd drove the goose on and
both disappeared into the crowd.

Susanna Clarke, "The Master of Nottingham's Daughter," in *Jonathan Strange &
Mr Norrell*, 2004.

The goose was bought by a man called John Ford who took it back to his house in the village of Fiskerton and the next day his wife, Margaret Ford, killed the goose, plucked it and drew out its innards. In its stomach she found a heavy silver ring set with a crooked piece of yellow amber. She put it down on a table near three hens' eggs that had been gathered that morning.

Immediately the eggs began to shake and then to crack open and from each egg something marvellous appeared. From the first egg came a stringed instrument like a viol, except that it had little arms and legs, and played sweet music upon itself with a tiny bow. From the next egg emerged a ship of purest ivory with sails of fine white linen and a set of silver oars. And from the last egg hatched a chick with strange red-and-gold plumage. This last was the only wonder to survive beyond the day. After an hour or two the viol cracked like an eggshell and fell into pieces and by sunset the ivory ship had set sail and rowed away through the air; but the bird grew up and later started a fire which destroyed most of Grantham. During the conflagration it was observed bathing itself in the flames. From this circumstance it was presumed to be a phoenix.

When Margaret Ford realized that a magic ring had somehow fallen into her possession, she was determined to do magic with it. Unfortunately she was a thoroughly malicious woman, who tyrannized over her gentle husband, and spent long hours pondering how to revenge herself upon her enemies. John Ford held the manor of Fiskerton, and in the months that followed he was loaded with lands and riches by greater lords who feared his wife's wicked magic.

Word of the wonders performed by Margaret Ford soon reached Nottingham, where the Master of Nottingham lay in bed waiting to die. So much of his power had gone into the ring that the loss of it had made him first melancholy, then despairing and finally sick. When news of his ring finally came he was too ill to do any thing about it.

His daughter, on the other hand, was thoroughly sorry for bringing this misfortune on her family and thought it her duty to try and get the ring back; so without telling any one what she intended she set off along the riverbank to the village of Fiskerton.

She had only got as far as Gunthorpe when she came upon a very dreadful sight. A little wood was burning steadily with fierce flames lapping every part of it. The black bitter smoke made her eyes sting and her throat ache, yet the wood was not consumed by the fire. A low moan issued from the trees as if they cried out at such unnatural torment. The Master's daughter looked round for someone to explain this wonder to her. A young woodsman, who was passing, told her, "Two weeks ago, Margaret Ford stopt in the wood on the road from Thurgarton. She rested under the shade of its branches, drank from its stream and ate its nuts and berries, but just as she was leaving a root caught her foot and made her fall, and when she rose from the ground a briar was so impertinent as to scratch her arm. So she cast a spell upon the wood and swore it would burn for ever."

The Master's daughter thanked him for the information and walked on for a while. She became thirsty and crouched down to scoop up some water from the river. All at once a woman—or something very like a woman—half-rose out of the water. There were fish-scales all over her body, her skin was as grey and spotted as a trout's and her hair had become an odd arrangement of spiny grey trout fins. She seemed to glare at the Master's daughter, but her round cold fish-eyes and stiff fishskin were not well adapted to reproduce human expressions and so it was hard to tell.

"Oh! I beg your pardon!" said the Master's daughter, startled.

The woman opened her mouth, shewing a fish throat and mouth full of ugly fish teeth, but she seemed unable to make a sound. Then she rolled over and plunged back into the water.

A woman who was washing clothes on the riverbank explained to the Master's daughter, "That is Joscelin Trent who is so unfortunate as to be the wife of a man that Margaret Ford likes. Out of jealousy Margaret Ford has cast a spell on her and she is forced, poor lady, to spend all her days and nights immersed in the shallows of the river to keep her enchanted skin and flesh from drying out, and as she cannot swim she lives in constant terror of drowning."

The Master's daughter thanked the woman for telling her this.

Next the Master's daughter came to the village of Hoveringham. A man and his wife who were both squeezed together atop a little pony advised her not to enter the village, but led her around it by narrow lanes and paths. From a little green knoll the Master's daughter looked down and saw that everyone in the village wore a thick blindfold round his eyes. They were not at all used to their self-created blindness and constantly banged their faces against walls, tripped over stools and carts, cut themselves on knives and tools and burnt themselves in the fire. As a consequence they were covered in gashes and wounds, yet not one of them removed his blindfold.

"Oh!" said the wife. "The priest of Hoveringham has been bold enough to denounce the wickedness of Margaret Ford from his pulpit. Bishops, abbots and canons have all been silent, but this frail old man defied her and so she has cursed the whole village. It is their fate to have vivid images of all their worst fears constantly before their eyes. These poor souls see their children starve, their parents go mad, their loved ones scorn and betray them. Wives and husbands see each other horribly murdered. And so, though these sights be nought but illusions, the villagers must blindfold themselves or else be driven mad by what they see."

Shaking her head over the appalling wickedness of Margaret Ford, the Master's daughter continued on her way to John Ford's manor, where she found Margaret and her maidservants, each with a wooden stick in her hand, driving the cows to their evening's milking.

The Master's daughter went boldly up to Margaret Ford. Upon the instant Margaret Ford turned and struck her with her stick. "Wicked girl!" she cried. "I know who you are! My ring has told me. I know that you plan to lie to me, who have never done you any harm at all, and ask to become my servant. I know that you plan to steal my ring. Well, know this! I have set strong spells upon my ring. If any thief were foolish enough to touch it, then within a very short space of time bees and wasps and all kinds of insects would fly up from the earth and sting him; eagles and hawks and all kinds of birds would fly down from the sky and peck at him; then bears and boars and all kinds of wild creatures would appear and tear and trample him to pieces!"

Then Margaret Ford beat the Master's daughter soundly, and told the maids to put her to work in the kitchen.

Margaret Ford's servants, a miserable, ill-treated lot, gave the Master's daughter the hardest work to do and whenever Margaret Ford beat them or raged at them—which happened very often—they relieved their feelings by doing the same to her. Yet the Master's daughter did not allow herself to become low-spirited. She stayed working in the kitchen for several months and thought very hard how she might trick Margaret Ford into dropping the ring or losing it.

Margaret Ford was a cruel woman, quick to take offence and her anger, once roused, could never be appeased. But for all that she adored little children; she took every opportunity to nurse babies and once she had a child in her arms she was gentleness itself. She had no child of her own and no one who knew her doubted that this was a source of great sorrow to her. It was widely supposed that she had expended a great deal of magic upon trying to conceive a child, but without success.

One day Margaret Ford was playing with a neighbour's little girl, and saying how if she ever were to have a child then she would rather it were a girl and how she would wish it to have a creamy white skin and green eyes and copper curls (this being Margaret Ford's own colouring). "Oh!" said the Master's daughter innocently "The wife of the Reeve in Epperstone has a baby of exactly that description, the prettiest little creature that ever you saw."

Then Margaret Ford made the Master's daughter take her to Epperstone and shew her the Reeve's wife's baby, and when Margaret Ford saw that the baby was indeed the sweetest, prettiest child that ever there was (just as the Master's daughter had said) she announced to the horrified mother her intention of taking the child away with her.

As soon as she had possession of the Reeve's wife's baby Margaret Ford became almost a different person. She spent her days in looking after the baby, playing with her and singing to her. Margaret Ford became contented with her lot. She used her magic ring a great deal less than she had before and scarcely ever lost her temper.

So things went on until the Master of Nottingham's daughter had lived in Margaret Ford's house for almost a year. Then one summer's day Margaret Ford, the Master's daughter, the baby and the other maids took their midday meal upon the banks of the river. After eating, Margaret Ford rested in the shade of a rose-bush. It was a hot day and they were all very sleepy.

As soon as she was certain that Margaret Ford was asleep the Master's daughter took out a sugar-plum and shewed it to the baby. The baby, knowing only too well what should be done to sugar-plums, opened its mouth wide and the Master's daughter popped it in. Then, as quick as she could and making sure that none of the other maids saw what she did, she slipped the magic ring from Margaret Ford's finger.

Then, "Oh! Oh!" she cried. "Wake up, madam! The baby has taken your ring and put it in her mouth! Oh, for the dear child's sake, undo the spell. Undo the spell!"

Margaret Ford awoke and saw the baby with its cheek bulging out, but for the moment she was too sleepy and surprised to understand what was happening.

A bee flew past and the Master's daughter pointed at it and screamed. All the other maids screamed too. "Quickly, madam, I beg you!" cried the Master's daughter. "Oh!" She looked up. "Here are the eagles and hawks approaching! Oh!" She looked into the distance. "Here are the bears and boars running to tear the poor little thing to pieces!"

Margaret Ford cried out to the ring to stop the magic which it did immediately, and almost at the same moment the baby swallowed the sugar-plum. While Margaret Ford and the maids begged and coaxed the baby and shook it to make it cough up the magic ring, the Master of Nottingham's daughter began to run along the riverbank towards Nottingham.

The rest of the story has all the usual devices. As soon as Margaret Ford discovered how she had been tricked she fetched horses and dogs to chase the Master's daughter. Upon several occasions the Master's daughter seemed lost for sure—the riders were almost upon her and the dogs just behind her. But the story tells how she was helped by all the victims of Margaret Ford's magic: how the villagers of Hoveringham tore off their blindfolds and, in spite of all the horrifying sights they saw, rushed to build barricades to prevent Margaret Ford from passing; how poor Joscelin Trent reached up out of the river and tried to pull Margaret Ford down into the muddy water; how the burning wood threw down flaming branches upon her.

The ring was returned to the Master of Nottingham who undid all the wrongs Margaret Ford had perpetrated and restored his own fortune and reputation.

There is another version of this story which contains no magic ring, no eternally-burning wood, no phoenix—no miracles at all, in fact. According to this version Margaret Ford and the Master of Nottingham's daughter (whose name was Donata Torel) were not enemies at all, but the leaders of a fellowship of female magicians that flourished in Nottinghamshire in the twelfth century. Hugh Torel, the Master of Nottingham, opposed the fellowship and took great pains to destroy it (though his own daughter was a member). He very nearly succeeded, until the women left their homes and fathers and husbands and went to live in the woods under the protection of Thomas Godbless, a much greater magician than Hugh Torel. This less colourful version of the story has never been as popular as the other but it is this version which Jonathan Strange said was the true one and which he included in *The History and Practice of English Magic*.

Notes on "The Master of Nottingham's Daughter" by Susanna Clarke (2004)

> A late interruption offers an invitation to question received notions of history.

The salient difference between *metanarrative* and *metafiction* in "The Master of Nottingham's Daughter" is that metanarrative techniques work to support and even enhance the mimetic illusion of a story. Metafictional techniques function to point out a narrative's status as fiction, its made-up-ness. In this case, metanarration works to further immerse the reader in the alternate-history storyworld by "proving" the truth claims of the tale within a tale within the novel. Yet it also has a distinct but subtle political effect.

This story appears as a footnote, a signifier of scholarly and therefore trustworthy and factual information, to a folktale that the character Mr Norrell intended to present as a true account of past historical events. Although its structure, flat characters, and repetitions belie its historicity, the metafictional move comes when the narrator truncates the telling and says that the "rest of the story has all the usual devices," thus slyly hinting that the story is fictional rather than historical, while also subtly undercutting Norrell's authority. The narrator's subsequent appeal to the expert opinion of magician Jonathan Strange and his scholarly tome *The History and Practice of English Magic* smoothly and effectively discredits Norrell's version of the story while also reinforcing the accuracy of Strange's.

This deceptively simple story produces a critique of the erasure of women's voices and of oppressive stereotypes by enacting that erasure, embedding the stereotypes and then, almost magically, completely undoing them all in just a few lines.

Neither of the women in the story is given a voice of her own, nor is she able to tell the story her way; their story is negotiated between men. Mr Norrell wanted to use the story as an example of how dangerous magic can be, particularly in the hands of women; but he never tells it. Jonathan Strange reads it as evidence of one of the ways women's magic, skills, and knowledge are erased in and by wonder tales, and his version is reproduced in the world of the novel. Does the fact that the women in Jonathan Strange's version need to turn to the male magician Thomas Godbless for protection detract from their power? And what of Jonathan Strange's reclamation of the story for his academic book?

Not only a means to create a surprise twist in the tail end of the tale, Clarke's metanarrative choices also have political implications. And this story is not alone in its metanarrative interruptions. In "Among the Thorns," "The Good Mother," and "Fairytales for Lost Children," the narrative choices of others have defined and entrapped or erased the protagonists from their own stories. Like Clarke's tale, they also, to a greater or lesser extent, expose those responsible for oppressive narrative acts, and they mark their own narrative choices as political acts.

Sources and Credits

Blackwell, Su. *Once Upon a Time*. 2016. © Su Blackwell.

Boyle. Shary. *Beast* (Highland Series). 2007. Purchased with the support of the Canada Council for the Arts Acquisition Assistance Program. Collection Musée d'art contemporain de Montréal. © Shary Boyle.

Boyle, Shary. *Untitled*. National Gallery of Canada, Ottawa. Photo: NGC. *Sans titre*. Musée des beaux-arts du Canada, Ottawa. Photo: MBAC. 2004. © Shary Boyle.

Clarke, Susanna. "The Master of Nottingham's Daughter." *Jonathan Strange & Mr Norrell*. Bloomsbury Publishing Plc, 240–43. 2004. © Susanna Clarke.

Donoghue, Emma. "The Tale of the Cottage." *Kissing the Witch*. HarperCollins, 133–41. 1997. © Emma Donoghue.

Ferré, Rosario. "A Poisoned Tale." Reprinted with permission from the publisher of *Short Stories by Latin American Women*, edited by Celia Correa de Zapata, 65–75. 1990. © Arte Público Press, University of Houston.

Hopkinson, Nalo. *Still Rather Fond of Red*. 2007. © Nalo Hopkinson.

Hyatt Orme, Rosalind. *Medusa*. 2018. © Rosalind Hyatt Orme.

Kamiya, Anne. *Burdens: They Must Always Be Carried*. 2010. © Anne Kamiya.

Kaplan, David. Stills from *Little Red Riding Hood*. 1997. © David Kaplan.

Kern, Maya. "How to Be a Mermaid." http://mayakern.com/cshort.html#htbam. 2012. © Maya Kern.

Kuwada, Bryan Kamaoli. "Of No Real Account." *Hawai'i Review* 81 (2015): 75–86. Student Media Board. © Bryan Kamaoli Kuwada.

Link, Kelly. "Swans." In *A Wolf at the Door and Other Retold Fairy Tales*, edited by Ellen Datlow and Terri Windling, 74–91. Simon & Schuster Books for Young Readers. 2000. © Kelly Link.

Osman, Diriye. "Fairytales for Lost Children." *Fairytales for Lost Children*. Team Angelica Entertainment, 15–30. 2013. © Diriye Osman.

Rock, Joellyn. "Bare Bones." Reprinted with Rock's permission from *Marvels & Tales: Journal of Fairy-Tale Studies* 16.2 (2002): 233–62. © Joellyn Rock.

Samatar, Sofia. "Selkie Stories Are for Losers." *Strange Horizons*. 2013. http://strangehorizons.com/fiction/selkie-stories-are-for-losers/. Also in *Tender: Stories*. Easthampton, MA: Small Beer Press, 1–9. 2017. © 2013 Sofia Samatar.

Schanoes, Veronica. "Among the Thorns." *Tor.com*. 2014. © Veronica Schanoes.

Shawl, Nisi. "Lupine." In *Once Upon a Time*, edited by Paula Guran, 185–88. Prime Books. 2013. © Nisi Shawl.

Tan, Shaun. *Birth of Commerce*. 2020. © Shaun Tan.

Tan, Shaun. *Shelter*. 2020. © Shaun Tan.

Tan, Shaun. "A Tale of a King." Previously unpublished. © Shaun Tan.

Taulapapa McMullin, Dan. *Aitu*. 2016. © Dan Taulapapa McMullin.

Wood, Danielle. "The Good Mother." *Mothers Grimm*. Allen & Unwin, 3–13. 2014. Reproduced with the permission of Allen & Unwin Pty Ltd.

Yanagi, Miwa. *Frau Trude*. 2005. © Miwa Yanagi.

Works Consulted and Further Readings

Bacchilega, Cristina. 2013. *Fairy Tales Transformed? Twenty-First-Century Adaptations and the Politics of Wonder*. Detroit, MI: Wayne State University Press.

———. 2018. "Adaptation and the Fairy-Tale Web." In *Routledge Companion to Media and Fairy-Tale Cultures*, edited by Pauline Greenhill, Jill Terry Rudy, Naomi Hamer, and Lauren Bosc, 145–53. New York: Routledge.

Bacchilega, Cristina, and Marie Alohalani Brown, eds. 2019. *The Penguin Book of Mermaids*. New York: Penguin.

Beckett, Sandra. 2002. *Recycling Red Riding Hood*. New York: Routledge.

———. 2008. *Red Riding Hood for All Ages: Fairy-Tale Icon in Cross-Cultural Contexts*. Detroit, MI: Wayne State University Press.

———. 2014. *Revisioning Red Riding Hood around the World: An Anthology of International Retellings*. Detroit, MI: Wayne State University Press.

Bernheimer, Kate, ed. 1998. *Mirror, Mirror, on the Wall: Women Writers Explore Their Favorite Fairy Tales*. New York: Anchor Books.

———, ed. 2007. *Brothers & Beasts: An Anthology of Men on Fairy Tales*. Detroit, MI: Wayne State University Press.

———, ed. 2010. *My Mother She Killed Me, My Father He Ate Me: Forty New Fairy Tales*. New York: Penguin.

Bettelheim, Bruno. 1976. *The Uses of Enchantment: The Meaning and Importance of Fairy Tales*. New York: Vintage Books.

Canavan, Gerry. 2014. "'There's Nothing New / Under The Sun, / But There Are New Suns': Recovering Octavia E. Butler's Lost Parables." *Los Angeles Review of Books*, June 9. https://lareviewofbooks.org/article/theres-nothing-new-sun-new-suns-recovering-octavia-e-butlers-lost-parables/

Carlson, Amy. 2019. "Kissing the Mermaid: Resistance, Adaptation, Popular Cultural Memory, and Maya Kern's Webcomic *How to Be a Mermaid*." *Marvels & Tales* 33 (1): 82–101.

Carter, Angela, ed. 1990. *The Old Wives' Fairy Tale Book*. New York: Pantheon.

Cook, Jacqueline. 1993. "Bibliography on Rosario Ferré." *Chasqui*, 22 (2): 129–49.

Datlow, Ellen, and Terry Windling, eds. 1993. *Snow White, Red Blood*. New York: HarperCollins.

———, eds. 1997. *Black Swan, White Raven*. New York: HarperCollins.

Desmond, John M., and Peter Hawkes. 2006. *Adaptation: Studying Film & Literature*. Boston: McGraw Hill.

Drouin-Brisebois, Josée, ed. 2013. *Shary Boyle: Music for Silence. Canada Pavilion, 55th Venice Biennale*. Ottawa: National Gallery of Canada.

Ferré, Rosario. 1994. "From Ire to Irony." Trans. Lizabeth Parvaisini-Gebert. *Callaloo* 17 (3): 900–904.

Fraser, Lucy. 2017. *The Pleasures of Metamorphosis: Japanese and English Fairy Tale Transformations of "The Little Mermaid."* Detroit, MI: Wayne State University Press.

Garland-Thomson, Rosemarie. 2005. "Feminist Disability Studies." *Signs* 30 (2): 1557–87.

Greenhill, Pauline. 2014. "Wanting (To Be) Animal: Fairy-Tale Transbiology in *The Storyteller*." *Feral Feminisms* 2:29–45. https://feralfeminisms.com/wanting-to-be-animal/

Greenhill, Pauline, Jill Terry Rudy, Naomi Hamer, and Lauren Bosc, eds. 2018. *Routledge Companion to Media and Fairy-Tale Cultures*. New York: Routledge.

Greenhill, Pauline, and Kay Turner. 2016. "Queer and Transgender Theory." In *Folktales and Fairy Tales: Traditions and Texts from around the World*, 2nd edition, 4 volumes, edited by Donald Haase and Anne E. Duggan, 3:843–46. Santa Barbara, CA: Greenwood.

Guran, Paula, ed. 2013. *Once Upon a Time: New Fairy Tales*. Germantown, MD: Prime Books.

———, ed. 2016. *Beyond the Woods: Fairy Tales Retold*. Germantown, MD: Prime Books.

Haase, Donald. 2006. "Hypertextual Gutenberg: The Textual and Hypertextual Life of Folk and Fairy Tales in English-Language Popular Print Editions." *Fabula* 47 (3–4): 222–30.

———. 2011. "Kiss and Tell: Orality, Narrative, and the Power of Words in 'Sleeping Beauty.'" *Des Fata aux Fées: regards croisés de l'Antiquité à nos jours*, edited by Martine Hennard Dutheil de la Rochère and Véronique Dasen, 3–4:279–94.

Haddawy, Husain, trans. 1990. *The Arabian Nights*. Based on the text edited by Muhsin Mahdi. New York: Norton.

Hallett, Martin, and Barbara Karasek. 2014. *Fairy Tales in Popular Culture*. Peterborough, ON: Broadview Press.

Heise, Ursula K. 2006. "The Hitchhiker's Guide to Ecocriticism." *PMLA*, 121 (2): 503–16.

hoʻomanawanui, kuʻualoha. 2018. "E Hoʻokikohoʻe iā Peʻapeʻamakawalu (Digitizing the Eight-Eyed Bat): Indigenous Wonder Tales, Culture, and Media." In *Routledge Companion to Media and Fairy-Tale Cultures*, edited by Pauline Greenhill, Jill Terry Rudy, Naomi Hamer, and Lauren Bosc, 122–32. New York: Routledge.

Jones, Stephen. 2013. *Faerie Tales: Stories of the Grimm and Gruesome*. New York: Jo Fletcher Books.

Joosen, Vanessa. 2011. *Critical and Creative Perspectives on Fairy Tales: An Intertextual Dialogue between Fairy-Tale Scholarship and Postmodern Retellings*. Detroit, MI: Wayne State University Press.

Justice, Daniel Heath. 2018. *Why Indigenous Literatures Matter*. Waterloo, ON: Wilfrid Laurier University Press.

Kamakawiwoʻole, Israel. 1993. "Maui, Hawaiian Sup'pa Man." Lyrics by Del Beazley. In *Facing Future*. Honolulu: Mountain Apple Company.

King, Thomas. 2008. *The Truth about Stories*. Minneapolis: University of Minnesota Press.

Kohn, Eric. 2009. "Exclusive Interview: David Kaplan on Seductive Fairy Tales." *Indiewire.com*, June 8.

Leavy, Barbara Fass. 1995. *In Search of the Swan Maiden: A Narrative on Folklore and Gender*. New York: New York University Press.

Lesuma, Caryn Kunz. 2016. "Living Moʻolelo for Young Adults: Story, Language, and Form in 'Of No Real Account.'" In *"In a Word": Proceedings 2015: Selected Papers from the Nineteenth College-Wide Conference for Students in Languages, Linguistics and Literature*, edited by Samuel Aguirre, Emily Gazda Plumb, and Kristyn Martin, 36–43. Honolulu: University of Hawaiʻi, National Foreign Language Resource Center. https://scholarspace.manoa.hawaii.edu/bitstream/10125/14578/RN53 -LLL2015.pdf

Link, Kelly. 2015. "Introduction." In *The Bloody Chamber and Other Stories*, by Angela Carter, vii–xiv. New York: Penguin.

The Little Mermaid. 1989. Dir. Ron Clements and John Musker. Walt Disney Home Video.

Maitland, Sara. 2013. *Gossip from the Forest: The Tangled Roots of Our Forests and Fairy Tales*. London: Granta Books.

McDougall, Brandy Nālani. 2012. "Ola (i) Nā Moʻolelo: Living Moʻolelo: Brandy McDougall at TEDx Mānoa." YouTube video, 16:57 min., October 25. https://www.youtube.com/watch?v=K69_kuqBiX

Møllegaard, Kirsten. 2014. "Global Flows in Global Contact Zones: Selkie Lore in Neil Jordan's *Ondine* and Solveig Eggerz's *Seal Woman*." In *Unsettling Assumptions: Tradition, Gender, Drag*, edited by Pauline Greenhill and Diane Tye, 93–111. Logan: Utah State University Press.

Murai, Mayako. 2013. "The Princess, the Witch, and the Fireside: Yanagi Miwa's Uncanny Restaging of Fairy Tales." *Marvels & Tales* 27 (2): 234–53.

———. 2015. *From Dog Bridegroom to Wolf Girl: Contemporary Japanese Fairy-Tale Adaptations in Conversation with the West*. Detroit, MI: Wayne State University Press.

Nünning, Ansgar. 2004. "On Metanarrative: Towards a Definition, a Typology and an Outline of the Functions of Metanarrative Commentary." In *The Dynamics of Narrative Form: Studies in Anglo-American Narratology*, edited by John Pier, 11–57. New York: Walter de Gruyter.

Orme, Jennifer. 2010. "Mouth to Mouth: Queer Desires in Emma Donoghue's *Kissing the Witch*." *Marvels & Tales* 24 (1): 116–30.

———. 2012. "Happily Ever After . . . According to Our Tastes: Jeanette Winterson's Twelve Dancing Princesses and Queer Possibility." In *Transgressive Tales: Queering the Grimms*, edited by Kay Turner and Pauline Greenhill, 140–60. Detroit, MI: Wayne State University Press.

———. 2015. "The Wolf's Queer Invitation: David Kaplan's *Little Red Riding Hood* and Queer Possibility." *Marvels & Tales* 29 (1): 87–109.

———. 2016. "'I'm Sure It All Wears Off by Midnight': Prince Cinders and a Queer Invitation." *Cinderella Across Cultures: New Directions and Interdisciplinary Perspectives*, edited by Martine Hennard Dutheil de la Rochère, Gillian Lathey, and Monika Wozniak, 215–31. Detroit, MI: Wayne State University Press.

Osman, Diriye. 2017. "The Queering of Sleeping Beauty." *diriyeosman.com*, October 17.

Parisien, Dominik, and Navah Wolfe, eds. 2016. *Starlit Wood: New Fairy Tales*. New York: Saga Press.

Parrish, Rhonda, ed. 2019. *Grimm, Grit, and Gasoline: Dieselpunk & Decopunk Fairy Tales*. Albuquerque, NM: World Weaver Press.

Propp, Vladimir. 1968. *Morphology of the Folktale*. 2nd edition. Translated by Laurence Scott. Austin: University of Texas Press.

Rigby, Kate. 2015. "Ecocriticism." In *Introducing Criticism in the 21st Century*, 2nd ed., ed. Julian Wolfreys, 122–54. Edinburgh: Edinburgh University Press.

Schanoes, Veronica. 2019. "Thorns into Gold: Contemporary Jewish American Responses to Antisemitism in Traditional Fairy Tales." *Journal of American Folklore* 132 (525): 291–309.

Schmiesing, Ann. 2014. *Disability, Deformity, and Disease in the Grimms' Fairy Tales*. Detroit, MI: Wayne State University Press.

———. 2018. "Disability." In *Routledge Companion to Media and Fairy-Tale Cultures*, edited by Pauline Greenhill, Jill Terry Rudy, Naomi Hamer, and Lauren Bosc, 104–12. New York: Routledge.

Seifert, Lewis. 2015. "Queer Time in Charles Perrault's 'Sleeping Beauty.'" *Marvels & Tales* 29 (1): 21–41.

Silver, Carole G. 2016. "Animal Bride, Animal Groom." In *Folktales and Fairy Tales: Traditions and Texts from around the World*, 2nd edition, 4 volumes, edited by Donald Haase and Anne E. Duggan, 1:40–42. Santa Barbara, CA: Greenwood.

Simpson, Leanne Betasamosake. 2011. *Dancing on Our Turtle's Back: Stories of Nishnaabeg Re-Creation, Resurgence, and a New Emergence*. Winnipeg, Manitoba: Arbeiter Ring Publishing.

Snyder, Sharon L., and David T. Mitchell. 2001. "Re-engaging the Body: Disability Studies and the Resistance to Embodiment." *Public Culture* 13 (3): 367–89.

Stam, Robert. 2000. "Beyond Fidelity: The Dialogics of Adaptation." In *Film Adaptation*, edited by James Naremore, 54–76. New Brunswick, NJ: Rutgers University Press.

Stamey, Emily. 2018. *Dread & Delight: Fairy Tales in an Anxious World*. Greensboro, NC: Weatherspoon Art Museum, UNC Greensboro.

Takahashi, Rumiko. 2004. *Mermaid Saga*. Vols. 1–4. San Francisco: Viz Media.

Tatar, Maria, trans. and ed. 2010. *The Grimm Reader: The Classic Fairy Tales of the Brothers Grimm*. New York: Norton.

Taulapapa McMullin, Dan. 2016a. *Aue Away: An Installation*. Special event in conjunction with the Margaret Mead Film Festival, American Museum of Natural History, New York City, October 13–16. https://www.amnh.org/explore/margaret-mead-film-festival/archives/2016/special-events

———. 2016b. *Aue Away: An Installation October 2016*. October 27. https://vimeo.com/189247497

———. 2019. "The Fag End of Fāgogo." *Narrative Culture* 6 (2): 216–28.

Taulapapa McMullin, Dan, and Yuki Kihara. 2018. *Queer Samoan Lives*. Auckland, NZ: Little Island Press.

Teverson, Andrew, ed. 2019. *The Fairy Tale World*. London: Routledge.

Turner, Kay. 2012. "Playing with Fire: Transgression as Truth in Grimms' 'Frau Trude.'" In *Transgressive Tales: Queering the Grimms*, edited by Kay Turner and Pauline Greenhill, 245–74. Detroit, MI: Wayne State University Press.

Turner, Kay, and Pauline Greenhill, eds. 2012. *Transgressive Tales: Queering the Grimms*. Detroit, MI: Wayne State University Press.

Uther, Hans-Jörg. 2004. *The Types of International Folktales: A Classification and Bibliography, Based on the System of Antti Aarne and Stith Thompson*. Helsinki: Academia Scientiarum Fennica.

Warner, Marina. 1991. "Absent Mothers: Women against Women in Old Wives' Tales." *History Today* (April): 22–28.

———. 2014. *Once Upon a Time: A Short History of the Fairy Tale*. Oxford: Oxford University Press.

"Yao Bikuni." 2019. Translated by Mayako Murai. In *The Penguin Book of Mermaids: Tales of Merfolk and Water Spirits from Around the World*, edited by Cristina Bacchilega and Marie Alohalani Brown, 210–11. New York: Penguin. Originally in 稲田浩二、小澤俊夫編『日本昔話通観 第11巻 富山・石川・福井』1981年、同朋舎出版. In *Nihon Mukashibanashi Tsūkan 11: Toyama, Ishikawa, Fukui*, edited by Koji Inada and Toshio Ozawa, 187–89. Kyoto: Dōhōsha, 1981.

Zipes, Jack, ed. 1987. *Don't Bet on the Prince: Contemporary Feminist Fairy Tales in North America and England*. New York: Methuen.

———, ed. 1993. *The Trials and Tribulations of Little Red Riding Hood*. 2nd ed. New York: Routledge.

———. 2012. *The Irresistible Fairy Tale: The Cultural and Social History of a Genre*. Princeton, NJ: Princeton University Press.

About the Authors, Artists, and Editors

Su Blackwell gives form to the images we imagine when we read literature. She cuts out the pages from secondhand books to create three-dimensional tableaux, which are then placed inside bespoke wood and glass cases.

Blackwell was born in Sheffield in 1975 and studied at the Royal College of Art in London in 2003. She has had solo exhibitions in London, Tokyo, and New York and has participated in international group exhibitions. Her work is in the collections of the National Museum of Wales and the Bronte Parsonage Museum in West Yorkshire. She has been commissioned by many clients including Crabtree and Evelyn, *The Guardian*, and *Vogue*. Su now lives and works on the south coast of England with her husband and daughter.

Shary Boyle works across diverse media, including sculpture, drawing, installation, and performance. She is known for her bold, fantastical explorations of the figure. Highly crafted and deeply imaginative, her practice is activated through collaboration and mentorship. Boyle's work considers the social history of ceramic figurines, animist mythologies, and folk-art forms to create a symbolic, feminist, and politically charged language uniquely her own.

Boyle is exhibited and collected internationally. In 2017, she cocurated and participated in the Esker Foundation–produced touring exhibition *Earthlings* and her sculptures were featured in both South Korea's Gyeonggi International Ceramic Biennale and the Phaidon publication *Vitamin C: Clay and Ceramic in Contemporary Art*. She is the recipient of the Hnatyshyn

Foundation Award and the Gershon Iskowitz Prize. She represented Canada with her project *Music for Silence* at the 55th Venice Biennale in 2013.

Boyle's public sculpture commission *Cracked Wheat* was installed in August 2018 on the front grounds of the Gardiner Museum in Toronto. Her work will be featured at the museum in a major solo exhibition opening January 2021.

Susanna Clarke was born in Nottingham in 1959, the eldest daughter of a Methodist minister. She was educated at St. Hilda's College, Oxford, and has worked in various areas of publishing. In 1990 she left London to teach English in Turin and Bilbao for two years, returning to England to work at Simon and Schuster as a cookery editor.

In 1992, she began working on *Jonathan Strange and Mr Norrell*, which was finally published in 2004 by Bloomsbury to widespread critical acclaim and commercial success. *Jonathan Strange and Mr Norrell* was filmed as a major BBC drama that aired in 2015. She followed with a collection of short stories, *The Ladies of Grace Adieu* (2006). Her short story "Mr Simonelli, or The Fairy Widower" was short-listed for a World Fantasy Award in 2001. Susanna lives in Cambridge with her partner, the novelist and reviewer Colin Greenland.

Born in Dublin in 1969, Emma Donoghue did a PhD in eighteenth-century literature at Cambridge before settling in Canada. A writer of fiction both short and long, as well as plays for stage and radio, screenplays, and literary history, she is best known for her international bestseller *Room* (short-listed for the Man Booker and Orange Prizes) and its film adaptation (for which she was nominated for an Oscar, a Golden Globe, and a Bafta). "The Tale of the Cottage" is one of a sequence of thirteen reimagined fairy tales entitled *Kissing the Witch*. Her novels include *Akin*, *The Wonder*, *Frog Music*, *The Sealed Letter*, *Life Mask*, and *Slammerkin*. She has published two books for young readers, *The Lotterys Plus One* and *The Lotterys More Or Less*. More information on Donoghue is available at www.emmadonoghue.com.

Puerto Rican author Rosario Ferré received a PhD in comparative literature from the University of Maryland. A magazine publisher, poet, short story writer, essayist, and literary critic, her first novel, *Maldito amor*, was published in 1986. She is the author of a collection of stories, *Papeles de Pandora* (1976); a poetry collection, *Fábulas de la garza desangrada* (1980); and a collection of feminist essays, *Sitio a Eros* (1980). Her children's stories include *El medio pollito* (1978), *La mona que le pisaron la cola* (1981), and *Los cuentos de Juan Bobo* (1982). She wrote in both Spanish and English, and her later works include *House on the Lagoon, Eccentric Neighborhoods*, and *Flight of the Swan*. Ferré died in 2016.

NALO HOPKINSON, a Jamaican Canadian, has published numerous novels, including *Brown Girl in the Ring* and *The Chaos*, and short stories collected in *Skin Folk* and *Falling in Love with Hominids*. Hopkinson has also coedited anthologies such as *So Long Been Dreaming: Postcolonial Science Fiction & Fantasy* and *People of Color Take Over Fantastic Stories of the Imagination*. She is the recipient of the World Fantasy Award, the John W. Campbell Award, the Andre Norton Award, the Inkpot Award, and the Octavia E. Butler Award for achievement in the field of science fiction. She is currently a professor of creative writing at the University of California, Riverside.

ROSALIND HYATT ORME is an eleven-year-old artist who enjoys exploring three-dimensional sculpture, figure, fashion drawing, and needlework. Her work has influences from her keen interest in animation. She says, "I don't think about it. I just do it." She is homeschooled and lives in Toronto with her parents and sister.

ANNE KAMIYA was born in Honolulu, Hawai'i. She is an artist, writer and scientist. Her stories and art combine elements from her life experiences, deep connection to family, and wonders from the natural and fantastical worlds. She is Okinawan on her mother's side and has traveled to Okinawa to deepen her connection to the arts, science, and her mother's family's roots. Her art is also viewable online at https://www.deviantart.com/boegeob.

DAVID KAPLAN has made several acclaimed short and feature-length films. Kaplan's short *Little Red Riding Hood* premiered at the 1997 Sundance Film Festival, was shown in theaters and on television throughout the world, and has been taught at many colleges and universities including Harvard, Oxford, and Columbia. "PLAY"—a collaboration with game designer Eric Zimmerman—won Best Short Film at the 2010 BiFan Fantastic Film Festival and was featured in the 2012 exhibition "Playtime—Videogame Mythologies" at the *Maison d'Ailleurs Musée* in Switzerland. His feature *Today's Special* was released theatrically by Reliance Mediaworks. His feature *Year of the Fish* premiered at the 2007 Sundance Film Festival and won Best Film at the 2007 Avignon Film Festival, Best Film at the 2007 Asheville Film Festival, and was nominated for the Piaget Producers Award at the 2009 Independent Spirit Awards. Kaplan has lectured at Scripps College in Claremont, California on "Fairy Tales into Film" and "Reimagining Fantastic Tales." His current projects include three horror films with fairy-tale underpinnings.

MAYA KERN is a self-employed comic artist, illustrator, and musician who has been publishing her web comics since 2011. *Monster Pop!* is her most extensive and ongoing comic with interactive elements (see www.mayakern.com). A graduate of the comic art program at the Minneapolis College of Art and Design, she lives in upstate New York with her wife and their two cats and dog. She grew up reading world mythology, the Grimms and other fairy tales, and YA retellings like *Ella Enchanted* and Robin McKinley's *Beauty*. In college, she successfully Kickstarted a project to self-publish a collection of three fairy-tale comics—*The Little Robot Girl*, *Fairyfail*, and *How to Be a Mermaid* (the only retelling in the trio)—and then created a comic retelling of "Little Red Riding Hood" called *Redden*. For Kern, the most important aspect of these comics, whether they are new tales or retellings, is to leave an impression of an atmosphere, as if the story itself was a character.

BRYAN KAMAOLI KUWADA, assistant professor of Moʻolelo ʻŌiwi at the Kamakakūokalani Center for Hawaiian Studies, University of Hawaiʻi at Mānoa, is a tiny part of a beautiful beloved community that fights every day for breath, for ea, for connection, for sovereignty. He is sometimes called tree, bear, Morris, hoa, Uncle Jacket, and more. He is also sometimes an academic (publishing on comics, Bluebeard, translation, and life writing, all in the context of Hawaiʻi and ʻōlelo Hawaiʻi); editor (*Hūlili: Multidisciplinary Research on Hawaiian Wellbeing*, and coeditor with Aiko

Yamashiro of the special issue of *Marvels & Tales* "Rooted in Wonder: Tales of Indigenous Activism and Community Organizing"); translator; blogger (hehiale.wordpress.com); poet (*The Offing, American Quarterly*); writer of dorky sci-fi and speculative fiction stories set in Hawai'i (*Black Marks on the White Page, Pacific Monsters, Hawai'i Review*); photographer; and/or videographer. What he mostly does is cook too much food and surf with his mother and a crew of fierce activist poet wahine who tease (and teach) him mercilessly.

KELLY LINK is the author of the collections *Get in Trouble* (a finalist for the 2016 Pulitzer Prize in Fiction), *Magic for Beginners, Stranger Things Happen,* and *Pretty Monsters.* She is the cofounder of Small Beer Press, along with her husband, Gavin J. Grant. Her short stories have been published in *Tin House, McSweeney's, A Public Space,* and *One Story* and reprinted in *The Best American Short Stories* and *Prize Stories: The O. Henry Awards.* She has received a grant from the National Endowment for the Arts, and in 2018 she was named a MacArthur Fellow. She lives with her husband and daughter in Northampton, Massachusetts.

DIRIYE OSMAN is a British Somali author, visual artist, critic, and essayist based in London. He is the author of the Polari Prize–winning collection of stories *Fairytales for Lost Children* (Team Angelica Press), and his writing has appeared in *The Guardian,* the *Financial Times,* the *Huffington Post, Vice, Poetry Review, Prospect, Time Out, Attitude,* and *Afropunk.* He lives on a diet of Disney cartoons, graphic novels, masala chai, and Missy Elliott records. More about his work is available at www.diriyeosman.com.

JOELLYN ROCK is an associate professor of art and design at the University of Minnesota Duluth. Her creative work includes digital print, interactive narrative, and experimental video. Revisiting fairy tales and myth, Rock seeks new ways to tell old tales. Hybridity (a mixing of artistic techniques and media) and distribution (the extension of the work across media platforms) are key components in her creative work. Rock collaborates with colleagues in the Motion and Media Across Disciplines Lab, where she ponders how emerging media is reshaping the ways that stories can be told. Interactive installations such as *Sophronia Project, Fishnetstockings,* and *Salt Immortal Sea* provide participatory space and multiple modes for the audience to play in the story. Exhibited regionally and internationally, Rock's multimedia projects have been included in *Northern Spark* at the Walker Arts Center in Minneapolis, Minnesota; *Hybridity and Synesthesia* at Lydgalleriet, Bergen, Norway; and the Electronic Literature Festival at Mosteiro de São Bento da Vitória, Porto, Portugal. "Bare Bones" owes a debt to Jack Zipes, who served as mentor during the project's development and whose fairy-tale scholarship continues to enlighten and inform. This current iteration of "Bare Bones" was resurrected with the help of her colleague David Short, assistant professor of art and design. An "Accidental Typographer," Short creates graphic design work that incorporates hand-lettering, type design, and illustration in both analog and digital media.

SOFIA SAMATAR is the author of the novels *A Stranger in Olondria* and *The Winged Histories*; the short story collection, *Tender*; and *Monster Portraits*, a collaboration with her brother, the artist Del Samatar. Her work has received several honors, including the Astounding Award (formerly the John W. Campbell Award), the British Fantasy Award, and the World Fantasy Award. She teaches African literature, Arabic literature, and speculative fiction at James Madison University.

VERONICA SCHANOES is a writer and scholar living in New York City. Her novella *Burning Girls*, a story inspired by "Rumpelstiltskin" and set during the great Jewish immigration waves of the early twentieth century, won the Shirley Jackson Award and was a finalist for the Nebula and World Fantasy Awards. Her stories have appeared on Tor.com and in various anthologies, including *Queen Victoria's Book of Spells*, edited by Ellen Datlow and Terri Windling, and *The Permanent Collection*, edited by Ellen Datlow.

Schanoes is also an associate professor in the Department of English at Queens College—CUNY, where she studies fairy tales and children's literature. Her book, *Fairy Tales, Myth, and Psychoanalysis: Feminism and Retelling the Tale*, published by Ashgate in 2014, is about the relationship between contemporary feminist revisions of fairy tales and contemporary feminist psychoanalytic theory. Her current project is on Jewish representation in the English-language fairy-tale tradition, an area in which she is also interested creatively.

NISI SHAWL wrote the 2016 Nebula Award finalist and Tiptree Honor novel *Everfair*, an alternate history in which the Congo overthrows King Leopold II's genocidal regime, and the 2008 Tiptree Award–winning story collection *Filter House*, which includes several stories based on African and Afro-diasporic folklore. In 2005 she cowrote *Writing the Other: A Practical Approach*, now the standard text on diverse character representation in the imaginative genres and the basis of her years of online and in-person classes of the same name. She has presented speeches at Duke University, Spelman College, the University of Hawai'i-Mānoa, and other educational institutions.

Shawl's dozens of acclaimed short stories have appeared in *Wired*, *Analog*, and *Asimov's Magazines*, among other publications; her "Everfair-adjacent" story "Vulcanization" was selected as one of twenty offered in Houghton Mifflin Harcourt's *Best American Science Fiction and Fantasy of 2017*. Recently she edited *New Suns: Original Speculative Fiction by People of Color*, which appeared in March 2019 from Solaris. In fall 2019, Lee and Low published *Speculation*, Shawl's middle grade historical fantasy novel. She lives in Seattle, where currently she is writing *Kinning*, a sequel to *Everfair* involving radio transmissions and infective empathy.

SHAUN TAN grew up in Perth, Western Australia, and works as an artist, writer, and filmmaker in Melbourne. He is best known for illustrated books that deal with social and historical subjects through dreamlike imagery: *The Rabbits*, *The Red Tree*, *Tales from Outer Suburbia*, and the graphic novel *The Arrival* have been widely translated throughout the world and enjoyed by readers of all ages. Tan has also worked as a theater designer, has been a concept artist for Pixar, and won an Academy Award for the short animated film *The Lost Thing*. In 2011 he received the prestigious Astrid Lindgren Memorial Award in Sweden. His most recent books are *Cicada* and *Tales from the Inner City*.

DAN TAULAPAPA MCMULLIN is an artist and poet from Sāmoa Amelika (American Samoa). His book of poems *Coconut Milk* (University of Arizona Press, 2013) was on the American Library Association Rainbow List Top Ten Books of the Year. In 2018, *Samoan Queer Lives*, coedited with Yuki Kihara and published by Little Island Press of Aotearoa, was named a best book of 2019 by Art Asia Pacific. Taulapapa's performance poem "The Bat" and other early works received a 1997 Poets & Writers Award from the Writers Loft. His artwork was on exhibit at the Metropolitan Museum, De Young Museum, Oakland Museum, Bishop Museum, NYU's /A/P/A Gallery, and the United Nations. His film *Sinalela* won the 2002 Honolulu Rainbow Film Festival Best Short Film Award. *100 Tikis*, an art appropriation video at the intersection of tiki kitsch and indigenous sovereignty, was the opening night film selection of the 2016 Présence Autochtone First Peoples Festival in Montreal as well as an Official Selection in the Fifo Tahiti International Oceania Documentary Film Festival and at the Pacifique Festival in Rochefort, France. Taulapapa's art studio and writing practice are based in Hudson, New York, where he lives with his partner. He is currently working on a novel and a queer history of Polynesia.

DANIELLE WOOD is the author of several works of fiction, including two collections with fairy-tale connections, *Rosie Little's Cautionary Tales for Girls* and *Mothers Grimm*. She has also written nonfiction and children's fiction and is the coeditor of two anthologies of Tasmanian writing (*Deep South: Stories from Tasmania* and *Island Story: Tasmania in Object and Text*). Her first novel, *The Alphabet of Light and Dark*, won *The Australian*/Vogel's Literary Prize in 2002 and the Dobbie Award for Australian women writers. She has twice been nominated a *Sydney Morning Herald* Best Young Novelist of the Year, and her shorter works have appeared in a range of literary and academic publications, including Australia's *Griffith Review* and *Island* magazines. She contributed to Routledge's compendium *The Fairy Tale World*; and an essay about, and an excerpt from, her work in progress, "The House on Legs," was published in *Marvels & Tales* (2019). This new work features a Baba Yaga-esque figure who lives in a rough hut in the Tasmanian bush and raises native animals that have been orphaned by road accidents. Wood teaches writing at the University of Tasmania, where her research interests include contemporary fairy-tale retellings and the literature of Australia's island state.

MIWA YANAGI first became famous in the 1990s with her photographic series *Elevator Girls*, which was followed by her two other major series *My Grandmothers* and *Fairy Tale*. She was commissioned to represent Japan at the 2009 Venice Biennale. After 2010, she began to focus on theater projects and directed a trilogy entitled *1924*. She also created a mobile stage truck and directed the traveling open-air performance *The Wings of the Sun*. In 2016, she launched her photographic series inspired by the motif of the peach tree in Japanese mythology. By going back and forth between visual and performing arts, Yanagi's recent work blends elements of documentary and spectacle and crosses the boundary between reality and fiction in a complex and multilayered manner. Her most recent major solo exhibition, *Myth Machines*, opened in 2019.

CRISTINA BACCHILEGA is a professor in the Department of English at the University of Hawai'i-Mānoa, where she teaches fairy tales and their adaptations, folklore and literature, and cultural studies. The author of *Fairy Tales Transformed? 21st-Century Adaptations and the Politics of Wonder* and other books, Bacchilega coedits *Marvels & Tales: Journal of Fairy-Tale Studies* with Anne Duggan. In 2019, she also coedited with Duggan special issues of the *Journal of American Folklore, Marvels & Tales*, and *Narrative Culture* focused on the theme "Thinking with Stories in Times of Trouble," and coedited, with Marie Alohalani Brown, *The Penguin Book of Mermaids*.

JENNIFER ORME is a narrative designer, writer, editor, and scholar in Toronto, Canada. She has taught at the University of Winnipeg, at Ryerson University, at the University of Hawai'i at Mānoa, and at York University. In addition to her fictional work as the Fabulist for The Mysterious Package Company and as the creator of the world of The Boundless Library, she has published in *New Approaches to Teaching Folk and Fairy Tales, Cinderella across Cultures: New Directions and Interdisciplinary Perspectives, Transgressive Tales: Queering the Grimms*, and *Marvels & Tales: Journal of Fairy Tale Studies*. She is extremely proud that her niece Rosalind Hyatt Orme's *Medusa* was chosen by Cristina Bacchilega and Wayne State University Press for the cover of this book.

CPSIA information can be obtained
at www.ICGtesting.com
Printed in the USA
LVHW071403230221
679746LV00029B/1077